EAST ANGLIAN ARCHAEOLOGY

Salt-Winning on the Lyn
Anglo-Saxon and Medieval Industry at Gaywood's North Marsh, King's Lynn

by Graeme Clarke

with contributions by
Sue Anderson, Matt Brudenell, Denise Druce,
Rachel Fosberry, Charles French, Frances
Green, Derek Hamilton, Nick Holder, Tom
Lane, Ted Levermore and Simon Timberlake

illustrations by
Séverine Bézie
with Gareth Rees and David Brown

edited for OA East by
Rachel Clarke

East Anglian Archaeology
Report No. 180, 2023

Oxford Archaeology

EAST ANGLIAN ARCHAEOLOGY
REPORT NO.180

Published by
Oxford Archaeology, Cambridge Office,
15 Trafalgar Way, Bar Hill
Cambridgeshire CB23 8SQ

in conjunction with ALGAO East
www.algao.org.uk/england/east_england

Editor: James Albone
Managing Editors: Jenny Glazebrook & Sue Anderson

Editorial Board:
James Albone, Historic England
Stewart Bryant, Archaeological Consultant
Andy Hutcheson, University of East Anglia
Maria Medlycott, Historic Environment, Essex County Council
Faye Minter, Historic Environment, Suffolk County Council
Zoe Outram, Historic England Science Adviser
John Percival, Head of Historic Environment, Norfolk County Council
Andy Thomas, Historic Environment, Cambridgeshire County Council
Alison Tinniswood, Historic Environment, Hertfordshire County Council
Jess Tipper, Historic England

Set in Times New Roman by Sue Anderson using Adobe InDesign
Printed by Henry Ling Limited, The Dorset Press

© OXFORD ARCHAEOLOGY
ISBN 978-1-907588-14-3

East Anglian Archaeology was established in 1975 by the Scole Committee for Archaeology in East Anglia. The scope of the series expanded in 2002 to include all six eastern counties. Responsibility for publication rests with the editorial board in partnership with the Association of Local Government Archaeological Officers, East of England (ALGAO East).

For details of *East Anglian Archaeology*, see last page

Cover illustrations
Front cover
The North Marsh *c*.1581 (Harrod 1874, pl. H; CUL Ll.32.47). Reproduced by kind permission of the Syndics of Cambridge University Library

Back cover
Line drawing of a filtration unit at Saltern 10, showing remnants of *in situ* turves

Contents

List of Figures	v
List of Tables	vii
Contributors	vii
Acknowledgements	viii
Abbreviations	viii
Summary/Résumé/Zusammenfassung	ix

Chapter 1. Introduction
I. Project background   1
II. Post-Roman salterns on the Wash: overview of previous work   1
III. The OA East excavation at Marsh Lane   5
IV. Lessons learned: formulating an excavation and reporting strategy   7
V. The developing research agenda   9
VI. Structure of this report   11

Chapter 2. Shaping an Anglo-Saxon Landscape on the Lyn
I. Archaeological overview of the Lyn and its Anglo-Saxon environs   13
II. Emerging 'gateway' and monastic communities on the Lyn   14
III. Discussion   16

Chapter 3. The Saltmarsh
I. A dynamic and coastal riverine environment   18
II. Saltmarsh formation   25
III. Transition from saltmarsh to 'reclaimed' pastureland   31
IV. Discussion   32

Chapter 4. The Salterns
I. Introduction   33
II. The process of sand-washing or *sleeching*   35
III. Dating framework   36
IV. Period 1: *Salters Waie* group (*c*.8th century to 10th century)   38
V. Period 2: *Bullcote Waie* group (*c*. late 10th to early 12th century)   52
VI. Discussion   73

Chapter 5. Salt-making in the Historical Narrative of Lynn
I. Domesday, charters and cartularies   80
II. The Gaywood Dragge of 1487: survey of a fossilised salt-making landscape   81
III. Discussion   87

Chapter 6. Overall Discussion and Conclusions
I. Overall discussion   91
II. The King's Lynn salterns: a view from Lincolnshire   95
III. General conclusions   97

Appendices
Appendix 1: Glossary   99
Appendix 2: Radiocarbon dating and chronological modelling   101
Appendix 3: Methodologies   104
Appendix 4: Translation of 'Encyclopédie'   106
Appendix 5: Extract from Dugdale *et al.* (1846) on the endowment of St Margaret's Priory, Bishop's Lynn   107

Bibliography   109
Index, by Sue Vaughan   116

List of Figures

Fig. 1.1	Location map showing Lynnsport and Greenpark Avenue School sites	2
Fig. 1.2	The Lynnsport 3 site, looking south	4
Fig. 1.3	The Greenpark Avenue School site, looking west towards Saltern 5	4
Fig. 1.4	Map showing location of NHER records with NNMP data, including salterns	6
Fig. 1.5	Schematic cross-section of a saltern	8
Fig. 1.6	Visualising the themes: the flow of a basic input and output model of a viable saltern	10
Fig. 2.1	Distribution of Anglo-Saxon pottery and undated metalworking slag in the environs of the Lyn	14
Fig. 3.1	Site location in relation to the Late Anglo-Saxon to medieval Norfolk coastline and rivers, with known post-Roman salt-making sites mapped by the NNMP (NHER)	18
Fig. 3.2	King's Lynn and the River Great Ouse, looking south-east	19
Fig. 3.3	Reclamation of the Lyn between the 10th and 19th centuries	20
Fig. 3.4	The Great River Ouse *c*.1725, based on a survey *c*.1604	21
Fig. 3.5	The proposed Eau Brink Cut, *c*.1724	22
Fig. 3.6	The North Marsh *c*.1581	23
Fig. 3.7	Gaywood 1838 Tithe map, with site locations shown	24

Fig. 3.8	Present-day saltmarsh at the mouth of the Great Ouse, looking north-west from the modern outflow of the Babingley river	24	Fig. 4.23	Plan of Salterns 4–7, and sections of salt-working features within Saltern 5 (*c.* late 10th to early 12th century) 61
Fig. 3.9	Reconstruction of the fossilised salt-making landscape	26	Fig. 4.24	Saltern 5: Hearth 1018 plan and section 62
Fig. 3.10	Saltwater creeks	27	Fig. 4.25	Saltern 5: Overhead view of hearth 1018 63
Fig. 3.11	Thin section photomicrograph. Alternating laminae of very fine quartz and humic very fine sand/silt, monolith Sample 421, fabric unit 2, context 1004, Saltern 5	29	Fig. 4.26	Saltern 5: Excavation of hearth 1018 64
			Fig. 4.27	Briquetage: brick pan supports with residues of accreted salt slag 64
			Fig. 4.28	Briquetage: brick pan supports with chamfered ends 65
Fig. 3.12	Thin section photomicrograph. Strongly sesquioxide-stained laminae of dusty clay and very fine sand, monolith Sample 421, fabric unit 2, context 1004, Saltern 5	29	Fig. 4.29	Briquetage: square brick with domed top 65
			Fig. 4.30	a) A salt-making slag cake of *c.*220mm diameter and b) Refitting pieces of a cake of *c.*180mm diameter 65
Fig. 3.13	Post-medieval Riley circles (hayricks) excavated on Saltern 4	31	Fig. 4.31	Three re-fitting pieces of vitrified clay melted in front of the tuyere hole of an iron-smithing (re-used saltern) hearth 66
Fig. 4.1	Evaluation trenches and excavation areas in relation to Salterns 1–12	34	Fig. 4.32	Saltern 11: Photogrammetry plan and section of salt-working features (*c.* late 10th to early 12th century) 67
Fig. 4.2	Relative chronology of Salterns 1–12 based on scientific and ceramic dating evidence	36	Fig. 4.33	Saltern 11: section through hearth waste 676 68
Fig. 4.3	A modern (1914) sketch map of Gaywood parish based on the 1487 Gaywood Dragge, showing waies into the North Marsh	36	Fig. 4.34	Habitat preferences of ostracods from Samples 402 and 404, clay-lined tanks 872 and 875, Saltern 5 69
Fig. 4.4	Aerial photograph of the North Marsh in 1946 showing *Salters Waie*, *Bullcote Waie* and Marsh Lane	37	Fig. 4.35	Habitat preferences of ostracods from Samples 419 and 420, clay-lined tank 942, Saltern 5 69
Fig. 4.5	Topographical model of the Lynnsport 4 & 5 development site (*Salters Waie* group)	38	Fig. 4.36	Habitat preferences of foraminifera from Samples 402 and 404, clay-lined tanks 872 and 875, Saltern 5 70
Fig. 4.6	Saltern 1: Plan and sections of salt-working features (*c.*8th to 10th century)	40	Fig. 4.37	Habitat preferences of foraminifera from Samples 419 and 420, clay-lined tank 942, Saltern 5 70
Fig. 4.7	Saltern 1: Area A, looking west	41	Fig. 4.38	Habitat preferences of ostracods from Samples 302 and 303, filtration unit 414 and clay-lined tank 423, Saltern 10 71
Fig. 4.8	Saltern 2: Plan and section of salt-working features (*c.*8th to 10th century)	42		
Fig. 4.9	Saltern 2: Area C, looking west	43	Fig. 4.39	Habitat preferences of ostracods from Sample 307, clay-lined tank 463, Saltern 11 71
Fig. 4.10	Saltern 1: Filtration unit 146	44		
Fig. 4.11	Saltern 2: Filtration unit 117	45		
Fig. 4.12	Saltern 1: Circular tanks, looking south	46	Fig. 4.40	Habitat preferences of foraminifera from Samples 302 and 303, filtration unit 414 and clay-lined tank 423, Saltern 10 72
Fig. 4.13	Saltern 1: Hearth 34, looking south-west	46		
Fig. 4.14	Saltern 1: Rake-out pit 83, looking west	47	Fig. 4.41	Habitat preferences of foraminifera from Sample 307, clay-lined tank 463, Saltern 11 72
Fig. 4.15	Saltern 1: Rake-out pit 128, looking west	48	Fig. 4.42	A French salicole 73
Fig. 4.16	Saltern 2: Excavation of rake-out pit 47, looking west	48	Fig. 4.43	Salt production in modern day Djègbadji, Benin 75
Fig. 4.17	Topographical survey of Greenpark Avenue School development site	53	Fig. 4.44	Reconstruction sketch of a salter's working area 78
Fig. 4.18	Saltern 10: Plan of salt-working features (*c.* late 10th to early 12th century)	55	Fig. 5.1	Assignment from William, prior of Holy Trinity, Norwich to John, bishop of Norwich, 1200–1214 80
Fig. 4.19	Saltern 10: Filtration unit 405	57		
Fig. 4.20	Saltern 10: Filtration unit 408	58		
Fig. 4.21	Saltern 10: Remnants of *in situ* turves in filtration unit 414	59	Fig. 5.2	Reconstructed map of the land holdings given on the Gaywood Dragge survey of 1487 81
Fig. 4.22	Saltern 12, photogrammetry plan and sections of salt-working features (*c.* late 10th to early 12th century)	60		

Fig. 5.3	Conveyance by John de Glynton rector of church of Hevingham to John Page de Wymondham, of 3 roods of salt meadow in Gaywood, 1330	87	Fig. 6.2	Anglo-Saxon or medieval salterns and related sites referred to in this volume	94
Fig. 5.4	Lease by Prior William Spynk of St Margaret's Church, Lynn, to Hewe Daye of Lynn of saltcote called Bulcote in marsh of Gaywood with grevas, hills *etc.*, 1481	87	Fig. A2.1	Chronological model for the salt production activity at *Salters Waie*, *Bullcote Waie*, and Marsh Lane	102
			Fig. A2.2	Span of the activity for each of the three sites in the primary model shown in Figure A2.1	102
Fig. 6.1	Interpretive map showing suggested reclamation of Gaywood's North Marsh	92	Fig. A2.3	The boundaries of the three site elements that form the chronological model presented in Figure A2.1	104

List of Tables

Table 1.1	Reporting of the Marsh Lane, Lynnsport and Greenpark Avenue School development sites	3	Table 4.9	Filtration unit elements, dimensions and associated deposits within salterns east of *Bullcote Waie*	56
Table 4.1	Excavation inventory of the Lynnsport and Greenpark Avenue School development sites	35	Table 5.1	Landholdings in the study area in *c*.1487	82
Table 4.2	Dating framework of *Salters Waie* group	39	Table 5.2	Documented tenants of Tenement 6, held by St Mary Magdalene Hospital, Gaywood	83
Table 4.3	*Salters Waie* filtration unit elements, dimensions and associated deposits	42	Table 5.3	Documented tenants of Tenement 7, known as Turnecole	83
Table 4.4	*Salters Waie* possible brine evaporation tank inventory	43	Table 5.4	Documented tenants of Tenement 10	83
			Table 5.5	Documented tenants of Tenement 18	83
Table 4.5	Sedimentology of Monolith 73 taken through hearth waste in rake-out pit 83	49	Table 5.6	Documented tenants of Tenement 19, known as Upgongacre	84
			Table 5.7	Documented tenants of Tenement 20	84
Table 4.6	Sedimentology of Monolith 98 taken through the profile of Saltern 2	52	Table 5.8	Summary of documentary and archaeological evidence for salterns in the study area	85
Table 4.7	Dating framework of *Bullcote Waie* group	54			
Table 4.8	Filtration unit elements, dimensions and associated deposits within salterns west of *Bullcote Waie*	56	Table A2.1	Radiocarbon dates from *Salters Waie*, *Bullcote Waie*, and Marsh Lane	103

Contributors

Sue Anderson
Freelance Pottery Specialist

Matt Brudenell
Former Senior Project Manager, OA East

Séverine Bézie
Illustrator, OA East

Graeme Clarke
Post-Excavation Project Officer, OA East

Rachel Clarke
Post-Excavation Editor, OA East

David Brown
Illustrator and former Surveyor, OA East

Denise Druce
Charcoal Specialist, OA North

Rachel Fosberry
Archaeobotanist, OA East

Charles French
Former Professor of Geoarchaeology, McBurney Laboratory, Department of Archaeology, University of Cambridge

Frances Green
Freelance Pollen and Sedimentology Specialist

Gareth Rees
Project Manager Geomatics (Topographic Models and Photogrammetry), OA East

Derek Hamilton
Senior Research Fellow, Scottish Universities Environmental Research Centre

Nick Holder
Freelance Historian

Tom Lane
Salt-working Specialist

Ted Levermore
Fired Clay Specialist, OA East

Simon Timberlake
Freelance Briquetage, Slag, Ostracod and Foraminifera Specialist

Acknowledgements

The Lynnsport and Greenpark Avenue School sites were owned by the Borough Council of King's Lynn and West Norfolk, and the projects were delivered in partnership with Lovell Partnerships Ltd and NPS Property Consultants Ltd respectively. OA East gratefully acknowledges the commissioning and funding of these projects.

James Albone monitored the works on behalf of Norfolk County Council and his advice and foresight was pivotal, along with Matt Brudenell, in the successful outcome of this project. Matt Brudenell managed both the fieldwork projects on behalf of Oxford Archaeology (OA) East, with post-excavation work co-managed by Rachel Clarke, both of whom are thanked for their support and guidance through the fieldwork and publication stages. In addition to Graeme Clarke, the sites were directed by Kathryn Blackbourn, Toby Knight and Malgorzata Kwiatkowska who are thanked for their contributions to the project, including compilation of the various site reports. They were supported on site by the following staff: Lindsey Kemp, Fergus Hooper, John Percival, Eben Cooper, Christof Heisterman, Brian Antoni, Anne Templeton, Paul Simkins, Frankie Wildmun, William Kelly, Rory Coduri, Francis Pitcher, Andrej Zanko and Edmund Cole. Gareth Rees, Dave Brown, Sarita Louzolo, Katie Hutton and Izzie Ward undertook the topographical and site surveys, alongside aerial photography using a polecam. The topographical models by Gareth Rees and Dave Brown were invaluable to informing the investigation and interpretation of the salterns and have been reproduced within this report. Denise Druce identified the charcoal sent for radiocarbon dating. Stuart Ladd produced the LIDAR base map used for Fig. 3.9. Lindsey Kemp took the archaeomagnetic dating samples from the *in situ* brine boiling hearth and the archaeomagnetic investigation report was written by A. Wilkinson and C.M. Batt at the University of Bradford's School of Archaeological and Forensic Sciences.

Thanks are extended to Alan Gillings of King's Lynn and West Norfolk Borough Council for assisting with site access and other logistical issues on the Greenpark Avenue development site. Darron Keen and Roger Bowers of Lovell are also thanked for their invaluable help in facilitating the archaeological works on the Lynnsport development sites. The various staff at the Norfolk Record Office, Norfolk Historic Environment Record, King's Lynn Borough Archives, Cambridge University Library and the National Archives are thanked for their assistance. Thanks are also extended to OA Staff who processed the finds and environmental assemblages and to Lawrence Billington, Ro Booth, Zoë Uí Choileáin, Martha Craven, Carole Fletcher, Christof Heisterman and Mairead Rutherford for contributing to the specialist reporting of the evaluation and assessment stages of each project. Katherine Hamilton prepared the project archives for deposition at Norwich Castle Museum.

Grateful acknowledgement is also due to the following organisations for permission to reproduce images in this report: to the Syndics of Cambridge University Library for the cover image and Figs 3.4–3.6; Norfolk Historic Environment Record (NHER) for Figs 1.4 and 4.4; and Norfolk Record Office for Figs 3.7, 4.3, 5.1 and 5.2–5.3. Séverine Bézie is thanked for translating the French text of *Encyclopédie* included in Appendix 4, detailing the brine boiling technique. The comments by James Albone and Tom Lane on the draft submitted to the EAA editorial board were also much appreciated. Tom Lane deserves particular thanks for his feedback on an early draft of this volume and for his insights into the archaeology of salt-working.

Abbreviations

BGS	British Geological Survey		Environment Service
CUL	Cambridge University Library	NHER	Norfolk Historic Environment Record
KLBA	King's Lynn Borough Archives	NNMP	Norfolk National Mapping Programme
NCCHES	Norfolk County Council Historic	NRO	Norfolk Record Office

OA East   Oxford Archaeology East
SUERC   Scottish Universities Environmental
          Research Centre
TLP   Total land pollen
WSI   Written Scheme of Investigation

Summary

Beneath the housing estates of Gaywood within the urban reach of modern King's Lynn lies a former saltmarsh — Gaywood's North Marsh — which once played an important role in the economic and physical development of this dynamic coastal and estuarine landscape. Focused on the eastern side of the Wash and to the north of an ancient inlet known as the Lyn, this marshland was rich in salt or 'white gold', gathered from the brine-saturated muds and processed using the post-Roman technique of sand-washing or *sleeching*. Often the only traces left behind of this once important coastal industry are the denuded hillocks or mounds representing the accumulated waste deposits associated with salt-winning, dozens of which have been mapped in this area. An opportunity to investigate several of these saltern mounds was prompted by the Lynnsport and Greenpark Avenue Primary School developments, leading to a three-year scheme of topographical survey, evaluation trenching and targeted excavation.

Building on previous work by OA East at Marsh Lane, this volume provides a synthetic overview of the salt-making evidence utilising a suite of scientific techniques underpinned by historical research and Bayesian modelling to reconstruct the saltmarsh environment and how this changed over time. One of the key results has been firmly to establish that the sand-washing method was in use on the east coast of England as early as the Middle Saxon period (8th to 9th century), continuing into the medieval period and beyond in some places. A possible association with the Middle Saxon 'productive' site at Bawsey is explored, as is the more definite connection with the East Anglian bishops and bishops of Norwich, who once owned this land. Linked to this are the provision of labour, methods of transport and access to fuel. The contribution of salt-working to the economy, notably trade, is assessed as is the impact that this industrial scale of salt production had on the physical environment which ultimately led to piecemeal reclamation and the development of valuable tracts of grazing land. By the 12th century, salt-winning on Gaywood's North Marsh was already in decline and by the 13th century its death knell was no doubt sounded by the diversion of the River Great Ouse into the Lyn: the fossilised salt-making landscape being recorded by the Gaywood Dragge survey of 1487. This narrative is further enhanced by comparison with similar records for sand-washing on the near continent, and a reconsideration of the evidence from the Lincolnshire side of the Wash.

Résumé

Les lotissements de Gaywood, à la périphérie urbaine de King's Lynn, reposent sur un ancien marais salé – Gaywood's North Marsh – qui jouait autrefois un rôle important dans le développement économique et physique de ce paysage côtier et estuarien dynamique. Situé sur la partie orientale du Wash et au nord d'une ancienne crique connue sous le nom de Lyn, ce marais était riche en sel ou « or blanc », recueilli à partir des boues saturées de saumure et traité à l'aide de la technique post-romaine du lavage et filtrage du sable. Souvent, les seules traces laissées de cette industrie côtière autrefois importante sont les buttes ou les monticules dénudés représentant les dépôts de déchets accumulés associés à l'extraction du sel, dont des dizaines ont été cartographiés dans cette zone. L'occasion d'enquêter sur plusieurs de ces monticules de sel a été incitée par les développements de l'école primaire Lynnsport et Greenpark Avenue, menant à un programme de trois ans, incluant relevés topographiques, fouilles préventives et programmées.

S'appuyant sur des travaux antérieurs d'Oxford Archaeology East à Marsh Lane, ce volume fournit un aperçu synthétique des preuves de la fabrication du sel en utilisant une suite de techniques scientifiques étayées par des recherches historiques et une modélisation bayésienne pour reconstruire l'environnement des marais salés et leur évolution au fil du temps. L'un des principaux résultats a été d'établir fermement que la méthode du lavage du sable était utilisée sur la côte est de l'Angleterre dès le milieu de la période anglo-saxonne (du VIIIe au IXe siècle), se poursuivant jusqu'à la période médiévale et au-delà à certains endroits. Une association possible avec le site « productif » de Bawsey, datant du milieu de la période anglo-saxonne, est explorée; tout comme le lien plus précis avec les évêques d'Est-Anglie et les évêques de Norwich, qui possédaient autrefois cette terre. La fourniture de main-d'œuvre, les méthodes de transport et l'approvisionnement en combustibles sont liés à cela. La contribution du travail du sel à l'économie, notamment à travers les échanges commerciaux, est ici évaluée; ainsi que l'impact de la production du sel a une échelle industrielle sur l'environnement physique, qui a finalement conduit à une récupération progressive et au développement de précieuses étendues de pâturage. Au XIIe siècle, l'extraction du sel dans le marais septentrional de Gaywood, était déjà en déclin, et, au XIIIe siècle, son abandon coïncida certainement avec le détournement de la rivière Great Ouse dans le Lyn: le paysage fossilisé lié à l'activité d'extraction du sel fut relevé lors de l'arpentage des terres faisant l'objet du Gaywood Dragge de 1487. En outre, cette étude s'appuie sur des éléments comparatifs observés sur des sites continentaux similaires, avec une activité liée à l'extraction du sel au moyen de la technique du lavage du sable; ainsi qu'un réexamen de la documentation du côté Lincolnshire du Wash.

(Traduction: Séverine Bézie)

Zusammenfassung

Unter den modernen Wohngebieten von Gaywood, im städtischen Einzugsgebiet von King's Lynn, liegt eine ehemalige Salzmarsch – Gaywoods *North Marsh* – die einst eine wichtige Rolle bei der wirtschaftlichen und naturräumlichen Entwicklung dieser dynamischen Küsten- und Mündungslandschaft spielte. Auf der Ostseite des Wash und nördlich einer als „*The Lyn*" bekannt alten Einbuchtung gelegen, war dieses Marschgebiet reich an Salz – dem "weißem Gold" – gewesen, das aus salzgesättigten Sedimenten gewonnen und mit der nachrömischen Technik des „Sandwaschens" hergestellt wurde. Oft sind die einzigen von dieser einst bedeutsamen Küstenindustrie zurückgelassenen Spuren die vegetationslosen Hügel oder „*mounds*", die die aufgehäuften Abfallprodukte der Salzgewinnung darstellen. Dutzende von ihnen wurden in diesem Gebiet kartiert. Die Gelegenheit zur Untersuchung mehrere dieser Salinenhügel ergab sich mit dem Bau der Lynnsport und Greenpark Avenue Primary School, was in einem dreijährigen Arbeitsprogramm mit topographischen Vermessungen, Suchgräben und gezielten Ausgrabungen resultierte.

Aufbauend auf früheren Arbeiten von Oxford Archaeology in der Marsh Lane, bietet der vorliegende Band einen synthetischen Überblick über die Nachweise der Salzgewinnung unter Einsatz naturwissenschaftlicher Techniken, die durch historische Forschungen und Bayessche Modellierung untermauert werden und zum Ziel haben, die natürliche Umwelt der Salzmarsch und ihre Veränderung im Laufe der Zeit zu rekonstruieren. Eines der Schlüsselergebnisse war der sichere Nachweis, dass die Methode des „Sandwaschens" oder „*Sleeching*" bereits in mittelsächsischen Zeit (8. bis 9. Jahrhundert) an der Ostküste Englands verwendet wurde und dann bis ins Mittelalter und stellenweise darüber hinaus gebräuchlich blieb. Eine mögliche Verbindung zu der "Produktionsstätte" von Bawsey aus der mittelsächsischen Zeit wird ebenso untersucht wie die eindeutigere Verbindung zu den Bischöfen von Ostanglien und Norwich, denen dieses Land einst gehörte. Damit verbunden waren die Bereitstellung von Arbeitskräften, Transportmitteln und der Zugang zu Brennstoff. Der Beitrag der Salzherstellung zur Wirtschaft, insbesondere zum Handel, wird ebenso bewertet wie die Auswirkungen, die diese Salzproduktion von industriellem Ausmaß auf die physische Umwelt hatte, was letztendlich zu einer zerstückelten Landgewinnung und zur Erschließung wertvoller Weideflächen führte. Im 12. Jahrhundert war die Salzgewinnung in Gaywoods *North Marsh* bereits rückläufig. Die Totenglocke läutete ihr zweifellos mit der Umleitung des Flusses *Great Ouse* in den *Lyn* im 13. Jahrhundert. Die nunmehr „fossile" Salzgewinnungslandschaft wurde im *Gaywood Dragge Survey* von 1487 aufgezeichnet. Die vorliegende Darstellung ist zusätzlich angereichert mit Vergleichen zu ähnlichen Quellen zur Salzgewinnung durch „*sandwashing*" vom nahen Kontinent, unter Einbeziehung der Nachweise von der in Lincolnshire gelegenen Seite des *Wash*.

(Übersetzung: Christof Heistermann)

Chapter 1. Introduction
by Graeme Clarke and Matt Brudenell, with Simon Timberlake

I. Project background
(Figs 1.1–1.4)

In 2020 Oxford Archaeology (OA) East was commissioned to publish the Anglo-Saxon and medieval salt-making remains (salterns) investigated at four adjacent development-led archaeological sites in Gaywood, King's Lynn. The projects were a partnership between the Borough Council of King's Lynn and West Norfolk, who owned the land, Lovell Partnerships Ltd (Lovell; Lynnsport sites) and NPS Property Consultants Ltd (NPS; Greenpark Avenue Primary School site). Located in areas of overgrown scrubland (c.4m OD) surrounded by modern residential development, the sites lay roughly 2.2km east of the current course of the River Great Ouse (Figs 1.1–1.3). They were all subject to evaluation trenching and excavation between February 2017 and September 2019 (Table 1.1). The Lynnsport excavations commissioned by Lovell took place on three sites at: Aconite Road (Lynnsport 1: ENF145343; Blackbourn 2019), Front Way (Lynnsport 3; ENF145065; Kwiatkowska 2020) and Greenpark Avenue (Lynnsport 4 & 5: ENF141949; Clarke 2017). Following further consultation, Lynnsport 2 was subsequently removed from the development plans. The investigation commissioned by NPS was undertaken at Greenpark Avenue Primary School site (ENF145594; Knight and Clarke 2019). This lay immediately adjacent to the Lynnsport sites and soon after the fieldwork was completed a decision was taken that these two projects should be published together, incorporating evidence from relevant surrounding excavations, notably Marsh Lane (Clarke and Clarke 2018). Both the Lynnsport sites and the Greenpark Avenue Primary School site archives will be deposited with Norfolk Castle Museum under a single umbrella Accession number: NWHCM 2018.151.

Once part of a saltmarsh known as the North Marsh in the lordship of Gaywood, the sites were located within a landscape focused on the Wash and to the north of an ancient coastal inlet ('Lena' meaning 'the Lyn' or 'Lin' from which the settlement at King's (formerly Bishop's) Lynn takes its name) where salt-making once flourished. Salt production was an important element of the economy of the Wash region from prehistoric times through to the Roman and medieval periods. This was a valuable commodity produced largely for domestic consumption and as a preservative for foodstuffs, as well as being a medium of exchange (Lane and Morris 2001, 402–4). The remains of this industry primarily take the form of saltern mounds (comprising waste sand from salt filtration in the 'sand-washing' process), some of which still survive as earthworks, or are visible on aerial photographs as pale oval or floriform soilmarks flanking the Lincolnshire and Norfolk Wash coastlines. A swathe of saltern mounds extends around North Lynn and Gaywood, where the current sites were located, and which were initially identified and recorded by the Norfolk National Mapping Programme (NNMP) survey (Fig. 1.4; Albone et al. 2007, 116). This group not only reflects the scale of the salt industry in this area, but also demonstrates how the associated land reclamation impacted this landscape.

Despite the large number of salterns identified around the Norfolk coast, relatively few have been excavated and fewer still have been published, especially in comparison with Lincolnshire. Until recently, most of the saltern mounds in the Gaywood/North Marsh area were thought to be predominantly medieval in origin; however, one of the key results of the Lynnsport project and adjacent investigation at Marsh Lane, Gaywood (Clarke and Clarke 2018) has been to demonstrate, largely through radiocarbon assay, that the origins of medieval salt production in this area lay in the Anglo-Saxon period, beginning as early as the c.8th century and continuing into the 12th or possibly 13th century. Together, these excavations make a significant contribution to the study of this once important coastal industry, particularly in terms of chronology and technology, but also in relation to understanding the wider economic, social and environmental context.

II. Post-Roman salterns on the Wash: overview of previous work
(Fig. 1.4)

Prior to the Lynnsport and Marsh Lane excavations, what was known of Anglo-Saxon salt production on the Norfolk Wash lay wholly within Domesday Book (Bell et al. 1999, ix–x). Recent excavations in Lincolnshire had, however, unearthed briquetage (a coarse ceramic material used to make evaporation vessels and supporting pillars used in extracting salt from brine or seawater) associated with an 8th/9th-century island settlement site at Fishtoft, which represents the main evidence for salt-making on the Lincolnshire Wash coastline during the Middle Anglo-Saxon period. Although this site did not reveal any salt-making features, the character of the briquetage recovered was suggestive of a late survival of Romano-British methods of salt production (Cope-Faulkner 2012; Lane 2018, 83–4).

It has long been recognised in Lincolnshire that a major evolution in the process of salt-making had come to pass at some point during the Anglo-Saxon period that broke with the Romano-British method of boiling seawater and instead employed a process

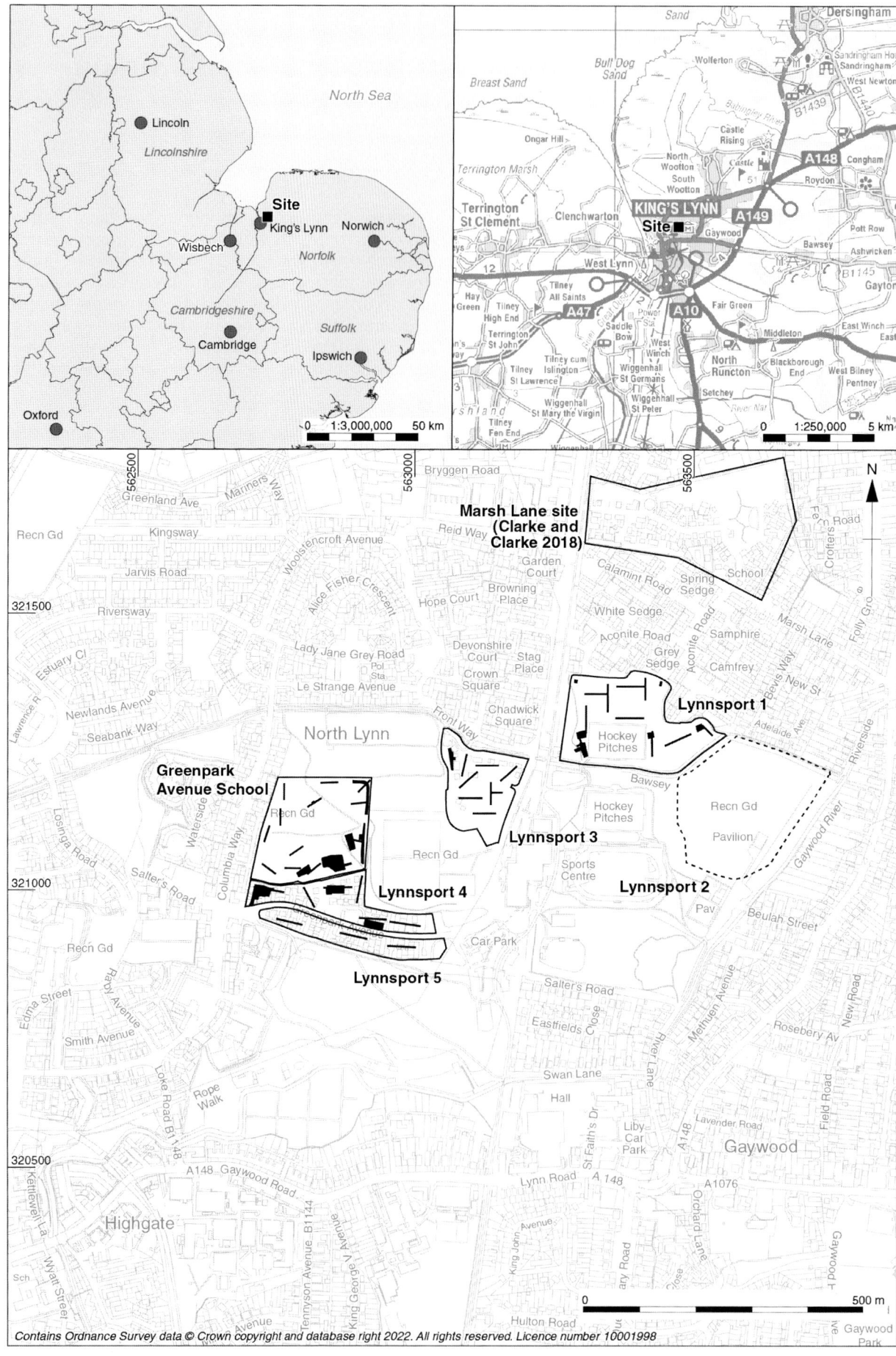

Figure 1.1 Location map showing Lynnsport and Greenpark Avenue School sites. Scale 1:10,000

Common name	Site name	Fieldwork date	National Grid Reference	Event number	OASIS	OA East Report No.	URL link to OA library	Archive receiving body
Marsh Lane	Marsh Lane watching brief	Dec. 2014 – Jan. 2015	TF 6349 2177	ENF135847	oxfordar3-219959	1820	https://eprints.oxfordarchaeology.com/3124/	Norfolk Castle Museum under Accession No.: NWHCM2016.201
	Marsh Lane evaluation	8–11 June 2015	TF 6352 2166	ENF137497	oxfordar3-210763	1799	https://eprints.oxfordarchaeology.com/3131/	
	Marsh Lane excavation	26 May – 28 July 2015	TF 6331 2163	ENF137496	oxfordar3-229639	1866	https://eprints.thehumanjourney.net/3125/	
Lynnsport	Lynnsport 1 evaluation	8–14 May 2018	TF 6337 2128	ENF139745	oxfordar3-238601	2213	https://eprints.oxfordarchaeology.com/4154/	Norfolk Castle Museum under Accession No.: NWHCM2018.151
	Lynnsport 1 excavation	14 Jan. – 1 Feb. 2019		ENF145343	oxfordar3-363781	2305	https://eprints.oxfordarchaeology.com/6044/	
	Lynnsport 3 evaluation	9–11 April 2018	TF 6313 2120	ENF138254	oxfordar3-215427	2197	https://eprints.oxfordarchaeology.com/6042/	
	Lynnsport 3 excavation	12–18 Sep. 2019		ENF145065	oxfordar3-379308	2380	https://eprints.oxfordarchaeology.com/6045/	
	Lynnsport 4 & 5 evaluation	27 Feb. – 3 March 2017	TF 6290 2097	ENF139746	oxfordar3-238605	2059	https://eprints.oxfordarchaeology.com/6046/	
	Lynnsport 4 & 5 excavation	3 April – 4 May 2017		ENF141949	oxfordar3-285004	2078	https://eprints.oxfordarchaeology.com/3468/	
Greenpark	Greenpark Avenue Primary School topographical survey and evaluation	15–23 Feb. 2018	TF 6278 2124	ENF143325-6	oxfordar3-308730	2194	https://eprints.oxfordarchaeology.com/3957/	Norfolk Castle Museum under Accession No.: NWHCM2018.151
	Greenpark Avenue Primary School excavation	4 Feb. – 5 March 2019		ENF145594	oxfordar3-371121	2308	https://eprints.oxfordarchaeology.com/6047/	

Table 1.1 Reporting of the Marsh Lane, Lynnsport and Greenpark Avenue School development sites

Figure 1.2 The Lynnsport 3 site, looking south

Figure 1.3 The Greenpark Avenue School site, looking west towards Saltern 5

of boiling a more salt-saturated liquor derived from sand-washing. Along the Lincolnshire Wash, the sand-washing method appears to have developed from at least the 11th century, although most of the excavated examples are later in date. These include the excavation of four 14th-century brine boiling hearths at Bicker Haven (Healey 1975; Healey 1999) and a series of 15th/16th-century filtration units (tanks within which coastal muds were 'washed' of their salt content) at Wainfleet St Mary (McAvoy 1994). These works, alongside smaller excavations of medieval salt-making features found in their vicinity, have recently been revisited in a report by Tom Lane (2018, 84–94). The latter also utilised LIDAR imagery further to demonstrate how the coastal advancement of this medieval industry has become fossilised in the topography as impressive groups of waste mounds — comprising desalinated sand — centred on the Holbeach Hurn/Gedney Dyke, Spalding area, Bicker Haven, and extending between Wrangle and Wainfleet St Mary (Lane 2018, fig. 19). The broadly uniform width of this salt-making zone aligns with a stretch of coastline devoid of any notable riverine influence, whereas the remaining zones (excluding the sheltered bay of Holbeach Hurn/Gedney Dyke) extend in a more amorphous fashion from the once tidal reaches of the Welland, Glen and (formerly navigable) Old Eau rivers (Lane 2018, 119).

Despite the plethora of saltern mounds recorded by the NNMP between Snettisham and King's Lynn, this Norfolk side of the Wash had until recently seen relatively little excavation of these relict features. Some 63 possible saltern mound sites are referred to in the Norfolk Historic Environment Record (NHER) extending in a roughly north-to-south swathe between South Wootton and the River Ouse (Fig. 1.4). The uneven distribution of known salterns on the former North Marsh (where the Lynnsport and Marsh Lane sites were located) that once flanked the Gaywood river north of King's Lynn probably reflects both the estuarine and shifting deltaic nature of this environment across the Anglo-Saxon and medieval periods. Although most of the saltern mounds were levelled in advance of housing development prior to 1975, some contemporary remains including briquetage, hearths and medieval (13th to 14th-century) pottery were recorded from the more northerly mounds (NHER sites 27122–27124 and 27127; Fig. 1.4). Limited excavation was undertaken in 1955 during house building on the Seabank Estate north of Bawsey Drain (and to the immediate north of the Greenpark Avenue School site), where two adjacent mounds were levelled and the traces of a furnace consisting of 'a structure of soft red brick and fused clay' were recorded during a watching brief undertaken by C. Lewton-Brain (NHER 5524). Another saltern mound (NHER 27897) at the north end of Hamburg Way was examined briefly by J. Wymer in 1989 (Johnson and Collcutt 2008, 8). In 2008 a desk-based assessment followed by a trench evaluation undertaken nearby at Hamburg Way, in the North Lynn Industrial Estate, revealed three superimposed saltern mounds (NHER 51419; Fig. 1.4; Timberlake 2008). The main mound was 1.9m thick in the centre and included laminae with traces of decomposed briquetage, charcoal/ash derived from peat burning on a hearth, and the remains of a possible sub-rectangular pit or water tank. A rim sherd of 14th/15th-century coarseware pottery was recovered from one of the smaller mounds, whilst from the earliest level, on a raised bank or small mound, were the remains of a briquetage structure similar to the pan supports described by Lane and Morris (2001). Evidence for medieval sand-washing has also recently come to light with the publication of a small investigation at the former Queen Mary's Nursing Home in King's Lynn, where the saltern appears to have been in operation during the 12th and 13th centuries (Cope-Faulkner 2014).

Of particular significance in terms of understanding the chronology of this industry on the Norfolk side of the Wash was the 2015 OA East excavation (ENF137496; Fig. 1.1; Table 1.1) of a saltern mound (NHER 27899; Fig. 1.4) at Marsh Lane, Gaywood. This revealed the same array of features typified at salterns excavated in both Lincolnshire and Norfolk, but demonstrated that the origins of this 'medieval' salt-winning tradition of sand-washing firmly lay in the Middle to Late Anglo-Saxon period (see below and Clarke and Clarke 2018).

III. The OA East excavation at Marsh Lane

The Middle to Late Anglo-Saxon salt-making site identified at Marsh Lane on Gaywood's North Marsh corroborated documentary evidence provided by Domesday Book for the existence of a well-developed salt-making industry within the estate of the bishops of East Anglia prior to the Norman Conquest (Clarke 2016; Clarke and Clarke 2018). The authors of the recently-published article postulated that, given the organisational ability of the church, control of salt-making could perhaps have stretched back to the first monastic boom of the late 7th century. Whether this resource was tied to the bishops prior to the Danish invasions of the 9th century or was part of a more localised exploitation controlled by the putative monastic 'productive' sites of West Norfolk was also considered. Radiocarbon determinations suggested that salt-winning may have commenced as early as the 8th or even late 7th century and continued until the mid-10th century at this site, followed by a period of abandonment of perhaps a century to around the time of the Norman Conquest, when the same salt-making processes were resumed.

The earliest group of features (filtration units) lay on the saltmarsh at a height of between 2.1–2.5m OD and were radiocarbon dated to 670–890 cal AD (95% confidence; SUERC–65063; 1225±35BP). Charcoal recovered from an overlying layer of relict soil was radiocarbon dated to 900–1040 cal AD (95% confidence; SUERC–65057; 1033±35BP) to provide a dating bracket for a possible hiatus in salt production. These layers were succeeded by a second, more extensive group of features (filtration units) radiocarbon dated to 1020–1170 cal AD (95% confidence; SUERC–65064; 952±26) which demonstrated a striking similarity in morphology and dimensions to the earlier phase of salt-working features (see Chapter 4 and Appendix 2 for a review of the chronology). Patches of red and black charcoal-

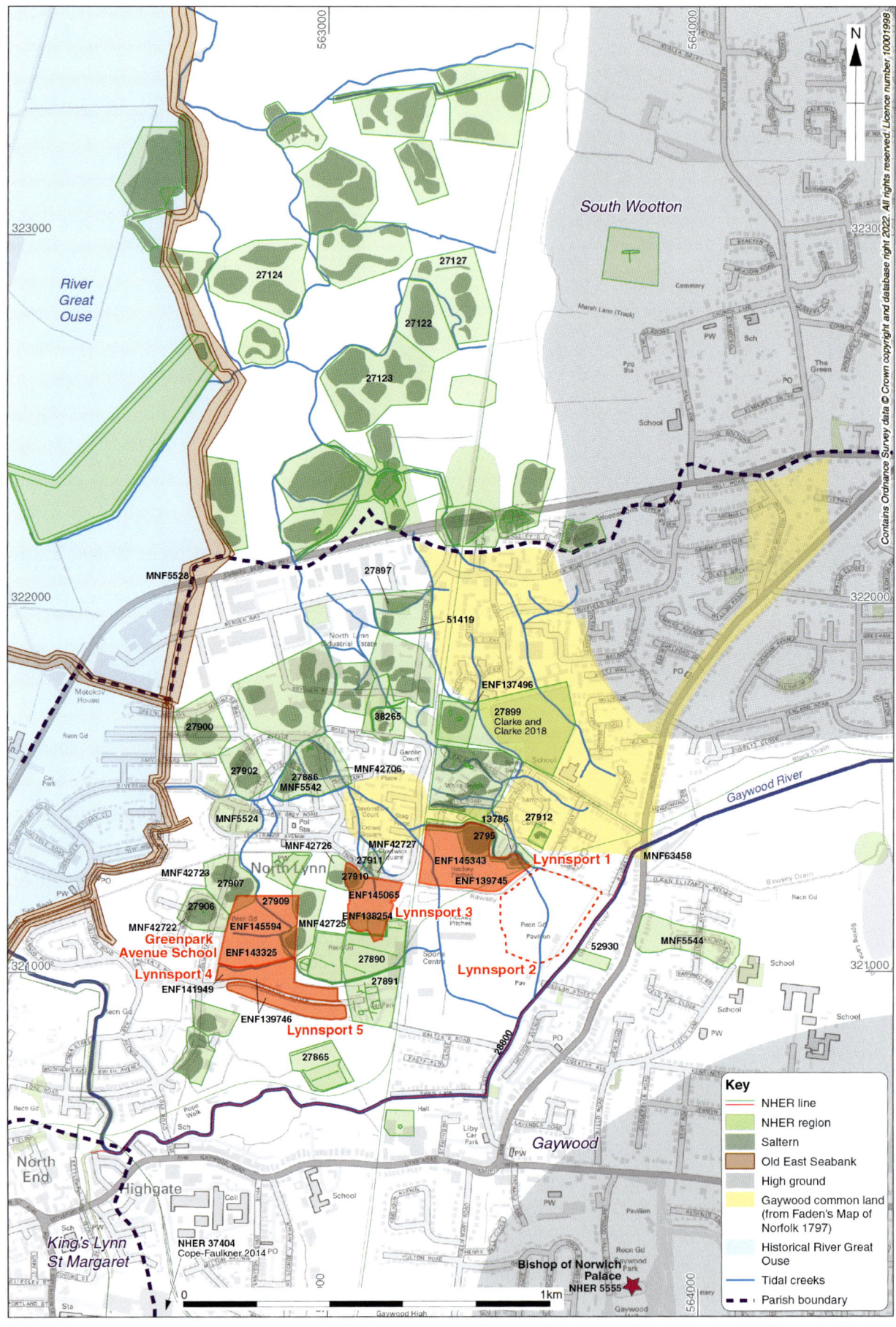

Figure 1.4 Map showing location of NHER records with NNMP data, including salterns (© Historic England National Mapping Programme, licensed to Norfolk County Council). Scale 1:15,000

rich earth interspersed between the filtration units produced a possible handmade clay wedge or support for a lead brine boiling pan. Associated sherds of Late Anglo-Saxon Thetford-type ware pottery (*c.* late 10th to 11th centuries) showed signs of burning with possible salt residues, suggesting that pots were also used in the salt-making process.

Within the upper part of the saltern were large amounts of slag and baked clay debris originating from decayed or deliberately broken-up brine boiling hearths, which included a soft-fired brick pan support. Sherds of early medieval ware (*c.*11th to 13th centuries) and Grimston coarseware pottery (*c.*12th to 13th centuries) were found which also displayed salt residues and signs of burning indicative of a continued use of pottery in the salt-making process during this later phase. There was no direct evidence for lead pans themselves (such as the lead scraps and off-cuts from repair), although chemical analysis of the slags and residues suggested their use on this site. Perhaps the most important discovery was the remains of four hearths immediately below the truncation level at *c.*3.2m OD. Two of the most well-preserved hearths displayed the same double-chambered morphology as the 13th-century example previously excavated at King's Lynn (Cope-Faulkner 2014). Early medieval ware pottery was recovered from the backfill of one of the two less well-preserved hearths, while the absence of any later pottery from this site indicates salt-making had ceased here by the mid-13th century.

IV. Lessons learned: formulating an excavation and reporting strategy
(Fig. 1.5)

To a large extent the Marsh Lane excavations were a learning process; a coming to terms with an approach of how best to examine saltern sites, how to map them, how to strip them, and how to excavate and sample them effectively. Though the geographic limits of the excavation were always set in relation to the development proposal and its impact on the archaeology, the process of undertaking the works was a steep learning curve – one in which flexibility and an experimental attitude of trial and error ultimately proved key to getting to grips with the complexity of the deposits and the features layered within them. In this process, the evolving strategy benefitted enormously from the input of James Albone (formerly Norfolk County Council Historic Environment Service), Steve Boreham (then of Cambridge University) and Mark Ruddy (then of Historic England), who encouraged a dynamic approach of 'seeing what worked' at Marsh Lane.

The space this afforded was crucial to building an understanding of the site and its sequence, though it must be stressed that this is never straightforward with salterns. Whilst salterns may be mapped or conceived as low-mounded earthworks with discernible summits and clearly defined edges, hinting at a measure of uniformity, the archaeological reality is far from this. Upon excavation, areas may present as having only thick bands of clean, sterile-looking dumps of weathered silts, sometimes with a visible laminated structure, at others, a homogenous mass hardly distinguishable from the natural mud flat deposits they sit upon. These silts have the habit of suddenly giving way to patches of blue-grey clay outlining pits and filtration units, or can be interrupted by tips of black ash and bright red hearth waste; these sometimes disappearing off at unexpected angles, occasionally with no relation to the wider gradient of the mound. In short, a somewhat chaotic arrangement of deposits often lies beneath the gentle time-weathered and plough-ravished profiles of the mound surfaces. This reflects their complex history of formation, tied to the shifting rhythms of working and relocation that occurred as waste silts accrued; the mounding in turn both constraining and enabling certain types of activity within the salt-winning process. The resulting architectures therefore have both 'slag heap' and 'Tell mound' qualities: a stratified mix of waste deposits and working areas, the ordering and location of which is unpredictable from the surface (Fig. 1.5).

As this realisation dawned during the excavations at Marsh Lane, it became apparent that careful machining was the key to an effective excavation strategy. The waste silts in the site were subsequently lowered in machined spits until features were revealed indicating working areas: pits, hearths, filtration units, substantial dumps of hearth waste *etc*. The methodology therefore moved from one of chasing individual deposits at a 'horizontal' level, which was proving futile, to the focus on a 'vertical' strategy aimed at exposing and recording the sequence of deposits down to the pre-mound surface, stopping to expose and hand excavate any working areas revealed in that downward progression. The skill and confidence of the machine watchers (and machine drivers) was vital to the success of this, as was their familiarity with the character of the deposits. As the wider Lynnsport project began to take shape (see below), the value of this prior experience proved critical in subsequent fieldwork stages. Of key importance was the continuity in the personnel that OA East was able to deploy to the salterns. And as knowledge and understanding of the archaeology grew, the fieldwork became more efficient and effectively targeted.

Building the Lynnsport project: approach and ethos
The concept and delivery of a wider project on the Lynnsport salterns was several years in the making. Although it became clear by the summer of 2015 that planned redevelopment of the Lynnsport land would potentially impact on a number of mapped saltern sites (recorded by the National Mapping Programme), and would require archaeological investigation, the possibility that these could be linked into a wider project only began to solidify in early 2017. This possibility emerged from a meeting at the Marsh Lane site between representatives from Lovell (Darron Keen, Michael Saunders and Roger Bowers), the Norfolk County Council Historic Environment Service (NCCHES, James Albone), Borough Council of King's Lynn and West Norfolk (the land owners, represented by Dale Gagen) and OA East (Matt Brudenell and Paul Spoerry), where the programme and approach to the work was outlined and discussed. By this stage OA East had already been commissioned by Lovell to produce Written Schemes of Investigation (WSIs) for the trial trench evaluation of Lynnsport

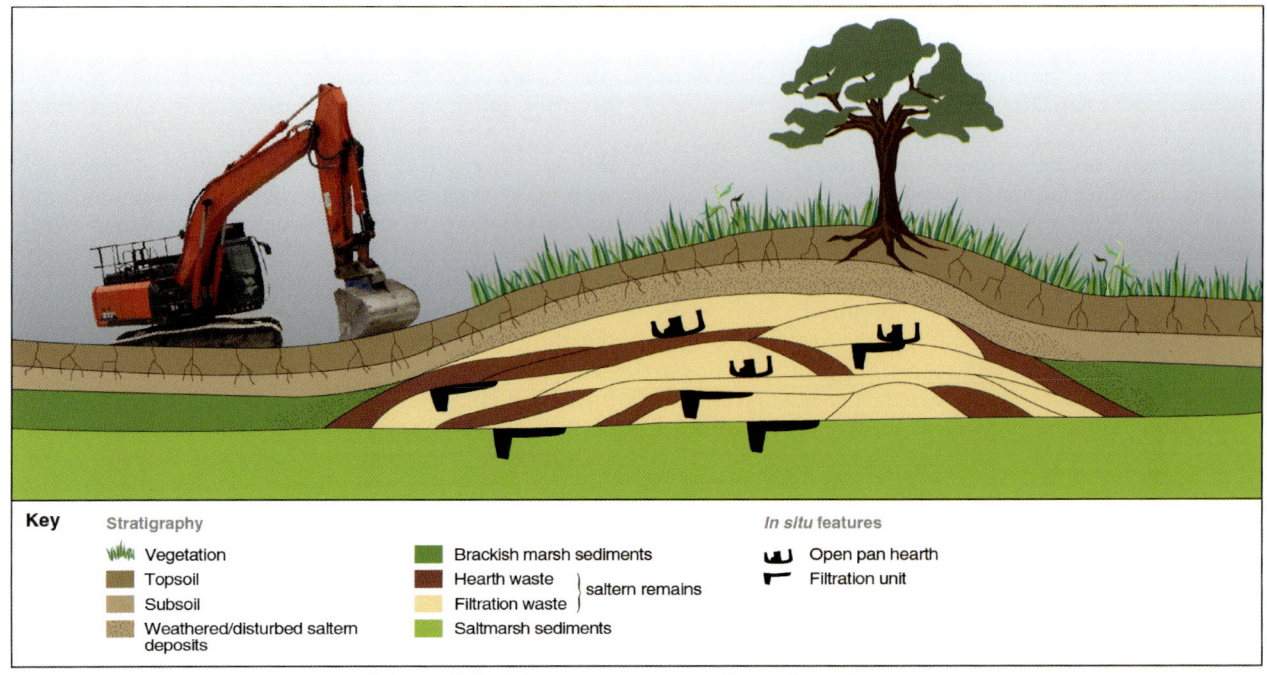

Figure 1.5 Schematic cross-section of a saltern

sites 1, 3, 4 & 5, all of which were approved by the NCCHES by the beginning of 2016. However, the Marsh Lane meeting made it clear that the sites were now likely to come forward for development in quick succession and would need to move from evaluation into mitigation, where needed, relatively rapidly.

By this stage, work on the Marsh Lane post-excavation was well advanced, with the assessment and archive report already completed and plans afoot to publish the results in *Norfolk Archaeology* journal (Clarke and Clarke 2018). Nonetheless, the research potential afforded by the opportunity to investigate a series of salterns in proximity was immediately apparent. Though none of the proposed development sites were vast, and therefore the individual investigations were always going to be relatively limited in scale, they still presented the opportunity to build a landscape picture of the salt-making industry and its development in the North Marsh area. As such, the combined value of an overarching project was recognised as being greater than the sum of its individual parts. Furthermore, there were cost-efficiencies to be gained by adopting a wider joined-up strategy, which was attractive to Lovell, who could see the financial benefits and appreciate the objectives and outcomes of works delivered under a coherent plan.

The first full expression of the wider Lynnsport project objectives were set out in an overarching WSI prepared in the autumn of 2017 (Brudenell and Clarke 2017), by which time the evaluation and excavation of Lynnsport 4 & 5 had already been undertaken (under their own WSIs). This overarching document was to frame the project as a whole (superseding earlier WSIs) and would sit above future site-specific WSIs going forward. The document also set out the ambition to publish a monograph on the collective results, with each site being reported to post-excavation assessment level first. Though it was originally envisaged that a combined archive report covering all sites would be produced prior to publication, it was subsequently agreed to expand the detail of each site assessment report instead (to include full reporting on results of analysis undertaken), and concentrate time and funds on the production of a synthetic monograph.

In 2018 the project expanded to include the Lynnsport Primary School site (adjacent to Lynnsport 4 & 5), which was being developed by NPS. Again, dialogue and a spirit of positive engagement between NPS (Richard Pollard), the NCCHES (James Albone) and OA East (Matt Brudenell), saw the archaeological works brought under the umbrella of the Lynnsport project and its wider objectives (and WSI). The excavations which followed ran in parallel with those at Lynnsport 1, with the final stages of work conducted at Lynnsport 3 in early autumn 2019. By the close of fieldwork, a total of twelve salterns had been examined by the project, seven of which were unknown just two years earlier.

Building on the overarching WSI, a publication synopsis was submitted to the EAA editorial board in May 2020 (Clarke and Clarke 2020), proposing the research-led focus and thematic structure of the publication: this was well received and culminated in the production of the present volume.

Upon reflection, the Lynnsport project was arguably born out of a serendipitous convergence of interests and opportunities that emerged in 2017. This could have been very different, and it is easy to imagine a situation where each of the Lynnsport sites would have been subject to excavation by different archaeological contractors instructed by different clients over a number of years. Such carving-up of landscapes in this manner is sadly commonplace, and would surely have produced a very different archaeological outcome had these been delivered as a series of stand-alone projects following the conventional excavation and reporting formats. Yet credit should be given to the foresight of the NCCHES, particularly James

Albone, for facilitating the emergence of the project and encouraging the joined-up framework ultimately adopted. The investigations which followed are testimony to what can be achieved by collaborative working in the industry (between clients, contractors and local authority archaeologists), seizing the opportunities, where presented, to bring forward projects at an early stage with thoughtful scopes. Here, the lessons learnt from Marsh Lane were obviously of benefit, and as each investigation unfolded, there was a feed-back loop in terms of what methods or approaches worked, and what could be tried differently next time. As such, the methodology was never tethered by an overly prescriptive adherence to a written strategy, but was guided by what might answer questions and what achieved the best results. The experimental 'ethos' of the Marsh Lane excavations was therefore carried forward in the Lynnsport project in a dynamic way by the field teams directed by Graeme Clarke, Kat Blackbourn, Toby Knight, and Malgorzata Kwiatkowska. It also saw OA East deploy a suite of scientific approaches and sampling methods to try to tease new details from the salterns, the results of which are synthesised in this volume. Not all were successful, but the picture that emerges from these collective endeavours is genuinely new, insightful, and exciting.

V. The developing research agenda
(Fig. 1.6)

Research aims and objectives
Informed by the previous OA East excavation of the saltern found at Marsh Lane described above, a comprehensive suite of site-specific research aims and objectives was formulated at the outset of the current investigations (Brudenell and Clarke 2017), which were updated as part of the reporting for each excavation stage (Table 1.1). The overarching aims being to:
- establish the date of the industry – both the overall date range of the salt-making industry at Lynn and the date that it was functioning at specific locations; and
- obtain a better understanding of the salt-making process and identify any methodological or technological changes over time.

Themes
The site-specific research objectives were sub-divided into a variety of categories relating to the salt-making industry. These were collated and refined as a series of themes (many of which inevitably overlap to some degree) for the publication synopsis (Clarke and Clarke 2020) and which can be used to draw together the various strands of evidence for Anglo-Saxon and early medieval salt-winning on the Lyn (Fig. 1.6).

Reconstructing the marshland environment
Although not a specific objective, the investigations have provided some insight into the development of the saltmarsh prior to and during the period of salt-winning. The combined analysis of pollen, ostracods, foraminifera, mollusca, micromorphology and geoarchaeology can help to reconstruct the immediate marshland environment prior to salt-winning and demonstrate how it changed as a result of both man-made and natural agencies.

Chronology
Establishing a chronology for the salterns was a key project aim and this has been achieved through a combination of ceramic dating, radiocarbon analysis and archaeomagnetic dating. This research is of particular significance as it has 'pushed back' the presumed date of salt-winning in this part of the Wash by several hundred years to the late 8th century (but perhaps focused on the 9th to 10th centuries), which may have implications for dating other salterns in the area and wider region.

Ownership and organisation
Exploring the influences behind the origin and development of salt-winning in this part of the Wash is a significant area of research, especially given the early date that the industry was established here. It is documented in Little Domesday that at the time of the Norman Conquest the town and lordship of Gaywode (Gaywood) — where the salterns lay — belonged to Almar, Bishop of Elmham, subsequently passing to the Bishop of Thetford and then Norwich (Blomefield 1808, 419). Understanding the scale of production will also help to elucidate the level of organisation involved and the range of additional resources required to make salt (fuel, transportation, labour *etc.*).

Process and technology
The salt-winning process via sand-washing or 'sleeching' is fairly well documented for medieval sites in the region, notably in Lincolnshire on the other side of the Wash Basin (*e.g.* McAvoy 1994) and closer-by at the former Queen Mary's Nursing Home (Cope-Faulkner 2014) and Marsh Lane sites (Clarke and Clarke 2018), although the Lynnsport excavations have demonstrated that some of the associated processes are perhaps earlier than previously thought. The morphology and layout of the features can be compared with similar evidence from other regional salt-working sites (and possibly the near continent) to help understand the processes and technologies involved, from where these may have originated and how they may have been adapted over time. Underpinning this is the analysis of the pollen, ostracods, foraminifera and other remains.

Continuity and change
A major consequence of the salt industry was the resultant reclamation of the marsh, creating valuable grazing land and altering the coastline forever. Salt-working would have been vulnerable to climate and environmental change, including sea level rises: with many documented storm surges occurring during the 11th century (Simmons 2015), evidence of marine incursions may be discernible within the mound sequences. Other changes included the creation of sea banks and channels, while political fluctuations would also have been a major factor, not least the Norman Conquest and the resultant changes in land ownership and organisation. The diversion of the Great Ouse to King's (Bishop's) Lynn in the 13th century would

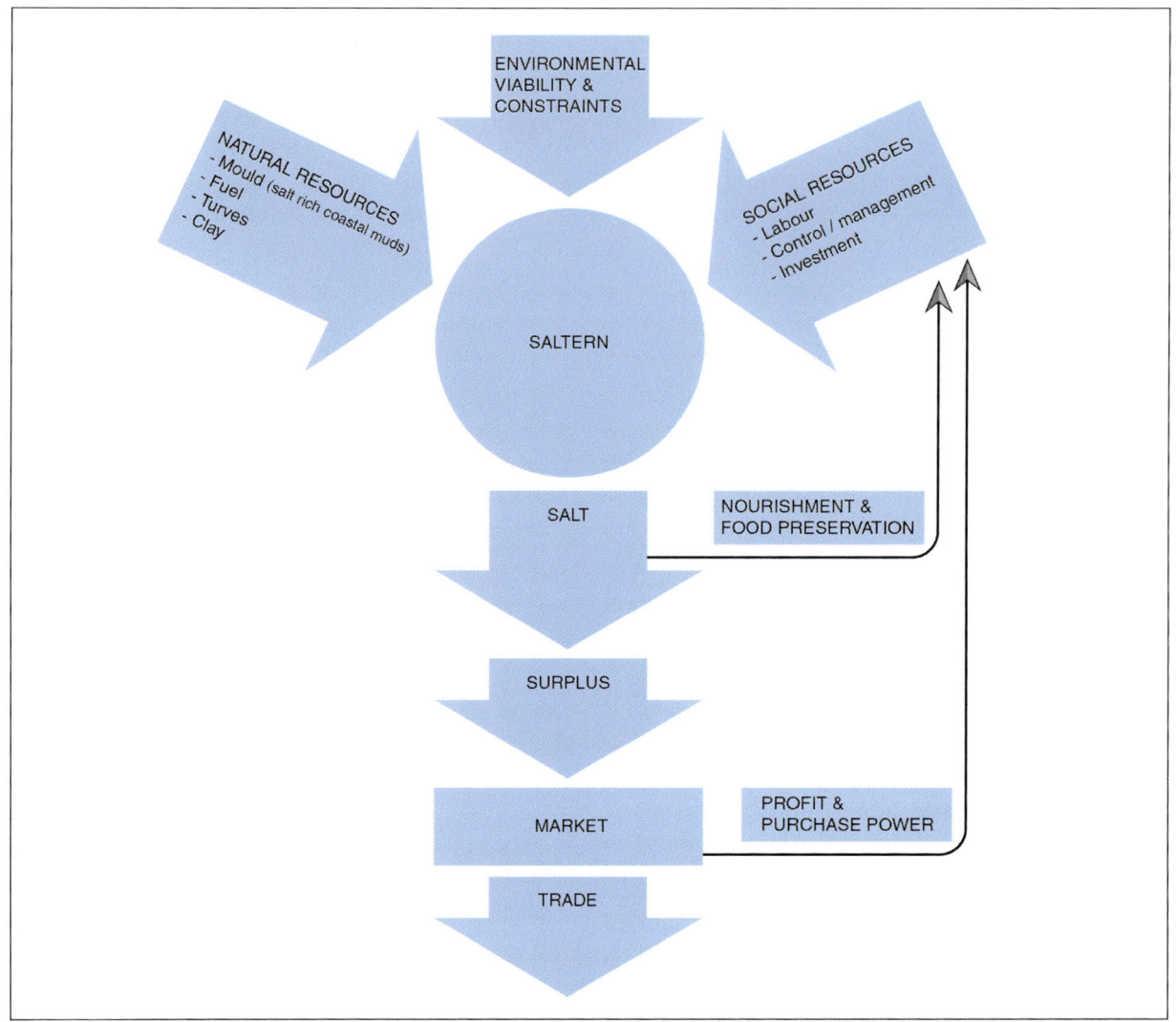

Figure 1.6 Visualising the themes: the flow of a basic input and output model of a viable saltern

probably have had a significant impact, while the raising of ramparts around the town may also have had a detrimental effect.

Social and historical context
Little is known about the salt workers themselves. For much or all of the period of operation of the excavated salterns, this area appears to have been under ecclesiastical ownership, although it is not clear if the salt workers were tenants or were required to work the salterns, presumably on a seasonal basis around other activities such as farming. Later documents suggest that whole families may have been involved in the process, and it is possible that this was the case for these early salterns.

Salt and the Late Anglo-Saxon and medieval economy
The importance of salt to the economy cannot be overstated and has been discussed elsewhere. Archaeology clearly has a role to play in terms of 'fleshing out' the historical sources and adding detail in terms of the technology, chronology and organisation of the industry on a more local scale. In particular, the relationship of this salt industry to the ecclesiastical houses and the development of the port at Bishop's Lynn is of particular interest in terms of its economic impact, as are potential links with Lincolnshire and the nearby continent.

Regional Research Frameworks
The related themes contribute to relevant goals of the Regional Research Frameworks pertinent to this area (Brown and Glazebrook 2000; Medlycott 2011). Specific themes drawn from these documents include:
- The need to increase understanding of the importance of this industry to the origin, economy and commerce of Bishop's (King's) Lynn
- To explore the extent to which the development of salt-making on the North Marsh was linked with the growing urban sphere of production within the town (and port) itself
- To examine how closely salt-making was allied with the needs of this town's growing number of inhabitants
- The need to consider the impact of changing political relationships between the town's burghers and church institutions (ecclesiastical see, priory, parochial church and hospitals) on salt-making
- To determine how pervasive the economic and organisational powers of the church were in

influencing the initiation, growth and maintenance of this industry
- Within the wider sphere of Norfolk, parallels may be drawn between the distribution of saltern mounds recorded by the Norfolk Coast and Broads NMP projects on the Wash with those of Breydon Water and the former Great Estuary
- The need for a wider, county-wide viewpoint on any commonality between the presence of more intensive/industrial-scale salt-making sites and the growth of early coastal towns or church foundations.

Research questions

Building on these themes and the site-specific research objectives, a series of related research questions was identified and these are summarised below.

The influence of the Church
- Given the scale of salt-winning and resources required, is there a link between the origin of salt-making at Gaywood and the postulated Middle Anglo-Saxon monastic foundation/high status site at Bawsey (Pestell 2004)?
- Did the associated process of mound building contribute to the decline of Bawsey and a possible shift of the settlement focused on the Gaywood river during the Late Anglo-Saxon period?
- Were the salterns in monastic ownership throughout their period of use?

Relationship with Gaywood and King's (Bishop's) Lynn
- How does this industry relate to the recently emerging evidence for a significant Middle Anglo-Saxon 'gateway' trading post/settlement on the Lyn (Collins 2018)?
- Did this salt industry contribute to the development of the major port and commercial centre at Lynn, first developed by the bishops of Norwich in the late 11th century?

The saltmarsh
- Can documentary sources, combined with the excavated evidence, including environmental indicators (pollen; foraminifera *etc.*), cast light on how environmental and man-made changes impacted this coastal community and the salt industry in particular?
- Using the same strands of evidence, is it possible to reconstruct the saltmarsh environment and how this landscape was managed?

Salt-making methods
- Building on previous work at Marsh Lane, how far does the uniformity in the salt-making process across these sites reflect a standard 'tool kit' approach?
- Can any evolution in terms of technology or approach be discerned in the stratigraphic sequence and associated evidence between the 8th and 12th centuries?
- Was this method imported from Lincolnshire or vice versa? Can contemporary parallels be found across the North Sea basin or was this method indigenous to the Wash?

Chronology
- Can additional radiocarbon dating and Bayesian modelling help to define a tighter chronological sequence within the salterns themselves?

Salt-makers and the North Marsh in the historical narrative
- What can the documented passing of rights over salterns between the bishop and his priory at the beginning of the 12th, and again at the beginning of the 13th centuries, reveal about the changing situation of salt-making in the North Marsh?
- To what extent does the Gaywood Dragge survey of these plots in 1487 preserve the topography of this now vanished industry?

Change
- When and why were the excavated salterns abandoned and what was their fate?

VI. Structure of this report

A review of the known evidence for Anglo-Saxon settlement (lay and ecclesiastical) on the Lyn inlet will be presented in Chapter 2. This will not be a comprehensive survey but an introduction to the record with the production of salt as a starting point: its relationship to the surrounding communities, the implications for the wider economy and possible apparatus of control by the church and aristocracy during this early period. Chapter 3 is a synthetic narrative focusing on the development of the natural saltmarsh upon which salt-making took place, largely gleaned from targeted scientific analysis. Chapter 4 provides a stratigraphic narrative for the saltern mounds in relation to the scientific dating, artefactual and ecofactual evidence. The few sherds of pottery recovered from these sites, along with radiocarbon determinations and archaeomagnetic dating, strongly suggest the salterns may represent two broadly chronologically distinct groups related to historic routes into the North Marsh. Within these two groups, the remains are described thematically in respect to each successive stage in the sand-washing process.

Chapter 5 focuses on the historical narrative of Lynn and outlines the establishment of the market and new town at the end of the 11th century, during the later heyday of salt-making on the North Marsh, and the major influence of the Bishop of Norwich in shaping this part of East Anglia. The arrival of the Great Ouse in the 13th century heralded the decline of the salt industry here, a major legacy of which was the creation of a valuable tract of reclaimed saltmarsh pasture. Each of the thematic chapters concludes with a discussion which feeds into an overarching consideration of the wider context in Chapter 6, including a review from the Lincolnshire side of the Wash. A glossary is included as Appendix 1, which explains the terminology used in this report with particular reference to the salt-winning process. Appendix 2 provides details of the radiocarbon dating analysis and Appendix 3 outlines the various methodologies employed by the contributing specialists. Appendix 4 includes a translation of an extract from Diderot *et al.*'s (1765) text describing the sand-washing process at the 18th-century coastal saltworks of Lower Normandy and Appendix 5 is an extract from William Dugdale's (1605–86) *Monasticon Anglicanum* (Dugdale *et al.* 1846) on the Endowment of St Margaret's Priory, Bishop's Lynn, including lands in Gaywood.

Chapter 2. Shaping an Anglo-Saxon Landscape on the Lyn

The auntient Brittaines called its name Le Hin
From many waters meeting, now called Lin,
The waters fresh and salt, doe both contende
Which shall espouse our Lyn, and yet no ende
Is put to their contention. Long armed Ouse
Many a mile travels her to espouse
Gathers an army in sundry shires, and comes
To carry her. Neptune still twice a day comes
To wash her shores...

(17th-century poem by Ben Adam, reproduced in Chambers (1829) from a book in Norwich Castle Museum entitled 'Lennae Redeuiua' [Rediviva])

I. Archaeological overview of the Lyn and its Anglo-Saxon environs
(Fig. 2.1)

Within the marine-laid siltlands of Norfolk to the west of the Lyn only a single Early Anglo-Saxon findspot is listed by the NHER, comprising sherds of handmade pottery recovered from fieldwalking at Tilney St Lawrence near to the northern margins of the peat fenland (Blinkhorn 2005, 213). This presumably reflects the situation during the initial post-Roman period when the coastal siltlands (marshland) were abandoned, with settlements initially being re-established on the fringes of the freshwater fen to the south (Rippon 2000, 177).

Several Ipswich ware pottery findspots have been recorded on the siltlands by the Fenland Survey that provide clear evidence for the colonisation of coastal saltmarshes during the Middle Anglo-Saxon period, between the mid 7th to 9th centuries (Silvester 1988, 158, fig. 113). Their distribution indicates that early settlement targeted banks of creeks naturally raised above the saltmarsh and the old riverbeds of more consolidated silts — roddons — which remained unaffected by marine inundation (Rippon 2000, 174). A notable concentration of nearly 1000 Ipswich-type ware sherds was recovered from investigations at Hay Green, Terrington St Clement (Rogerson and Silvester 1986, 320–2). Subsequent excavation of the sites of these scatters was carried out as part of the English Heritage funded Fenland Management Project in the Lincolnshire and Norfolk siltlands (Crowson *et al.* 2005). The evidence from this body of work showed that these pioneer communities practised a mixed farming system of both arable agriculture and the raising of cattle and sheep. The most salt-tolerant species of barley (six-row hulled barley) was grown alongside horse bean, pea and flax/linseed (Crowson *et al.* 2005, 95–6). Despite these sites being situated on tidal saltmarsh (Rippon 2000, 174), there was only slight evidence for salt-making at the site of Chopdike Drove, Gosberton in Lincolnshire. Here an 'industrial' phase of pits and ditches was revealed that contained ash and evidence of burning, including mauve-grey fired clay indicative of contact with saltwater at high temperatures (Crowson *et al.* 2005, 76; 294). Within the Norfolk siltlands permanent settlements were established within the six long narrow estates of Emneth, Walsoken, Walton, Walpole, Terrington and Islington/Tilney which extended between the coast and peat fen (Rippon 2000, 174).

Only a limited number of sites across the fenland appear to have witnessed continued occupation between the Middle and Late Anglo-Saxon periods (Crowson *et al.* 2005, 97). It has been proposed, based on the distribution of Middle Anglo-Saxon pottery findspots, that the Middle Anglo-Saxon settlements on the siltlands were all abandoned between the later 9th to early 10th centuries and the 11th century, with the populations relocated to new sites (Blinkhorn 2005, 213). The distribution of Late Anglo-Saxon pottery findspots suggests that these new settlements were advancing towards the coastal saltmarshes (Fig. 2.1). The former saltmarsh was first embanked by the Bardike sea wall (see below and Chapter 3) probably during the 10th century and later by the Sea Bank, which protruded further into the saltmarsh north of the Lyn to encompass the 10th-century foundation of Clenchwarton. The Late Anglo-Saxon settlement remains excavated at Terrington St Clement and West Walton were found to lie in wholly freshwater environments having been enveloped by sea defences by this time. The southern margins of the Lyn surrounding the parishes of Wiggenhall St Germans and Wiggenhall St Mary Magdalen were also probably later reclaimed portions of siltland. Domesday records that by the 11th century this extensive tract of protected siltland was a well-populated zone used for agriculture and pasture (Rippon 2000, 169 and 175).

To the east of the Lyn lay the very different landscape of Norfolk's Western Escarpment (see Pestell 2004, 14 fig. 3), a low chalk escarpment sloping west to east that forms a plateau of brown rendzina soils with a small number of shallow river valleys emptying into the Wash. An outcrop of Lower Greensand separates this area from the coastal strip along the eastern edge of the Wash, which includes a ridge of orange-brown 'carstone', a type of

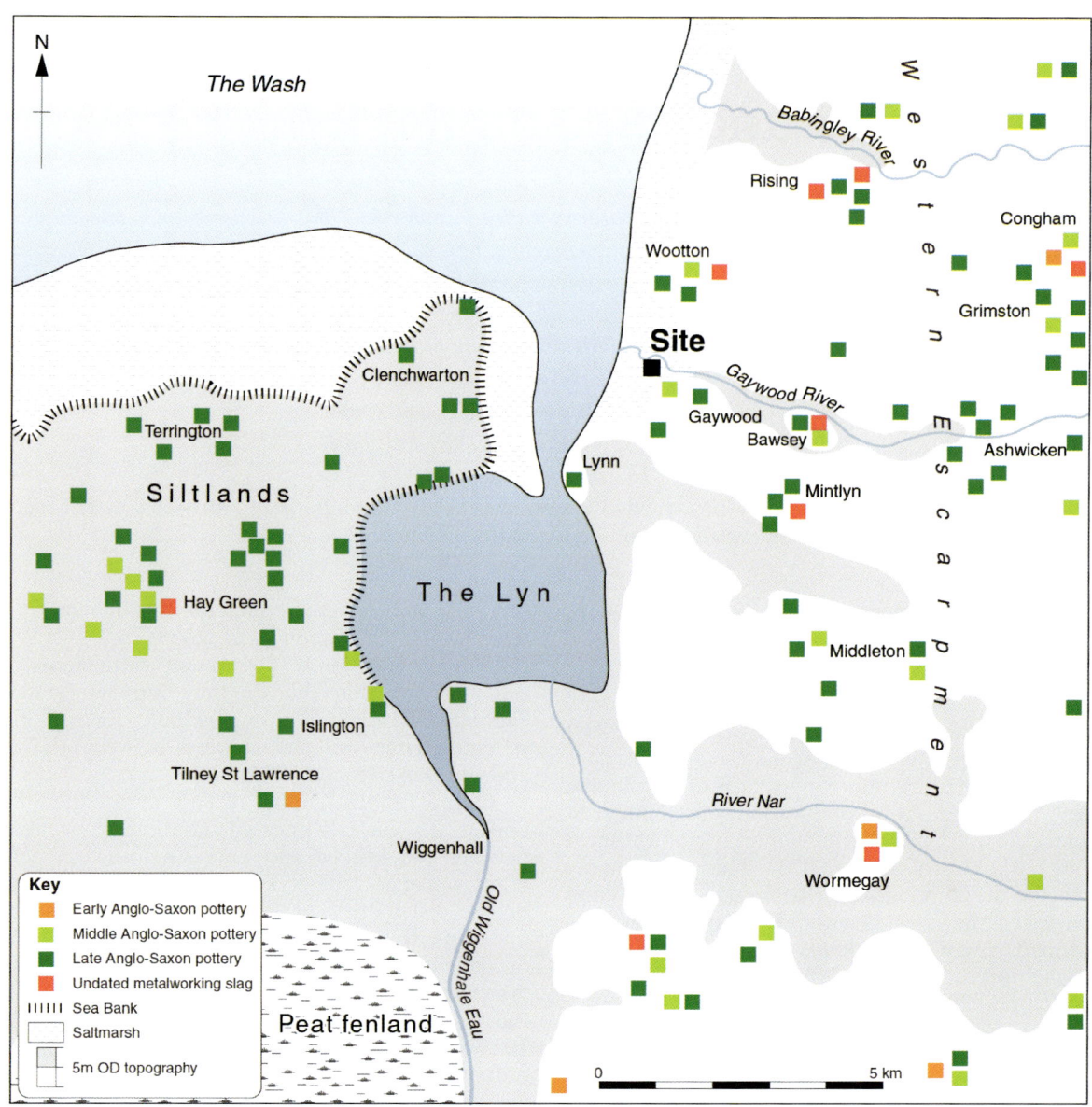

Figure 2.1 Distribution of Anglo-Saxon pottery and undated metalworking slag in the environs of the Lyn (based on information from www.heritagegateway.org.uk and https://magic.defra.gov.uk). Scale 1:125,000.

ferruginous sandstone (Chris Blandford Associates 2007, 10). The distribution of Anglo-Saxon pottery generally indicates a continuity of settlement across its later date span, congregating mainly around the present-day villages of Castle Rising, Grimston, Bawsey, North Wootton, Gaywood, Mintlyn, Middleton and Wormegay (Fig. 2.1). Undated surface findspots of iron-rich slag have also been recorded at many of these settlements, suggesting that the smelting of iron may have been an inherited skill from the Romans who are known to have dug ore from the widespread outcrops of Sandringham Sands in this part of Norfolk (Gallois *et al.* 1994, 1). A number of small Roman shaft furnaces that produced iron by direct smelting were revealed near Holt House Farm in the Ashwicken area to the south of the Gaywood river in the eastern part of this zone. Some unroasted nodules of limonite ore were also discovered, which is commonly found only on the Snettisham Clay with the nearest outcrops to the furnaces being at Brow-of-the-Hill and Ashwicken (Gallois *et al.* 1994, 180; Tylecote and Owles 1960, 142–62). The Mintlyn Beds sands and clays also contain bands of clay ironstone with sandy ironstone found in the Leziate Beds and Carstone (Gallois *et al.* 1994, 1).

II. Emerging 'gateway' and 'monastic' communities on the Lyn

'Gateway' Communities
(Fig. 2.1)

With its extensive river systems extending inland to the West Anglian Plain, the Wash was a natural highway for Early Anglo-Saxon incomers. The geological and soil make-up of each locality exploited by these early settlers would have had an important influence on the emerging Anglo-Saxon settlements. On entering the Lyn, incoming peoples would have been presented with a choice of settling the expanse of rich coastal siltlands to the west, turning east to the equally rich loamy soils of the Babingley, Gaywood and Nar valleys or continuing south into the peat fenland. Their choice may in part have been determined by the presence of remaining Romano-British settlements in the landscape. Within the Norfolk siltlands, the names of present-day villages such as Walpole, Walsoken and West Walton are thought to originate from the Anglo-Saxon term 'Welsh (*Walh*)-man' for Britons (Coles and Hall 1998, 66). Oosthuizen (2017, 43–46) has also dismissed — on chronological grounds — this group of sites having been named after the protective 'Sea Bank' (utilising the Anglo-Saxon *weall* for wall) which was probably constructed around the siltland in the 10th century. Furthermore, the notable Roman pottery concentrations found in the Norfolk siltlands, indicative of pre-existing scattered farming communities, are largely confined to these same parishes and are absent to the east (Waller 1994, 267; Silvester 1988).

It appears from the distribution of Early Anglo-Saxon settlement remains and findspots that the more sheltered edge of the peat fen and relatively higher spots on the siltland were preferred during this time of fairly stable sea levels. As the Early Anglo-Saxon centuries progressed into the Middle Anglo-Saxon period (*c.*AD 650–850) there was a deterioration in the stability of sea levels which may have driven a change in settlement pattern (Waller 1994, 61). The excavated farmsteads and surveyed surface scatters of debris attributed to this period are confined to roddons which presumably also provided sufficiently elevated land for agriculture (examples given in Silvester 1988, 158). The small quantity of metalwork items recovered from them has been taken as evidence for their low status (Waller 1994, 64). It was probably the peak rise in sea levels towards the end of the 9th century (which also marks the beginning of the Late Saxon period) that drove the construction of sea defences such as the Bardike and the Sea Bank on the western side of the Lyn. These large-scale flood defences (erroneously attributed 'Roman Bank' in the past) surrounded the whole of the Norfolk siltlands. Such impressive earthworks allowed for the full development of the siltland and successfully maintained this area as agricultural land into the medieval period (Waller 1994, 67).

In contrast to the siltland, Early Anglo-Saxons arriving to the east of the Lyn below the Norfolk escarpment would have encountered a patchwork of heathland, woodland, arable farmland and river valley environments due to this zone's more varied geology and surface topography (Gallois *et al.* 1994, 1). Early agricultural settlements may have first targeted the belt of free-draining sandy loam soils which underlie (from north to south) the present-day villages of Snettisham, Castle Rising, North Wootton, South Wootton and Gaywood. Hutcheson (2006, 101) noted that all of the pre-AD850 Anglo-Saxon finds in the area around King's Lynn came from the Gaywood area and included an 8th- or 9th-century brooch associated with an undated cemetery (Fig. 1.4, MNF5544). The rich peaty loam soils that fringe the rivers between these settlements would also have provided the necessary meadows for livestock. Further inland are successive belts of coarse acidic sand and thin lime-rich soils less suitable for agriculture. In particular, the broad swathe of this ground to the east of the Woottons probably remained forest, which at its southern end, within the parish of Gaywood, would emerge as the historical Reffley Wood (British Geological Survey 2023).

Although the present-day geography of Gaywood is much removed from this past Anglo-Saxon landscape, this period witnessed the exploitation of an extensive saltmarsh — the North Marsh — which encompassed the whole of the current Lynnsport and Greenpark School development sites. This saltmarsh would have provided Anglo-Saxon communities with the valuable commodity of salt. Salt was essential for the preserving of food from earliest times, principally fish along with meat and certain vegetables, as well as in the production of foodstuffs including bread, butter and cheese. Salt was also used as a medium of exchange (Lane and Morris 2001, 402–404).

Possible early church influence on salt-making at the 'gateway'

The formation of the Anglo-Saxon landscape within the environs of the Lyn may have been heavily influenced by the archaeologically-significant 'productive' sites of Bawsey and Wormegay, situated upon their respective island-promontories overlooking the floodplains of the rivers Gaywood and Nar respectively (Fig. 2.1). These sites probably represent centres of administration during the Middle Anglo-Saxon period and may therefore have been early instigators of a well-organised salt-making landscape on the Norfolk Wash coast, including Gaywood's North Marsh. Surface finds at these sites, such as the quantity of 7th- and 8th-century coins (*sceattas*), the quality of metalwork and the discovery of styli (associated with writing and literacy) has been taken as evidence for these centres having been monasteries, although there also remains the possibility that these finds originated from an aristocratic or royal *villae regiae* (Pestell 2004, 54 and 59–62; Blair 2005, 208–11). Access to a reliable supply of salt would have been a fundamental requirement for a monastic community. However, Pestell (2004, 54 and 59–60) is keen to stress that the dominant land holders across this period were secular aristocratic rulers: valuable tracts of saltmarsh would have been equally desirable for incorporation into their estates.

Any possible early involvement of the Church in salt-making should also consider the Anglo-Saxon diocese of Elmham (which roughly corresponds with present-day Norfolk), especially given the emergence of Gaywood as one of the East Anglian See's capital manors by Domesday (see Chapter 5). Having been established in the region from AD 630/631, bishops played a part in the foundation of monasteries within their diocese, with some known examples carved out of episcopal land (Blair 2005, 93). This See was extinguished during the Danish invasions of the 9th century. After the English re-conquest of East Anglia, the bishops were re-established at their seat of North Elmham from AD 950, located approximately 30km to the east of the Lyn. It has been postulated that Gaywood was perhaps the vestige of a pre-Viking ecclesiastical (possibly monastic) estate centred on the confluence of the Gaywood and Nar valleys (Hutcheson 2009, 289). Within this context, this act of renewal and continuity of the parochial church may also have led to the reclaiming of pre-Viking church lands such as Gaywood, including its important saltmarsh.

The role of emerging trade in the supply of salt

The recent discovery of a large quantity of Ipswich ware pottery excavated from garden test pits along Wootton Road near to Gaywood Bridge (Collins 2018) suggests the early role of trade between *Gipeswic* and West Norfolk may have played a part in shaping the landscape of the Lyn. At this point of entry may have lain one of Hodges' 'gateway communities' for this utilitarian ware (Hodges 1982, 50–52; Blinkhorn 2012, fig. 36; Blair 2018, 49). Working back from this landscape's documented role as a major salt-producing centre by Domesday, it is not unreasonable to postulate that the production of this commodity during the Middle Anglo-Saxon period may also have acted as a stimulus for regional trade during this early period.

The inhabitants of the farmsteads of the siltlands west of the Lyn and those of the farmsteads within the river valleys to the east would no doubt have congregated at seasonal markets to sell surplus agricultural produce and manufactured goods. Both the Gaywood river and Wormegay on the River Nar contain the Middle English 'key' element for 'quay', alluding to their early role in waterborne trade. The early importance of the Gaywood river has been previously suggested, in particular for providing a sheltered anchorage where trade in commodities could take place (Owen 1980, 146). It is possible that during the Middle Anglo-Saxon period the river was navigable as far as Bawsey where the quantity of *sceattas* found has been taken to suggest this site also acted as a market during the 8th and 9th centuries (Pestell 2004, 33). However, the Ipswich ware find near to Gaywood Bridge suggests that bulk goods may have been set down and traded from a port-settlement further downstream from the 8th century. Dense scatters of this pottery type have previously been suggested to correlate to important centres (Pestell 2004, 29). Dispersed from the *emporium* of *Gipeswic* (Ipswich), this ware has been found throughout East Anglia and is thought possibly to have played a part in the social and cultural identity of this Middle Anglo-Saxon kingdom (Blinkhorn 2005, 211). The large quantity of this pottery at Gaywood strongly suggests trade on the Lyn was integrated into the regional network in the Middle Anglo-Saxon period. The arrival of pottery and other goods, which perhaps included luxury items for consumption at the higher status centres of Bawsey and Wormegay, would have acted as a stimulus for the production of surplus salt (and other commodities) with which to trade in return. An early trading centre at Gaywood may conceivably have taken the form of Hodges' Type A model, where 'the earliest and most vestigial of gateway communities' conducted coastal fairs where foreign traders visited for 'short periods annually or perhaps seasonally' (Hodges 1989, summarised in Hill and Cowie 2001, 6). Although only speculative, perhaps there was a polyfocal dimension to trade which links the possible port-settlement at Gaywood and the probable administrative centre at Bawsey. A similar situation may have emerged for the neighbouring riverine 'productive' sites of Congham and Wormegay on the Babingley and Nar rivers respectively. Not forgetting the landward distribution routes for trade, Congham lay at a significant junction in the landscape between the seaward access via its river and the important overland communication route of the Icknield Way.

III. Discussion

Situated at the northern end of the Lyn, the settlements at Gaywood encompassed the range of ploughland, meadow and woodland environments necessary to supply the needs of its populace. The ploughland produced cereals to make bread and beer and provided stubble after each harvest to help fatten cattle and sheep. Fields could also be turned to other crops such as peas or flax. The well-watered meadows on the valley floor either side of the promontory were available for grazing livestock or could be harvested for hay to feed livestock over winter. The forests upon the acidic escarpment soils would have been a necessary source of wood for fuel and constructing buildings, as well as providing a feeding ground for pigs. Vegetables, herbs, nuts and fruits were probably grown in tended gardens and orchards nearer to the home/farmsteads and estate centres or harvested from nearby hedgerows or woodland. The escarpment to the east of the Lyn had widespread beds of clay and sand ironstone ore which had been exploited for iron production since Roman times (Gallois *et al.* 1994, 180; Tylecote and Owles 1960). These resources (excepting iron ore) were common to the fully-developed estates of Anglo-Saxon East Anglia.

A central concern for the people extracting the wide variety of resources from this landscape was the supply of salt as the primary method to preserve meat, fish or dairy products until their consumption. In the medieval period domestic households were fed with animals slaughtered and salted in the autumn along with quantities of fish, mostly herring. Herring could be cured either through salting to produce white herring or smoked to produce red herring (Keen 1987, 25; 1988). Keen (1987, 26) highlighted a correlation between the large number of salterns listed in Domesday on the east coast of England with the importance of the local fishing industries. The medieval Latin term of *allec* (*alecium, allecum, etc.*) was in widespread use across northern Europe to refer to herring whether salted, smoked or otherwise preserved (*e.g.* dried as 'stockfish'). The scale of this medieval industry even warranted a factory for salting herring near Durham, and herring merchants (Curtis 1984, 147). Medieval religious houses were both consumers and producers of salt. Early medieval Welsh monks used it to season their simple food: 'at supper their food was bread, with roots, or herbs, seasoned with salt' (Dugdale *et al.* 1846, vol. 6, part 3, 1629). Later church communities could meet their needs directly through tithes of salted meat and fish (*ibid.*, vol. 5, 619) or through endowment of coastal saltworks to produce their own salt. Dugdale's great monastic survey includes examples of endowed saltworks at Stallingborough, Lincolnshire on the Humber (*ibid.*, vol. 3, 494) and near the estuary of the River Tees at Coatham, North Yorkshire (*ibid.*, vol. 4, 316). It is conceivable that the same modes of tribute and endowment supplied the salt needs of the preceding Anglo-Saxon religious communities. It is also possible that herring played a similar role in stimulating salt production during this earlier time as in the medieval period as, for example, there is a possible 8th-century reference to a herring fishery at Yarmouth in the records of the monastery of Evesham (Curtis 1984, 147, n.1).

The well-suited environment of the West Norfolk coast for the laying down of a predictable supply of salt with each spring tide would have been welcomed as a boon by the inhabitants. A spring tide is a common historical term not associated with the season but which conveys the concept of the tide 'springing forth'. Spring tides occur twice each lunar month all year long (National Ocean Service 2021). The ready availability of this vital resource probably marked out the Lyn as a destination for traders from *Gipeswic* and elsewhere to peddle their wares in exchange for this 'white gold'. This would push back into the Middle Anglo-Saxon period the possible importance of locally-produced salt to regional trade previously suggested by Owen (1984, 7) for the period immediately prior to the Norman Conquest. Even at this early date, salt-making may have resulted in a 'production-orientated community' requiring a level of organisation greater than mere opportunistic salt-winning activity at a household level. It is likely that, as in medieval times, salt production at a surplus level was probably controlled by Anglo-Saxon elites from aristocratic or monastic centres, who had the ability to coordinate the required resources of fuel and labour.

As touched upon above, the success of a salt-winning campaign was closely tied to the availability and rights to woodland and/or peat to fuel brine-boiling along with turf to filter. Minor beds of peat and turf were widespread across East Anglia with the most extensive tracts of peat lying within the area which later became the Norfolk Broads (Rackham 1996, 359). Whatever the nature of the string of 'productive' river valley sites within the hinterland of the Wash and the Lyn, they remain the most likely candidates for the organisation and control of salt production from the end of the 7th century onwards. It is unknowable if this scenario holds true as no charters or grants of Middle Anglo-Saxon salterns survive from this part of Norfolk. However, Blair (2005, 256) argues that minsters/monasteries may have been the best placed proprietors of new ventures such as specialised salt-making during these centuries in terms of their scale in land holdings, ability to amass labour and resources for investment. There is documentary evidence from other parts of the country of late 7th- and 8th-century minsters/monasteries involved in specialised industries including salt; Blair provides the examples of religious houses at Lyminge, Kent and Taunton, Somerset holding salt pans on tidal marshes (Blair 2005, 258, n.58). Other examples include documentary evidence in Dorset of Aethelmoth, Bishop of Sherborne being granted a parcel of land from King Cynewulf in AD 774 for saltworks on the west bank of the River Lym (Keen 1987, 25). Keen considered the wider association of saltworks and religious houses in the 8th-century documentary record as unexceptional when taking into account similar continental records from this period. The mention by Brushfield (1890, 41) of a charter of King Edward the Confessor granting a saltern at Teignmouth, Devon to his chaplain Leofric highlights that transactions passing wholly between the hands of secular lords were possibly as equally commonplace. The close association in medieval records between the church and salt production on the Atlantic coasts is discussed by Hocquet (1984, 57) who discounts an earlier assertion that 'the monks actually built the salt marshes', with saltworks probably being donated by lay owners to the monasteries they founded.

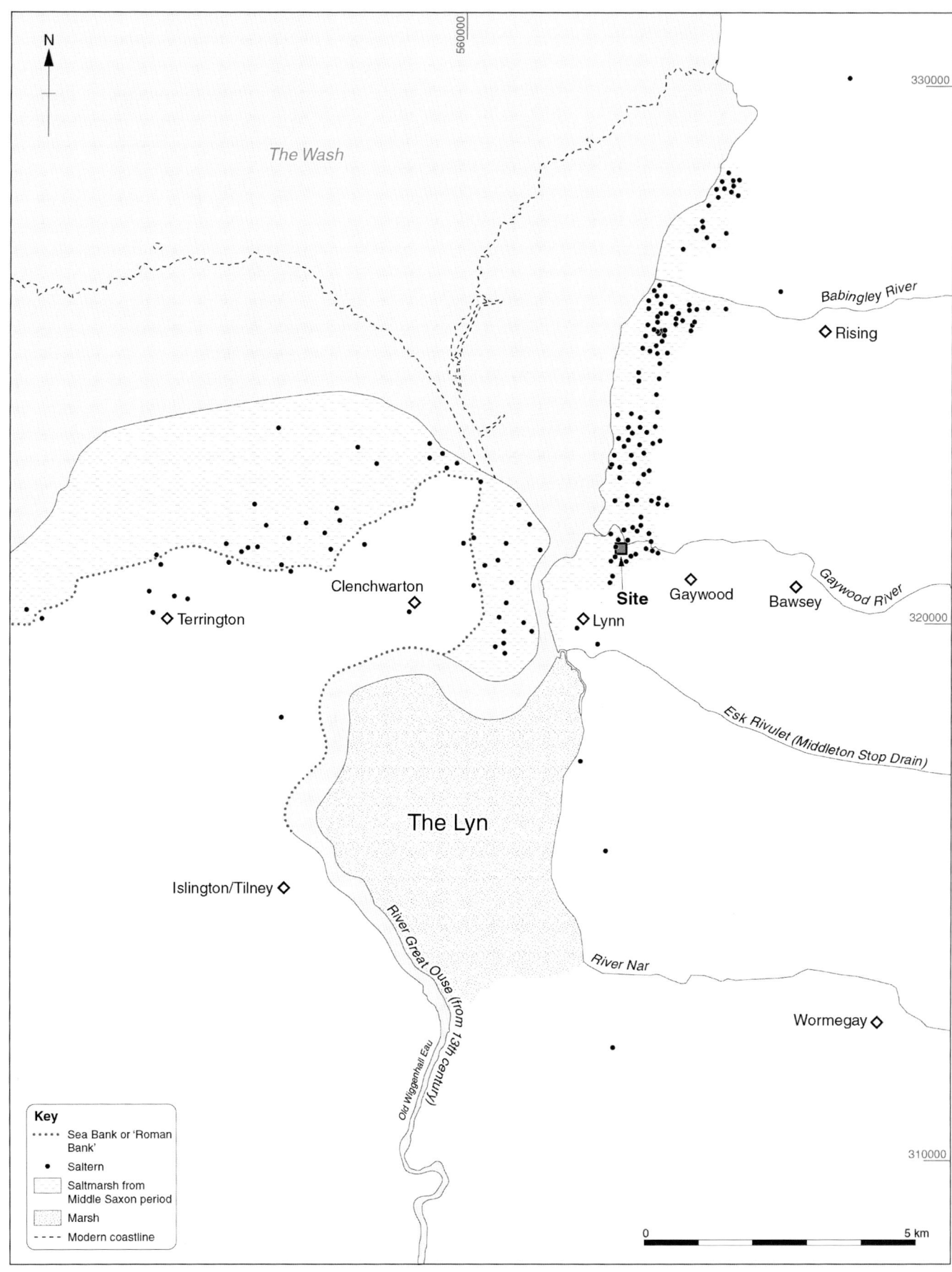

Figure 3.1 Site location in relation to the Late Anglo-Saxon to medieval Norfolk coastline and rivers, with known post-Roman salt-making sites mapped by the NNMP (NHER). Scale 1:1,000

Chapter 3. The Saltmarsh

…the wind was so violent, and the sea stormy, at Yarmouth, Dunwich, Ipswich, and other places in England, as well as on the coasts of other countries bordering on the sea, that many buildings were thrown down, especially in that part of England called the Fens; nearly the whole district was converted into a lake, and, unhappily, great numbers of men were overtaken by the floods and drowned.

(Florence of Worcester's entry for AD 1287, reproduced from Forester 1854, 375)

I. A dynamic coastal and riverine environment

Introduction
(Figs 3.1–3.2)

Present day King's Lynn lies at the south-eastern corner of the Wash embayment. Its suburb of Gaywood and the focus of this study — the North Marsh — have witnessed significant changes to their topography over the last 1000 years and more (Figs 3.1–3.2). It is essentially a story of continued landward retreat from a more prominent coastal situation during the Anglo-Saxon period through a process of land reclamation, the progression of which was indirectly influenced by the salt-winning industry: a theme underpinning this volume. The historical North Marsh was a saltmarsh which lay to the north of the entrance to the Lyn. This inlet is now a swathe of reclaimed arable farmland, but when the North Marsh was being exploited in the Anglo-Saxon period as a source of salt it was a shallow coastal inlet whose tidal reach extended to the present-day parishes of Wiggenhall St Germans and Wiggenhall St Mary Magdalen, encompassing an area of approximately 24km^2. The Lyn lay between the opposing environments of the fertile flat Norfolk siltlands to the west and the more varied topography of Norfolk's western escarpment to the east with its patchwork of sandy heathland, arable clay land, chalk downland, and loam-filled valleys. Whereas in Anglo-Saxon times the Gaywood and Babingley rivers would have drained directly into the Wash, the Lyn would have received from the east the waters of the Middleton Stop Drain (a canalised natural rivulet formerly known as the Esk) and the River Nar and from the south an outflow of water from the peat fenland via the Old Wiggenhall Eau (Fig. 3.1).

The Lyn
(Figs 3.3–3.5)

Although there is much speculation on the date of reclamation and construction of sea defences, the western margins of the Lyn were probably embanked by the Bardike during the 10th century as part of the Late Anglo-Saxon colonisation of the siltlands (Fig. 3.3 and see Chapter 2). The line of this bank was superimposed in the 11th century by the Sea Bank (formerly known as 'Roman Bank') which was extended along the northern side of the Lyn to encompass the newly reclaimed parish of Clenchwarton (Rippon 2000, 175 and fig. 59). To the south this bank extended as far as Eau Brink. A continuation of the Sea Bank may have then extended eastwards to enclose the southern side of the Lyn around this date, along the line of North Sea Bank, which extends between Islington Lodge and the River

Figure 3.2 King's Lynn and the River Great Ouse, looking south-east (photo by Katie Denham; licensed with CC BY 2.0. https://creativecommons.org/licenses/by/2.0/)

Nar at Whitehouse Farm then onward along an old bank to the higher ground at West Winch (Gallois *et al.* 1994, 172, fig. 55). The rising ground to the east negated the need for a bank on that side and so the waters were kept at bay within its fixed extent during any subsequent sea level rise or storm surge, into the medieval period. The only remaining low ground east of the Lyn leads into the wide valley of the Middleton Stop Drain (former Esk) where partly along its course the marine silts give way to an expanse of peat at its upper reaches. Therefore, the southern parts of the Lyn south of the North Sea Bank surrounding the parishes of Wiggenhall were also probably drained around the 10th to 11th centuries (Rippon 2000, 175). Domesday shows that by the 11th century this extensive tract of protected siltland surrounding the Lyn was a rich and well-populated zone used for agriculture and pasture (Rippon 2000, 169). Thereafter, expansion of Wiggenhall St Mary Magdalen into the peat fen to the south of the Lyn is documented with the raising of the

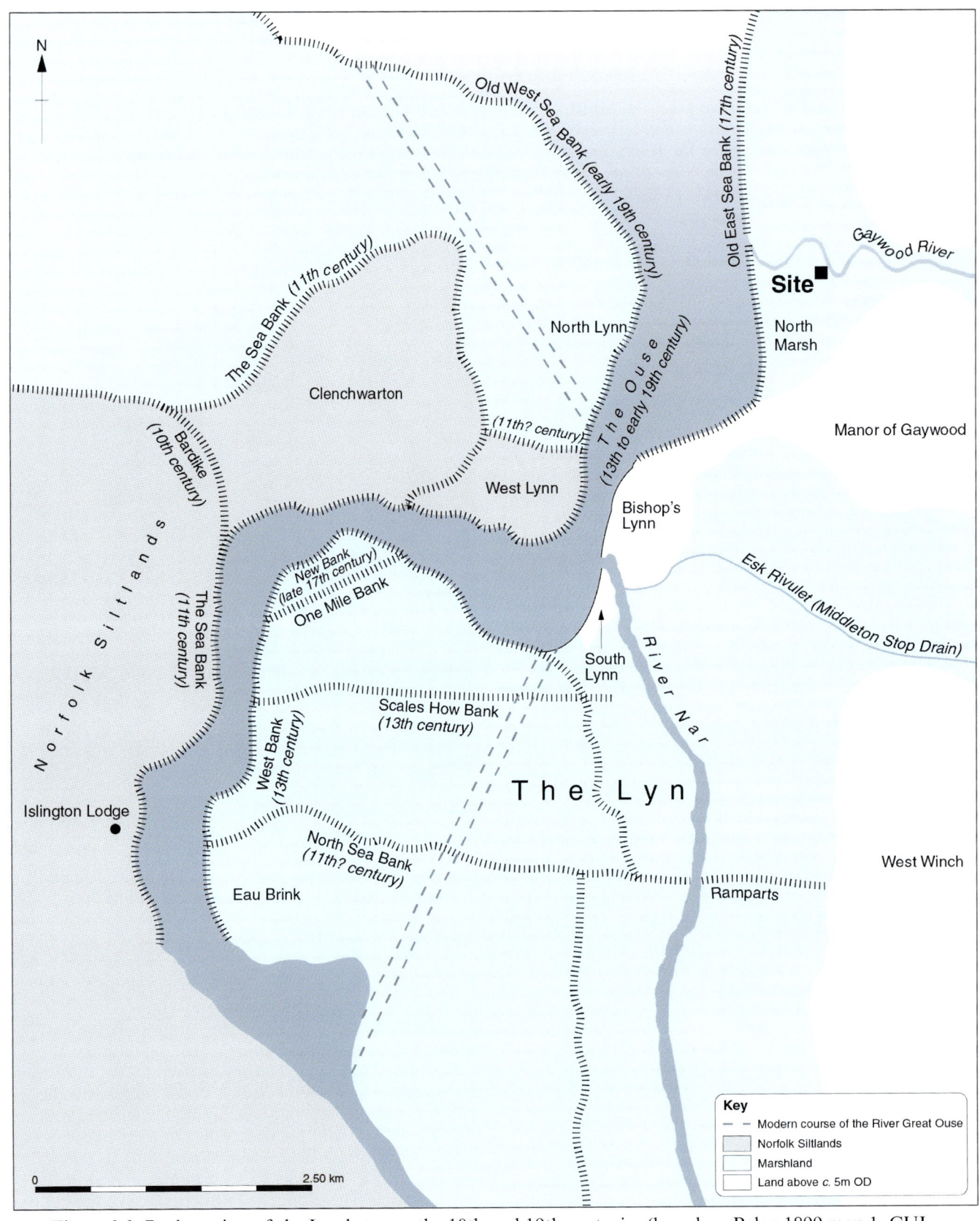

Figure 3.3 Reclamation of the Lyn between the 10th and 19th centuries (based on Beloe 1899 map 1. CUL, RC.25.70. Reproduced by kind permission of the Syndics of Cambridge University Library). Scale 1:50,000

Figure 3.4 The Great River Ouse *c*.1725, based on a survey *c*.1604 (Armstrong 1725, historical maps: a) page between 6 and 7, and b) page between 72 and 73; CUL, Cam.a.725.1. Reproduced by kind permission of the Syndics of Cambridge University Library). North to the right

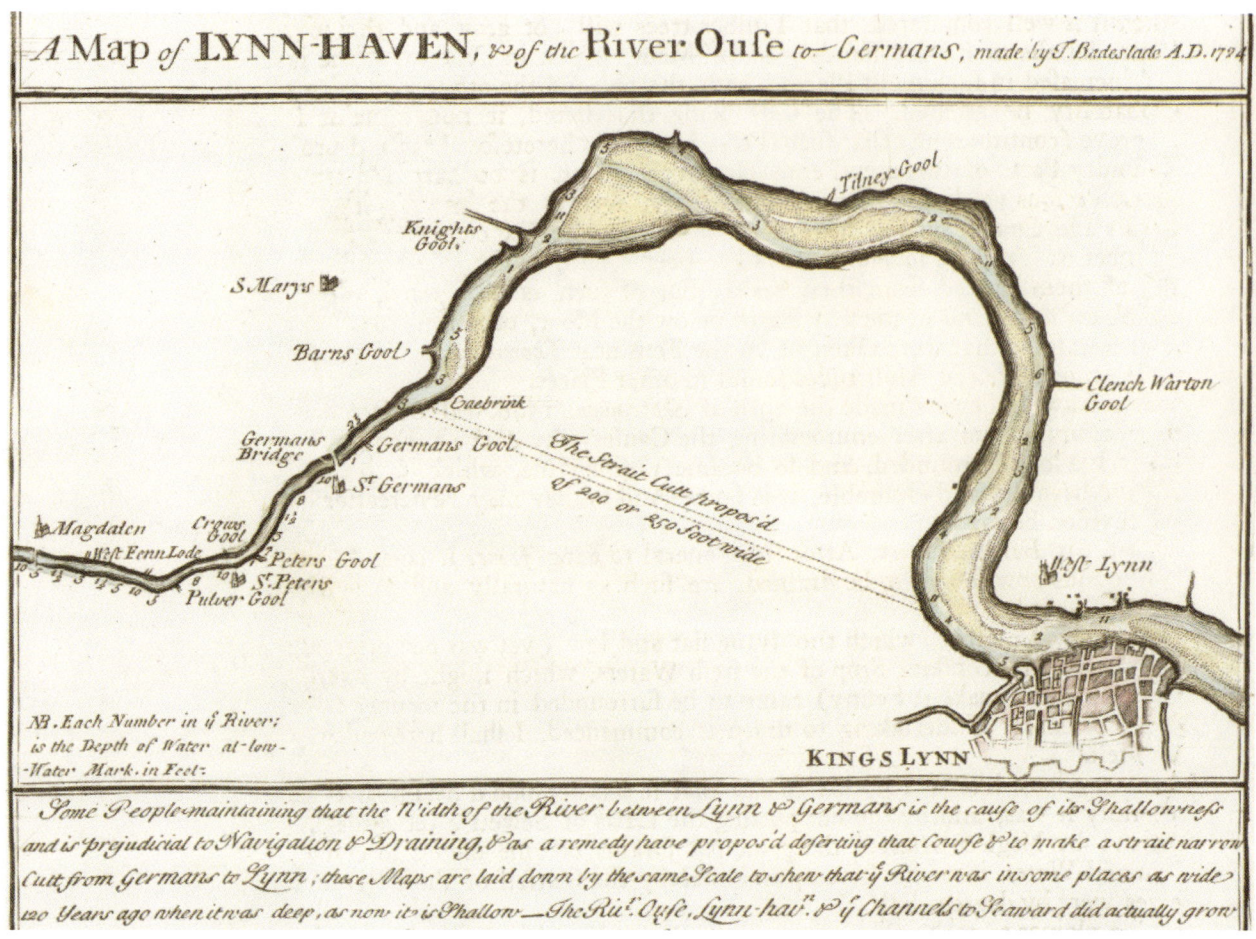

Figure 3.5 The proposed Eau Brink Cut, c.1724 (Armstrong 1725, historical maps, page between 14 and 15. CUL, Cam.a.725.1. Reproduced by kind permission of the Syndics of Cambridge University Library). North to the right

Podike in the vicinity of Crabhouse Nunnery in about the year 1223 (Darby 1940, 47); although it is possible this dyke is much older (Hallam 1988, 157).

The diversion of the River Great Ouse to King's Lynn in the 13th century would have had a great impact on the evolving medieval topography of the Lyn. This salt-water inlet described variously by antiquarian sources as 'but six poles, or about an hundred feet wide' or 'to flow between banks 12 perches apart' at its mouth became a substantial freshwater estuary up to 'a mile in breadth' (Richards 1812, 22–3; Hillen 1907, 335; Silvester 1988, 22). The average salinity of the Wash in the recent period is 33:1000. At the mouth of the River Nene this salinity has been recorded to fall to as little as 18–20:1000 which may be roughly comparable to that of the River Great Ouse (Healey 1999, 98). This would have had a detrimental impact on the potential for the raw material of the salt-making industry — the salt encrusted muds laid down by the spring tides — to accumulate to an economically viable extent. Early maps of the siltlands south of King's Lynn show the sweeping bends of this estuary along the Lyn's western shore (Fig. 3.4). Defensive ramparts were raised around King's Lynn from c.1266, possibly due to rising sea levels and probably also as a response to the new river's outflow. Within the Lyn itself, reclamation of its extent north of the North Sea Bank was only achieved much later. The central and northern reaches of the Lyn remained a series of marshes until each was embanked; a piecemeal process which continued from the 13th century through to the late 17th century when the River Great Ouse became hemmed in to the east as well as to the west (Silvester 1988, 22; fig. 10; Beloe 1899, map 1). In response to flooding and difficulties in navigating its shifting channel, a new cutting of the river (Eau Brink Cut) was completed in 1852 which allowed for the remaining part of this inlet-estuary to be filled in and reclaimed (Fig. 3.5).

The Gaywood Valley and North Marsh
(Figs 3.6–3.7)
To the north-east of the Lyn, the valley of the River Gaywood extends approximately 10km inland between the North Marsh and its headwaters between Gayton and Grimston. This river is fed by springs emanating from the chalk escarpment. It is one of a series of west-facing valleys carved into Norfolk's Western Escarpment by glacial and periglacial river activity during the preceding ice ages, which accounts for its disproportionate width in relation to the size of its river (Gallois *et al.* 1994, figs 42 and 44). The course of the river has been canalised along much of its length to facilitate drainage of the agricultural land and would historically have been more sinuous. The former meandering course of the river prior to 1425, which passed through the North Marsh as 'le Seadyke' or 'Seadyek', can be inferred from old maps of Gaywood

Figure 3.6 The North Marsh c.1581 (Harrod 1874, plate H. CUL, Ll.32.47. Reproduced by kind permission of the Syndics of Cambridge University Library)

parish (NRO, DN/TA 137 (Fig. 3.7); see also BL 55/1 (below, Fig. 4.3) and Chapter 6), while a map dated c.1581 shows the rivers bisecting and flanking the marsh and emptying into the Great Ouse (Fig. 3.6). The superficial geological deposits underlying the North Marsh form part of the same unit of tidal silt deposits as the Norfolk siltlands and the Lyn. These deposits are commonly known as the Terrington Beds and/or the Iron Age silts and are believed to have been laid down between c.1300 BC and the 2nd or 1st centuries BC. Later deposits of post-Roman date were added to this unit largely by short-lived flooding and marine transgressions and are still classed as Terrington Beds by the British Geological Survey. The Fenland Survey identified these later deposits as post-Roman silt to avoid confusion (Silvester 1988, 7).

The historical period witnessed the development of the lower reaches of the Gaywood valley as a saltmarsh environment. The Anglo-Saxon incomers would have recognised the North Marsh then, as today, as a highly attractive ecosystem for gathering wild food resources ranging from fish to migratory shorebirds and waterfowl. The creeks also provide shelter for juvenile fish with abundant shellfish resources

Figure 3.7 Gaywood 1838 Tithe map, with site locations shown (NRO, DN/TA 137. Reproduced by kind permission of the Norfolk Record Office)

Figure 3.8 Present-day saltmarsh at the mouth of the Great Ouse, looking north-west from the modern outflow of the Babingley River

within the adjacent mudflats (Davidson-Arnott *et al.* 2019, 395 and 398). Nevertheless, this productive environment has historically been impacted by human activity through the establishment of defensive sea banks and land reclamation for agriculture such as on the Norfolk siltlands during the Late Anglo-Saxon period (Waller 1994, 37–8; Davidson-Arnott *et al.* 2019, 395). Pastoral activity has also played its part, with the drier reaches of the upper saltmarshes being left unbanked and exploited for their valuable herbaceous grassland by the grazing of sheep and sometimes cattle (Tansley 1939, 840). Saltmarshes in Essex and Kent were already viewed in Anglo-Saxon times as prized tracts of pasture for sheep (Rackham 1996, 386); therefore, it is not unreasonable to suggest Gaywood's North Marsh was similarly utilised at this time. Added to this array of resources were the salt-rich muds laid down by the spring tides across the upper reaches of the saltmarsh that would become the focus of a major salt-making industry across the later Anglo-Saxon and early medieval periods.

The lower reaches of the River Gaywood were dammed in the early medieval period, the first probably dating to AD 1101 (Neville 2014), although earlier undocumented mills may have existed. The arrival of the substantial freshwater estuary of the Great Ouse in the 13th century probably had an immediate effect in lowering the salinity of the North Marsh; impacting the salt-making industry here. An even more dramatic event was the separation of the North Marsh from the sea by the raising of the Old East Sea Bank flood defences of King's Lynn in the 17th century (Figs 3.3 and 3.7; see also Fig. 1.4, NHER MNF5528). These changes probably heralded the end of salt-making at an industrial level of production on the North Marsh. This area became a highly fragmented patchwork of smallholdings utilised as pasture which straddled the former course of the River Gaywood after its diversion along the southern margins of the marsh in 1425 (NRO, BL 55/1, Fig. 4.3; NRO, DN/TA 137, Fig. 3.7). Based on a 1487 survey of the North Marsh (Gaywood Dragge; NRO, BL/MA/2/1–2; see Chapter 5 and Fig. 5.2) the erection of this sea defence also fossilised this landscape into the modern period by protecting it from rising sea levels; especially considering the modern tidal range of the Wash (see below). Further reclamations of land were probably made on the seaward side of the Sea Bank, but these were presumably lost during a period of relatively high sea level which coincided with the diversion of the River Great Ouse in the 13th century (Gallois *et al.* 1994, 174). The record of post-17th-century land reclamation is better documented and summarised within the British Geological Society (BGS) memoir for the King's Lynn district which shows that the piecemeal reclamation of the former course of the River Ouse did not end until the 1950s (Gallois *et al.* 1994, fig. 55). Saltmarshes still border the coast of the Wash under a macrotidal regime (defined as a 4–6m tidal range; Davidson-Arnott *et al.* 2019, 402) with many still strongly affected by land reclamation and sea defence programmes (Wheeler 1995, 139; Fig. 3.8).

II. Saltmarsh formation

Introduction
(Fig. 3.9)
Saltmarshes are a type of wetland that forms in the intertidal zone of a sheltered coast, notably in bays, lagoons, deltas and estuaries (Davidson-Arnott *et al.* 2019, 395). Located within the relatively sheltered south-eastern corner of the Wash embayment, the larger number of salterns mapped by the NNMP along the coast to the north of King's Lynn and the more scattered examples mapped on the siltlands to the west (Fig. 3.1) clearly indicate the pre-existing extent of the early medieval and presumably later Anglo-Saxon saltmarsh of West Norfolk. At the entrance to the Lyn inlet the distribution of fossilised salterns indicate that this saltmarsh zone was in the region of *c.*1km wide (Fig. 3.9). Coincidentally, this is also the measurement indicated for a stable saltmarsh width in the present southern Wash environment (Gallois *et al.* 1994). This observation is supported by Kestner's work on the history of saltmarsh advancement on the Wash, which determined that the foreshore becomes stabilised when a saltmarsh reaches between 0.5–0.8km in width ('1/3 to 1/2 miles wide'; Kestner 1962, 457). The steady advancement of land reclamation for arable agriculture into the Wash over the succeeding centuries has left this fossilised saltmarsh up to *c.*5km from the present coastline. The greatest concentration of salterns lay to the east of the Lyn, either side of the medieval courses of the Gaywood and Babingley rivers. A more dispersed group of salterns lay on the wider expanse of saltmarsh on the seaward side of the Sea Dyke (the old 'Roman Bank'), west of the Lyn stretching to the River Nene estuary (Fig. 3.1). This wider stretch of saltmarsh is explained by Kestner (1962, 469) as having resulted from the diversion of the River Great Ouse from its outfall at Wisbech to King's Lynn in the 13th century, which left the high mudbanks either side of its old course less susceptible to erosion by the lower amplitude fluctuations of the River Nene alone, and this land continued to rise to become saltmarsh.

Within the coastal marshland zone of the Wash it has previously been recognised that the *natural* build-up of a saltmarsh will eventually act as a barrier to freshwater discharge during low tides, creating an area of quiet brackish water behind (Wheeler 1995, 144). However, the contribution of *artificial* movement of saltmarsh muds through salt-making may yet be an under-appreciated cause for coastal change. Although a significant stretch of the Norfolk Wash coastline is studded with relict saltern mounds, the part played by the movement of this great quantity of coastal sediment on the advancement of the Wash coastline has been somewhat 'skipped over' in the past. For example, in the early 19th century, prior to the knowledge that the 'Roman Bank' was actually of Anglo-Saxon origin, Borer's discussion of coastal change in the Wash stated that 'from that [Roman] time until the 17th century there is no record of anything being done to help the natural process of accretion' (Borer 1939, 491). This discourse nevertheless fully recognised that the very slow natural process of accretion — the continuous deposition of sediments from suspension

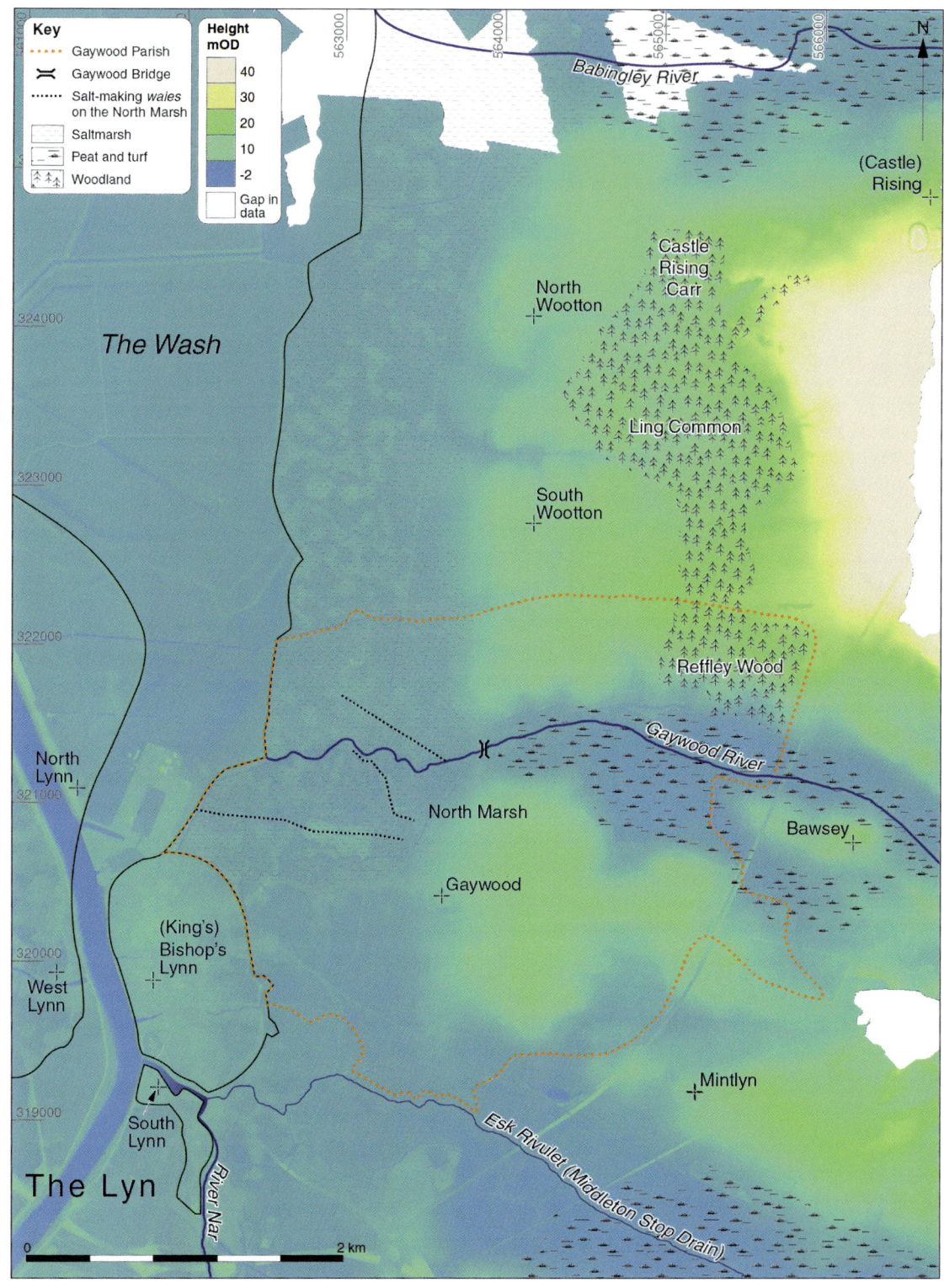

Figure 3.9 Reconstruction of the fossilised salt-making landscape (contains Environment Agency LIDAR data licensed under the Open Government Licence v3.0). Scale 1:40,000

— can be hastened by artificial means (Borer 1939, 492). In the early 1960s, the leading edges of old saltmarshes were traced by Kestner (1962) in his study of the old Wash coastline. Kestner's study deliberately avoided reclaimed ploughland when seeking evidence for old saltmarsh foreshores and only surveyed the intervening unreclaimed stretches of surviving saltmarsh. Both these geographical studies clearly did not recognise the topographical (and archaeological) potential of saltern mounds to map pre-existing saltmarsh zones, at least at a local level. Kestner nevertheless reiterated Borer's observation that the very gradual accretion processes on the Wash can be interrupted by rapid leaps of coastal advancement when the delicate balance of accretion and erosion on the foreshore are disturbed (Kestner 1962, 465). It was during the 1979 Battle Conference on Anglo-Norman studies that the historian Dorothy Owen explored the

Figure 3.10 Saltwater creeks

possibly wide-ranging effects of man-made coastal change through salt-making, being central to her discourse on the origins of King's Lynn. This lecture presented a model whereby the heaps of salt-making waste — the salterns — raised the level of the land, which progressively pushed the high spring tides and the salt-making sites seaward. A combination of field observation and research had led her to conclude that Bishop's (later King's) Lynn and certain villages on the Norfolk siltlands such as North Lynn, Clenchwarton and Terrington All Saints had been established upon land reclaimed directly by this process (Owen 1980, 142–3). The Fenland Project of the 1980s conceded this to be true of West Lynn and probably of King's Lynn but warned against the blanket interpretation for the siltland villages having been established in this way. Instead, these are more likely to have been sited upon roddons (Silvester 1988, 165).

Sea level
The upper horizon of the natural sediments upon which the salterns were placed lay at differing heights across the North Marsh: Marsh Lane at between 1.5–2m OD (Clarke and Clarke 2020); Lynnsport 1 at 1.7–2.29m OD; Lynnsport 3 at 1.75–1.9m OD; Lynnsport 4 & 5 at 2m OD and Greenpark School at 1.4–2m OD. In the modern tidal regime this saltmarsh would be within the daily tidal range and be characterised by mudflats or lower marsh. At Hunstanton the lowest high water (Mean High Water Neap (MHWN)) is currently 1.85m OD and the highest high water (Mean High Water Spring (MHWS)) is 3.65m OD (the lowest tides are MLWS -2.85m OD and MLWN -1.25m OD) (East Anglian Coastal Group 2010, C34). The modern tide levels for King's Lynn are MHWN 1.97m OD and MHWS 3.77m OD (the lowest tides for King's Lynn are MLWS -2.03m OD and MHWN -1.23m OD). The estuary at King's Lynn is highly modified, meaning that comparison to Hunstanton is perhaps more appropriate. If exposed to modern sea levels, the North Marsh would be covered by virtually all tides, suggesting that Middle to Late Anglo-Saxon sea levels were lower than today. Such lowering of relative sea level is in accord with the somewhat debated sea-level curve of the southern North Sea proposed by Behre (2007, fig. 7), where Early and Middle Anglo-Saxon sea levels are shown as still receding after the Roman sea-level rise to a low point in c.AD 1000 (see also Waller 1994, 14, citing Shennan 1986; Simmons 2015).

Minerogenic sediments
(Fig. 3.10)
Waller, in his volume on Flandrian environmental change in the fenland, describes the sediment sequence to be expected within this brackish zone between the freshwater coastal reedswamp environment studded with creeks and the lower saltmarsh environment characterised by dendritic saltwater creeks (Fig. 3.10). The lower altitudes towards the coastal mudflats are laminated with a fine sand content up to c.10%. At higher altitudes, the silt fraction dominates with fine sand virtually absent and a gradually increasing content of clay towards the coastal reedswamp environment. These sediments contain organic matter of mostly rootlets with some seeds of saltmarsh taxa (Waller 1994, 39). Periodically immersed by tides, these saltmarsh deposits were lain between the mean high-water neap tide (tides of least range) to above the mean high-water spring tide (tides of greatest range). The accretion of sediment is classed by the BGS as forming part of the Terrington Beds (Gallois *et al.* 1994, 163–5).

Each of the Lynnsport and Greenpark School, excavations encountered natural sediments of silty sand in hues varying between yellow, brown and grey. The abundant supply of sediment to the North Marsh from the coastal mudflats of the Wash and from the River Gaywood has produced a saltmarsh made up of minerogenic deposits with only scant evidence for the accretion of organic material. A large volume of this sediment is ultimately generated by coastal erosion of fine-grained rocks. Study into the vertical growth rate of saltmarshes dominated by this sediment has been shown to be rapid at first until a mature saltmarsh has been established, after which the growth rate is very slow. Study into the deposition of sediment during a single tide has shown this tended to decrease with distance from the main creek channels (Davidson-Arnott *et al.* 2019, 404; 417).

Sedimentology
by Frances Green
The underlying natural deposit of the (presumed) saltmarsh environment exploited by the Middle and

Late Anglo-Saxon salt-workers was characterised during the excavations of Salterns 1 and 2 (Lynnsport 4 & 5). During excavation these deposits (*e.g.* context 141) were described in the field as a varied mix of pale yellow, green, orange, brown and grey silty sands. The top of these deposits was encountered at a height of approximately 2m OD in both these excavations. A 50cm-long monolith sample was taken across the upper surface of this sediment beneath Saltern 2. This sample allowed the underlying sediment to be logged using the Tröels-Smith (1955) classification scheme (see Chapter 4; Fig. 4.8, section 75, Monolith 98):

Saltmarsh deposit (context 141): fine pale brown very fine sand with a composition suggestive of deposition on a sandflat in a relatively high energy environment exposed to all tides.

Nascent surface soil development
With each inundation silt is trapped by plants which has the effect of gradually raising the ground surface until brought to a level above the highest tides. From this level the ground surface is raised further by the build-up (vertical accretion) of dead (humic) vegetable matter. The anaerobic conditions of saltmarsh soils from only a few millimetres below the surface greatly slows the rate of breakdown of organic matter (Davidson-Arnott *et al.* 2019, 411). In this way saltmarshes act as sinks in the landscape for both fine sediments carried in from the tidal mudflats and sediment transported from upland by rivers to the coast, augmenting the build-up of organic matter. With these processes a saltmarsh has the potential to be raised further in level from between a few millimetres to several centimetres a year. However, the gradual compaction of sediments generally lessens the rate of growth (Davidson-Arnott *et al.* 2019, 395; Tansley 1939, 819–21). Studies of marsh growth have shown accretion rates over decades and centuries can range from <1mm to 10–15mm per year due to the varied locations of saltmarshes and taking into account the effect of rising and falling sea levels (Davidson-Arnott *et al.* 2019, 420–21). A discussion by Borer of coastal change in the Wash provides a useful description of the natural accumulation of deposits around its tidal limit. Warping — the deposition of loamy particles — takes place above *c.*1.5m OD. From a height of the neap tide at *c.*2.4m OD samphire (*Salicornia*) grows to a height of *c.*3m OD. Above this level samphire is gradually replaced by grasses. In this way a new saltmarsh attains a height of *c.*3.35m OD with old marshes reaching a maximum height of *c.*4m OD, just beyond the upper limit of the spring tides at *c.*3.8m OD. It is only above this height that soil consists largely of warp or loamy particles with the exclusion of waterborne siliceous silt and sand (Borer 1939, 492).

The excavations of Salterns 2, 5 and 11 encountered intermittent thin horizons of darker deposits beneath their bases which were variously interpreted during the site work as possible patches of organic/humic build-up or even nascent soils on the pre-existing saltmarsh surface. However, it must be emphasised that these horizons were absent from beneath most of the salterns and across the excavated areas which strongly suggests that the excavated salterns were placed at an elevation below that of the highest tides.

A layer of soil-like sediment (context 481=628) between *c.*0.2–0.25m thick overlay the minerogenic deposits beneath Saltern 11 from a height of *c.*1.75m OD (see Chapter 4, Fig. 4.32, Section 142). This sediment was logged on site as greyish blue sandy clay with orange mottling. Significantly, it produced two sherds (55g) of Ipswich ware pottery, tentatively suggesting that the earliest use of this site for salt-making lay somewhere between the 8th to 9th centuries (see Chapter 4).

Sedimentology
by Frances Green
An intermittent sediment horizon (context 142) measuring a maximum *c.*0.05m thick and containing occasional charcoal fragments was revealed beneath Saltern 2 at a height of *c.*2m OD (see Chapter 4, Fig. 4.8, Section 75, Monolith 98). This deposit was logged using the Tröels-Smith (1955) classification scheme:

Saltmarsh surface (context 142): firm dark brown structureless clayey silt with some sand, rare fine charcoal. Ag3, Gamin1, As1, sharp boundary with below. Its composition and the presence of charcoal is considered indicative of the saltern's establishment within an upper saltmarsh environment rarely influenced by tides.

This clayey silt lay directly over the fine sands sampled by Monolith 98 characterised as having probably been deposited within the lower saltmarsh (see above), which is indicative of a relative lowering of sea level at the time of the commencement of salt-making activity at this site.

Micromorphology
by Charles French
(Figs 3.11–12)
A test pit was excavated into the northern end of Saltern 5 (Greenpark Avenue School site) that revealed a *c.*0.05m-thick horizon (contexts 1004/1005) of finely laminar sediment at a height of *c.*1.7m OD (Fig. 4.23, Section 222, Monolith 421). Consisting of dark greyish brown silty clay and sand, this horizon extended over the natural saltmarsh deposits beneath the northern part of the saltern. A soil block sub-sampled from Monolith 421 across this horizon was provided for micromorphological analysis that was able to characterise the components of the sediments and the nature of their depositionary processes:

Thin section analysis:
Fabric unit 1 (context 1005): very fine quartz sand with minor very fine charcoal fragments and 10% micro-sparite calcium carbonate, with some micro-laminae of slightly wavy silty clay crusts and horizontal organisation of the very fine sand grains;
distinct horizontal boundary with
Fabric unit 2 (context 1004): multiple finely laminar silty clay crusts alternating with very fine quartz sand lenses, with either amorphous humic (Fig. 3.11) or amorphous sesquioxide staining (Fig. 3.12).

This sequence is composed of either laminae of very fine to fine sand or silty clay crusts with greater to lesser impregnation with amorphous iron oxides. This suggests that there were short, episodic influxes of eroded fine material which were then subject to rapid drying out (Lindbo *et al.* 2010), a sequence repeated over and over again. This would be expected to be found on the edge of an active body of water, such as a small stream or marsh.

Detailed micromorphological description:
Fabric unit 1 (context 1005): predominantly (90%) very fine quartz sand, 50–100μm, sub-rounded; 10% micro-sparite calcium carbonate, <50μm; pale greyish brown (CPL/PPL); 5% fine charcoal, <75μm;

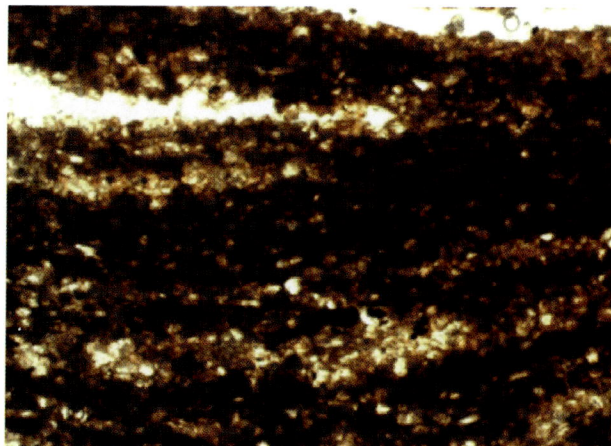

Figure 3.11 Thin section photomicrograph. Alternating laminae of very fine quartz and humic very fine sand/silt, monolith Sample 421, fabric unit 2, context 1004, Saltern 5. Frame width = 4.5mm; plane polarized light

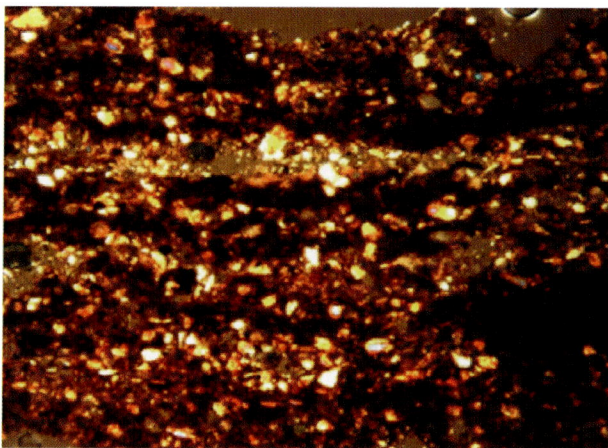

Figure 3.12 Thin section photomicrograph. Strongly sesquioxide-stained laminae of dusty clay and very fine sand, monolith Sample 421, fabric unit 2, context 1004, Saltern 5. Frame width = 4.5mm; cross polarized light

distinct horizontal boundary with
Fabric unit 2 (context 1004): all finely laminar; alternating laminae of brown humic silt and very fine quartz sand, or very fine quartz sand and strongly amorphous sesquioxide stained silty clay; pale brown/brown (PPL/CPL) and pale brown/reddish brown (PPL/CPL).

Salinity
As the lower saltmarsh zone is flooded twice daily by the tides its salinity is similar to that of the ocean waters. In contrast, the salinity of water within the upper saltmarsh may increase due to less flooding, poorer drainage and greater evaporation (Davidson-Arnott *et al.* 2019, 400). Conversely where saltmarshes lie alongside the deltaic distributaries of rivers (such as the Gaywood river) there may be periods of low salinity due to freshwater flooding (*ibid.*, 396). During the summer months the surface soil of a saltmarsh can become very dry. It was proposed prior to the Lynnsport excavations that this upper crust of salt-rich sediment was the raw material — *muldfange* — gathered up from individual *grevas* to be stripped in *kinches* of salt content (see Chapter 4 and Appendix 1: Glossary). Micropalaeontology, including the identification of ostracods and foraminifera, are useful indicators in determining levels of salinity and the types of habitat environments represented.

Ostracods and foraminifera
by Simon Timberlake
Sediment Sample 108 was taken from the unworked silts of the natural saltmarsh revealed by the excavation at Lynnsport 4 & 5 (see Chapter 4, Fig. 4.6, context 170). During the course of processing this sample for archaeobotanical remains ostracods were also recovered from the flot fractions, although in theory (at least) most of the adult valves and carapaces and instars should have passed through the 0.3mm mesh sieve into the residues. Despite the relatively poor recovery of ostracods from this sample the results appear reasonable in terms of what they indicate about the salinity ranges and habitat preferences of the identified fauna.

Sample 108 contained 37 ostracods within the total flot of 0.5g. Marginally the most abundant ostracod present is *Loxoconcha elliptica* (Brady 1868) which is represented by eleven individuals (four adults (two carapaces + two valves) and four juveniles) and is perhaps most typical of the sandy-muddy mudflat littoral palaeoenvironment located just seaward of the salterns. *Loxoconcha rhomboidea,* with quite similar habitat preferences, is represented here by just two adults and a juvenile. By contrast *Cyprideis torosa* is noticeably sparse (one adult and two juveniles), being an ostracod which in this environment is more closely associated with the salterns and brine tanks (see Chapter 4). *Limnocythere inopinata* (six juveniles) is similarly allochthonous to the mudflats, as are the freshwater (oligohaline) ostracods *Candona candida* (ten juveniles) and *Cypria opthalmica* (four juveniles). The latter are present here in larger numbers, suggesting freshwater inlets close-by, the most likely candidate being the contemporary course of the River Gaywood which until 1425 passed to the north of this site. The tidal flat/submerged saltmarsh context of these sediments is confirmed by the paucity of terrestrial snails and by greatly increased numbers of saltmarsh species (*Hydrobia ventrosa*), as well as by a large and more diverse assemblage of marine foraminifera; mostly rotaliines such as *Elphidium* sp. and *Ammonia* sp., and miliolines such as *Triloculina* sp, and rarely the planktonic foram *Globigerina* sp..

Vegetation
A saltmarsh is characterised by its salt-tolerant (halophytic) grass and herb habitat, dominated by one or two species at the lower levels inundated most by seawater and by an increasing variety of vegetation towards the highest intertidal reaches (Davidson-Arnott *et al.* 2019, 395). Saltmarshes generally comprise two zones of 'lower' and 'upper' ecological environments comprising different plant communities. The more mobile muds of the lower saltmarsh are covered by the sea for longer periods with the seaward edge submerged for six hours or more by every tide. The more stable silts of the upper saltmarsh are inundated for far shorter periods with the uppermost

reaches only affected by the spring tides (*ibid.*, 396 and 398). A study at Scolt Head Island on the North Norfolk coast measured that the uppermost reaches of the saltmarsh were only submerged for approximately three hours per month (Tansley 1939, 819–21). The highest tides reach the uppermost saltmarsh twice a year in a predictable cycle during the spring and autumn equinoxes. However, unpredictable storm surge events may also reach this far inland and submerge a saltmarsh for hours or even days at a time (Davidson-Arnott *et al.* 2019, 400). Above the mudflats grows a sequence of halophytic (salt-loving) plants typically ranging from *Spartina* spp. (cord grass) on the lowest part to *Salicornia* spp. (succulents including marsh samphire) and *Puccinellia maritima* (grasses such seaside alkaligrass, common saltmarsh-grass or sea poa grass) on the low saltmarsh (Gardiner 2005, 73).

Pollen
by Frances Green
A sample of sediment from the thin horizon of possible nascent soil with evident charcoal beneath the base of Saltern 1 (Lynnsport 1) was assessed for the presence of pollen and diatoms. Although no diatoms were found the pollen was characterised by plants of the upper saltmarsh. However, the low pollen counts are not statistically valid and allow only a tentative interpretation. Pollen of the Poaceae (grasses) contribute almost 40% of total land pollen (TLP) and the saltmarsh is envisaged as being predominantly grassy with herbaceous plants, some of which would have been salt tolerant. Pollen of the Chenopodiaceae is frequent (*c.*30% TLP) and although undifferentiated this pollen type is typical of saltmarsh pollen diagrams (*cf.* zone WGA6 Wiggenhall St Germans; Waller 1994) as the family includes many saltmarsh species such as *Atriplex potulacoides* (sea purslane) and *Atriplex prostrata* (spear-leafed orache). Pollen of other typical saltmarsh plants includes *Plantago maritima* (sea plantain). Pollen of Taraxacum-type pollen (20% TLP) includes plants such as *Taraxacum* (dandelion), *Leontodon* (hawkbits) and *Hieracium* (hawkweeds) which would have grown on disturbed ground typical of the upper saltmarsh. A mosaic of environments on the upper marsh is envisaged, with marginal freshwater wet areas supporting aquatic plants such as *Typha latifolia* (bulrush) and Cyperaceae (sedges). The presence of *Glomus*-type bodies (mycorrhizal fungi) is indicative of aerobic bioactive soils (Bagyaraj and Varma 1995). Tree pollen was found at less than 5% TLP indicating an absence of local trees with woodland or isolated trees of pine, birch and alder at some distance.

Creeks and pans
Saltmarshes develop as nearly flat or gently sloping platforms (Davidson-Arnott *et al.* 2019, 396). They are never uniformly sloped down to the coastal mudflats and the relative widths of the upper and lower saltmarsh will vary considerably due to the presence of other physical features such as the many tidal creeks of carrying size passing through it (Tansley 1939, 819–21). At first shallow and highly mobile in their courses, these creeks deepen over time as the saltmarsh develops and become fixed conduits for the incoming waters of the rising tides. Within an old saltmarsh, large well-developed systems of dendritic creeks and their tributaries have all the appearance of a river system but with freshwater passing down and saltwater passing up and continuing out onto the intertidal mudflats (Davidson-Arnott *et al.* 2019, 396 and 405; Figs 3.8 and 3.10). When the creek is full the water pours over its banks into the surrounding marsh with the silt suspended in this water trapped by the vegetation along the creek bank. In this way the level of the creek banks become more elevated in relation to the intervening flats between the creeks. Consequently, narrow zones of more passable, better drained land emerge to wind their way through the saltmarsh (Tansley 1939, 835). The effect of different communities of plants on the trapping of silt and their unequal growth further accentuates the unevenness of a saltmarsh environment. Hummocks appear which can deflect the courses of creeks around them and can coalesce into ridges and continuous raised areas. Depressions can become marooned within a surrounding ridge of hummocks to form poorly-drained pans (or 'pannes'). Saltwater trapped within these pans can form pools of highly saline water that are a much higher concentration than the 3.5% saline concentration of seawater. Within a developed and stable saltmarsh some of these pans can become relatively permanent fixtures in the environment as small lagoons, with their high salinity causing vegetation to die back (Davidson-Arnott *et al.* 2019, 396). Salinity within some of them may even exceed 80% (*ibid.*, 400). Others eventually become eroded and drained by newer creeks. Pans of stagnant highly saline water may also form along the beds of blocked-up channels (Tansley 1939, 841).

Fixed creek patterns have also been shown to be very persistent within the context of an evolving saltmarsh. There is evidence that creeks have often been canalised into larger drainage channels or to act as boundaries, alterations that have failed to be recognised by archaeologists (Gardiner 2005, 74). Navigable channels through the saltmarsh would no doubt have greatly benefitted the movement of salt-workers and their equipment through the North Marsh and complemented the three '*waies*' (trackways) that also led into the marsh (see Chapters 4 & 5). A probably navigable creek (known as a fleet) was revealed adjacent to the previous saltern excavated by OA East at Marsh Lane which measured *c.*6.5m wide: a width that would have adequately served this purpose, although it was not proven to be a contemporary feature (Clarke 2016, 28). Using a 1946 aerial photograph of the North Marsh, taken prior to the extensive housing scheme developments of the 1950s, it has been possible to map at least part of the pre-existing tidal creek network from cropmark evidence (Fig. 1.4). A few of the tidal creek names evidenced from historical sources (notably the Gaywood Dragge survey of 1487; see Chapter 5) incorporated elements such as '-flete' and 'salt' to suggest that a number of their courses traversing the saltmarsh were navigable, for example: le Dale, le Marish (near Marsh Lane?), le Bull (near *Bullcote Waie*?), le Goole, le Salt Ea (possibly the estuary of the River Gaywood?), Reluflete and Salt Rivallett.

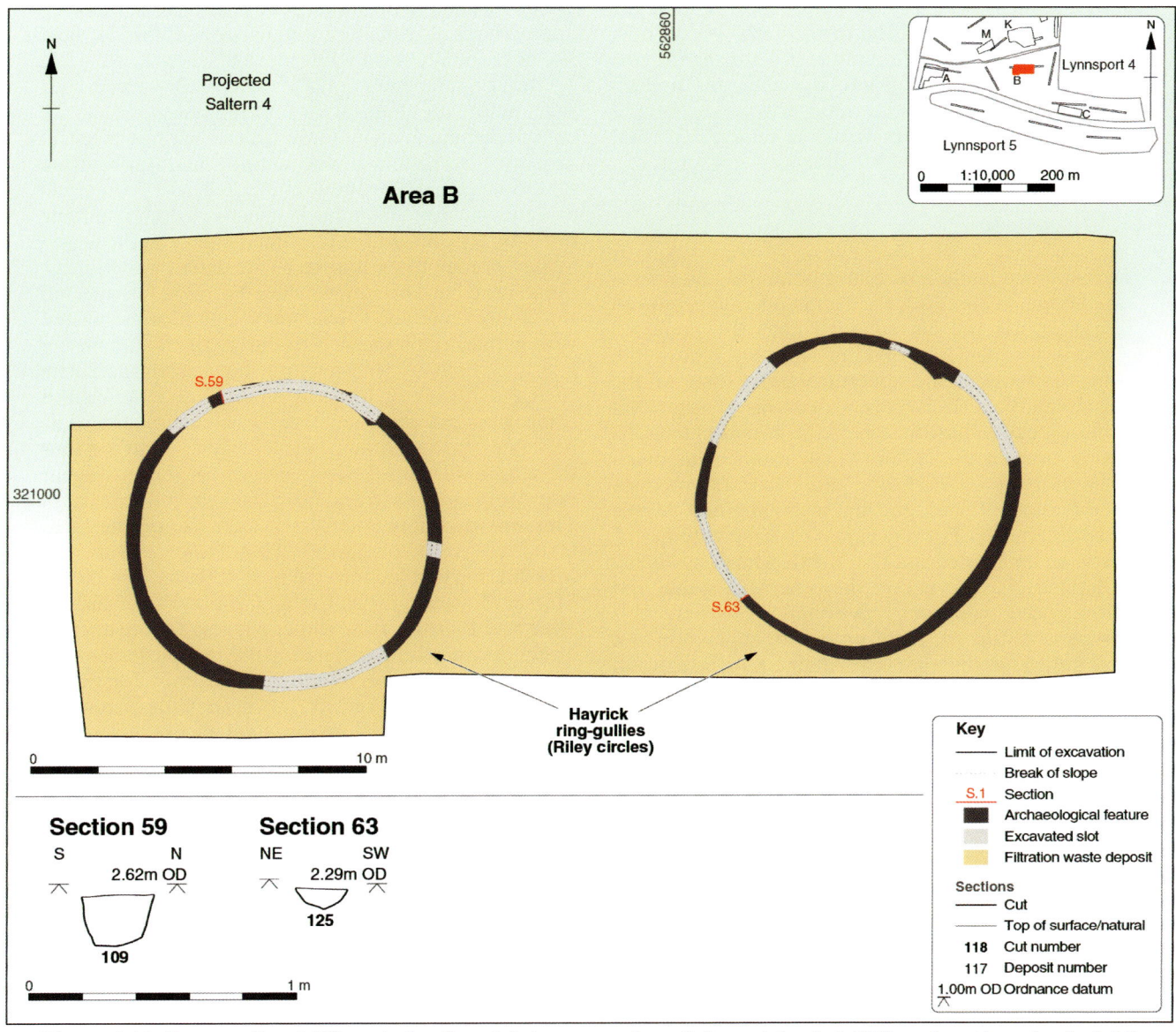

Figure 3.13 Post-medieval Riley circles (hayricks) excavated on Saltern 4 (scale 1:200) and sections (scale 1:25)

Despite this, no direct association was established between any of these creeks and the salterns during the current suite of archaeological investigations on the North Marsh.

III. Transition from saltmarsh to 'reclaimed' pastureland
(Fig. 3.13)

It remains open for debate whether any of the numerous drains mapped on the enclosure map of 1810 (see Chapter 5) delineate the courses of any of the early medieval creeks or fleets. This system of drainage is perhaps more likely to have been associated with the later medieval and post-medieval use of Gaywood's North Marsh as pasture. The drainage network would have ultimately linked with the River Gaywood, the course of which was diverted from the central part of the marsh to its present course in 1425. Earthworks of possible medieval banks, ditches and drains in the area attributed to the process of land reclamation are listed by the NHER (Fig. 1.4, NHERs 13785 and 27891). The raising of the level of the saltmarsh by the waste silts discarded by the Anglo-Saxon and early medieval salt-makers directly resulted in the creation of the many parcels of pasture mapped by the Gaywood Dragge of 1487. The North Marsh had evolved by that time from an intertidal salt-making zone to a valuable belt of 'reclaimed' coastal pastureland, further discussed in Chapter 5. Remnant ridge and furrow or 'lazybedding' agricultural features are also recorded by the NHER on the North Marsh, demonstrating the continued transition to farmland (Fig. 1.4, NHERs 27890 and 27865). Evidence for the harvesting of hay was located upon the southern slope of Saltern 4 (Lynnsport 4; Fig. 3.13), comprising the remains of two hayricks ('Riley circles'), each represented by a complete *c.*10m-diameter circular ring gully (*c.*0.3m wide and 0.5m deep with U-shaped profiles) that yielded a tobacco pipe bowl dated to *c.*1680–1710. Part of a curved gully was also observed extending across the top of the sequence of salt-making deposits of Saltern 5 (Greenpark Avenue School site), which may represent a further hayrick (not illustrated). Later activity was also found at the Lynnsport 4 & 5 site in the form of the burial of a horse, with a small iron horseshoe still attached to one of the hooves, the latter of a type in use from the 19th century onwards. This, and other uses of the former saltern mounds and saltmarsh, are discernible from documentary sources and are discussed in Chapter 5.

IV. Discussion

The combined analysis of micro-botanical and micro-faunal remains alongside the sediments that produced them supports the current view that the preferred locations for new salt-making sites lay within the saltmarsh zone, at the uppermost tidal limit of the coastal mudflats. It is hoped that this chapter will enable a greater appreciation of the potential for salt-making to alter the saltmarsh environment as much as the more recognised (and more recent) processes of embankment and grazing is highlighted in the current literature. The movement of large volumes of coastal sediments across the North Marsh probably accelerated changes within the otherwise stable and well-balanced saltmarsh environments. Where this balance is disturbed, rapid growth or regression can occur until a new balance is maintained. Although still speculation, it is conceivable that the environmental effect of the gradual fall in sea level to *c.*AD 1000 was exacerbated by changes to the physical environment of the Gaywood estuary through saltern mound accumulation which had potential to cut off direct riverine access to both the 'productive site' of Bawsey and perhaps also the recently discovered possible port site near to Gaywood Bridge (see Chapter 2).

Mark Gardiner (2005, 73–83) recognised that landscape analysis of saltmarshes could be complemented by the study of the natural physical processes operating on and within them during their development. His study compared the landscape evidence gathered from both an active saltmarsh in the north of Norfolk with a reclaimed marsh on the Kent–Sussex border to demonstrate the extent past human impact can have on saltmarshes. As might be expected this study concluded that many activities associated with gathering of the rich resources of the marsh are invisible, such as wild-fowling, but certain activities such as salt-making have the potential to leave behind some physical evidence for the archaeologist. The presence of drove roads — trackways — that led into the saltmarsh was taken as evidence for the movement of grazing animals to and from their coastal pasturage. This was probably true of the later use of the three identified 'waies' of *Salters Waie*, *Bullcote Waie* and Marsh Lane that led into the post-13th-century North Marsh. However, the salt-related toponyms of *Salters Waie* and *Bullcote Waie* rather suggest a more ancient origin, primarily associated with the movement of workers and materials to and from salterns. The tracks would have been linked to the village with causeways and bridges over the many tidal creeks extending across the marsh.

Chapter 4. The Salterns

Teacher: Salter, how do we benefit from your craft?
Student "Salter": My craft is of great use to you all. None of you eats lunch or dinner happily unless he is amenable to my craft.
Teacher: How?
Student "Salter": Which man fully enjoys very sweet food without the taste of salt? Who can fill his cellar or storehouse without my craft? Look, you lose butter and cheese curd unless I am present as a preservative for you; you couldn't even enjoy your herbs.
(Colloquy of Ælfric (c.955–1010), reproduced from Harris 2003, 122)

I. Introduction
(Fig. 4.1)

The archaeological evidence for salt-making was gathered from four separate investigations on the Lynnsport housing developments and adjacent Greenpark Avenue School development site. The results of each of these investigations was reported on separately (see Chapter 1; Table 1.1) focusing on the following elements: Saltmarsh formation; Mid to Late Anglo-Saxon to early medieval salt-making remains; and later features and deposits. Whereas Chapter 3 describes the saltmarsh deposits (originally assigned to Period 1 in the previous reports), the current chapter will deal solely with the salt-working remains. These were previously described under Period 2 in the reports, as they relate to the distinctive salt-making tradition of *sleeching* and brine boiling using the open pan method, which continued to be employed both before and after the Norman Conquest. Following additional analysis, underpinned by Bayesian modeling, the salterns have been separated into two spatially and chronologically distinct but possibly overlapping groups named for the associated routes that lay adjacent to them: *Salters Waie* (Period 1) and *Bullcote Waie* (Period 2; also known as Salters Lode (NRO, BL14-41; see Chapter 5)).

A total of twelve salterns lay partly or wholly within the bounds of the investigation areas, which represents a significant portion of the $c.50$ salterns mapped by the NNMP in Gaywood (Figs 1.4 and 4.1). Each of these salterns comprised upstanding mounds of varying size which were initially investigated by evaluation trenches and boreholes to determine their spatial extents and depositional sequences. Topographical surveys were also carried out at both the Lynnsport 4 and 5 and Greenpark School development sites which proved to be a reliable predictive tool for identifying salt-making sites. The projected saltern mound outlines are illustrated on the relevant figures, while the estimated volumes and depths of deposits are included in Table 4.1.

Due to the relative rarity of intact brine boiling hearths in the archaeological record in comparison with the greater numbers of filtration units found, any areas of intensively burnt ground indicative of nearby hearths were one of the main targets of the subsequent excavations. Salt-making activities are likely to have migrated between different locations upon each saltern from season to season. Although the drier crests of mounds were probably repeatedly visited as the safest location for brine boiling above the saltmarsh (along with a helpful exposure to the prevailing wind), these locations are unfortunately also the most susceptible to later disturbance and truncation.

It is important further to emphasise that this project was driven by the requirements of the planning process which resulted in only those small fractions of each saltern mound susceptible to impact by the proposed developments being investigated (see Chapter 1 and Table 4.1). Consequently, the features uncovered alongside the associated waste products effectively represent 'snap shots' into the salt-making industry here. Each saltern comprised approximately circular areas of between $c.50m$ and $c.150m$ in diameter which contained salt-making deposits between $c.1m$ and $c.1.7m$ thick, not including the disturbed and rooted topsoil overburden. The comparative size of each excavation in relation to the salterns and the numbers of *in situ* features encountered is given in Table 4.1. Even allowing for the wider coverage of features and deposits provided by the evaluation trenches, together these investigations essentially represent a partial survey with all the limitations in interpretation that this entails. Furthermore, the industrial, non-domestic setting (and probable seasonal use) of these sites is reflected in the paucity of finds and general cultural debris normally found on settlement sites.

Rather than presenting a feature-by-feature stratigraphic description, the following narrative focuses on those elements such as the hearths, filtration units and other pertinent features identified within the salterns and the associated processes that most inform and advance the study of salt-winning on the Lyn. This is underpinned by tabulated data (Tables 4.3–4 and 4.8–9), with further details of individual features and related deposits available in the relevant reports, links to which are provided in Table 1.1 (Chapter 1). Pertinent analysis relating to the small quantity of pottery is included below as an aid to dating, while further details of this and the other assemblages can also be found in the relevant 'grey-literature' (unpublished) client reports. Specialist reporting has been integrated within the site narrative, with specific methodologies included as Appendix 3. Despite the limitations outlined above, the suite of scientific analyses combined with a more process- and landscape-driven approach to the saltern remains has provided a solid foundation for understanding the chronology and evolution of salt-working on Gaywood's North Marsh.

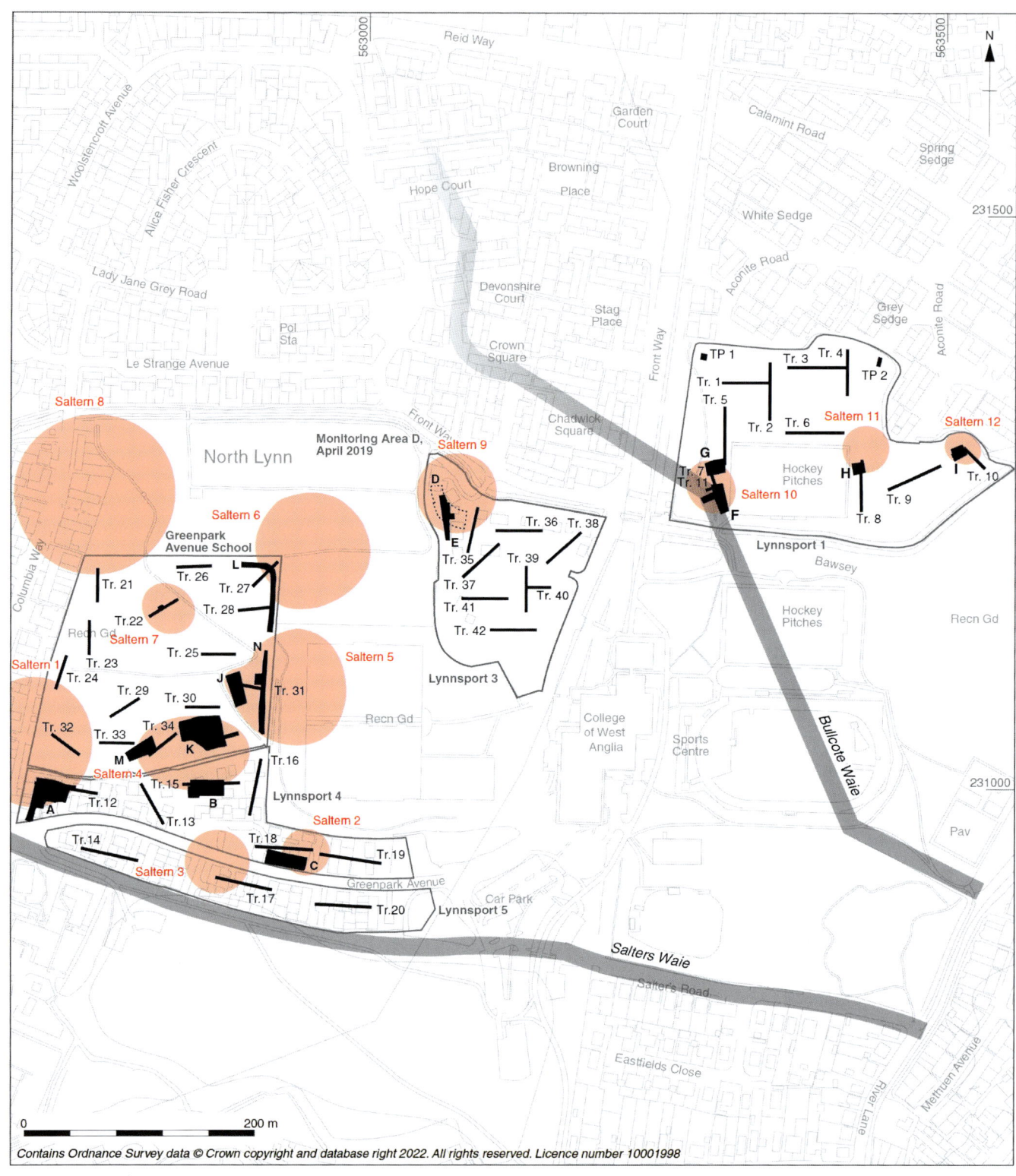

Figure 4.1 Evaluation trenches and excavation areas in relation to Salterns 1–12. Scale 1:5000

A note on nomenclature

The nomenclature used in this chapter to describe the features and deposits follows that used within previous reports on salterns in King's Lynn (see Cope-Faulkner 2014; Clarke and Clarke 2018) and on the Lincolnshire Wash (see McAvoy 1994; Healey 1975 and 1999; Lane 2018). It is hoped that this consistent approach will provide clarity when comparing this site with similar evidence within the wider archaeological record (see Appendix 1 for a Glossary). The 'open pan hearths' are the brine boiling sites constructed out of (fired) clay which was also moulded into pan supports. A 'filtration unit' is used to describe a recognisable clay-lined tank used to process the salt-impregnated coastal muds (the Anglo-Norman *mould*), whether surviving whole or in part. The broader umbrella term of 'clay-lined tank' is used to describe water-holding cisterns of less certain morphology and purpose. The 'filtration process/waste' may equally be described as '*sleeching* process/waste' which constitutes the bulk

Saltern	Saltern area (m²)	Estimated Saltern volume (m³)	Maximum thickness of salt-making deposits (m)	Excavation	Excavation area (m²)	Evaluation trenches	Estimated % of saltern area excavated	No. clay-lined features	No. hearths
1	c.3,317	c.9,654	1.2	A	684	12, 24, 32	21	9	1
2	c.1,256	c.1,022	1.2	C	401	18, 19	32	2	-
3	c.3,317	c.2,106	?	-	-	17	-	-	-
4	c.7,085	c.2,800	1.2	B, K, M	1,619	15, 34	23	4	-
5	c.7,850	c.5,183	1.7	J, N	791	31	10	10	1
6	c.7,850	-	1.5	L	475	27	6	-	-
7	c.3,847	c.1,027	?	-	-	22	-	1	-
8	c.13,267	c.10,624	?	-	-	21	-	-	-
9	c.4,416	c.1,108	1.45	D, E	216	35	5	3	-
10	c.1,962	-	1	F, G	488	7, 11	25	10	-
11	c.1,590	c.1,650	1	H	119	8	7	1	-
12	c.962	c.996	1.5	I	110	10	11	5	-

Table 4.1 Excavation inventory of the Lynnsport and Greenpark Avenue School development sites

of the salterns' make-up and represents the discarded salt-depleted sand. The term 'hearth waste' is self-explanatory, comprising fuel-ash and fragments of fired clay and salt-slag which have been heat affected and broken off the hearth structure. Three of the salterns also contained highly stratified fuel-ash waste deposits which appeared to have been tidied away from nearby hearths into either natural depressions or deliberately-excavated pits. These features are given the name 'rake-out pits' to describe their suggested function adjacent to an open pan hearth.

II. The process of sand-washing or *sleeching*

Previous excavations on the Wash coast have brought to light a method of making salt which differs from that of the prehistoric and Roman periods. Within post-Roman salterns, the remains of heavily truncated clay-lined features have commonly been identified *in situ* either laid in 'chains' between the waste heaps, as found at Wainfleet St Mary, Lincolnshire (McAvoy 1994) or at multiple heights within a saltern mound, as was found at two previous excavations at King's Lynn (Cope-Faulkner 2014; Clarke and Clarke 2018). The surviving complete examples share a distinct morphology, known as a *kinch* in medieval times, but usually described in the archaeological record as a filtration unit. Their use in salt-making has been described in depth by historical sources, notably Brownrigg (1748), Diderot *et al.* (1765; see Appendix 4), Duncan (1812, cited in McAvoy 1994) and more recently by Fielding and Fielding (2006, 8–9) and Went (2011, 2). To summarise, each filtration unit comprised a rectangular flat-based filtration tank that was lined with a watertight membrane of puddled clay and filled with turves. This tank was then filled with coastal muds (known as *mould*) deposited during the high spring tides which had dried in the summer heat to form a salt-rich crust. Despite their name, spring tides occur fortnightly throughout the year, meaning that salt-workers could collect material throughout the year if required.

A study in the early 1960s concluded that it was possible to obtain muds with salt content as high as between 50–75% (Seppings 1961, cited in Healey 1999, 98). This sand was then saturated within the watertight tank (probably by sea water) to allow the finer salt particles to filter out of the silt through the turf layer. This mud was gathered from nearby coastal plots allotted to each salter — strikes — known to the Anglo-Normans as *grevas* or *greves* (Keen 1988, 143). The presence of such strikes of sand on the North Marsh of Gaywood is strongly suggested by the granting of '*quandam grevam*' to St Margaret's Priory, Bishop's Lynn by Bishop Turbe during the reign of Henry II (Dugdale *et al.* 1846, 462; Appendix 5). A narrow clay-lined channel drained the brine from one end into a deeper, circular lined collection tank or cistern. This sand-washing process was known as *sleeching* on the Cumbrian/Lancashire coastline and *muldefange* in Lincolnshire. The resulting solution could then be re-processed through these filtration units to obtain the correct strength of brine. Once a sufficiently strong solution was achieved (the specific gravity of which could be tested by floating an egg) this liquor was taken to a hearth to extract the salt by boiling. Filtration units would be emptied of the de-salted sands, which were discarded in an adjacent heap, and then refilled with a new batch of sleech. At Wainfleet St Mary, indications of the presence of wooden frames or boxes were recognised in nearly all of the filtration tank ends of these units. These removable superstructures would have retained each batch of sleech being washed and stopped silt from flowing into the collection vat (McAvoy 1994, 141).

Brine-boiling was known to have been carried out using lead pans (*plumba*) placed over specially-constructed clay hearths presumably fueled by locally sourced peat and/or wood: the open pan method. Examples of hearths have been found at a saltern on the Lincolnshire Wash at Bicker Haven (Healey 1975; 1999) and at two salterns excavated at King's Lynn (Cope-Faulkner 2014; Clarke and Clarke 2018). These are presumed to have been housed within purpose-built shelters known as salt-cotes to protect this

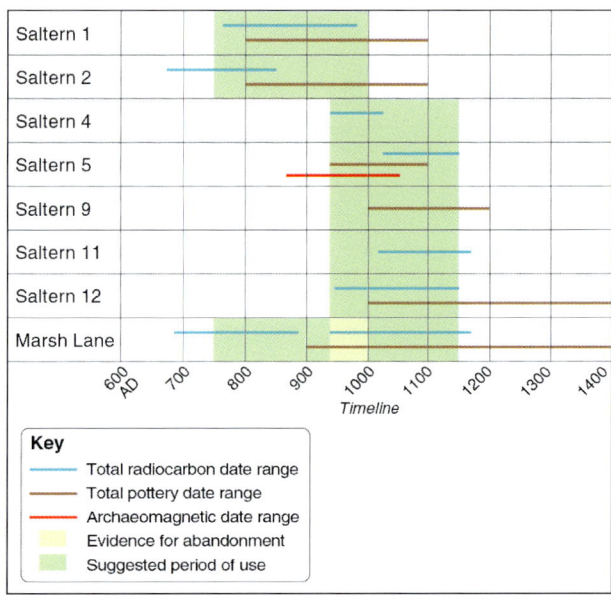

Figure 4.2 Relative chronology of Salterns 1–12 based on scientific and ceramic dating evidence

volatile activity from any adverse weather, although open-air examples may also have operated. The final stage in the process was to drain off any remaining liquor, dry the salt, and prepare it for storage or shipment (Fielding and Fielding 2006, 9–10; Went 2011, 2). Basketwork was probably used to drain the finished product (example shown on Fig.4.42 below, and see Discussion).

It was as a result of the filtration and brine boiling processes that each saltern grew out of the marsh as an accumulating heap of successive tips of salt-depleted sleech and fuel-ash, known to the Anglo-Normans as a *hogga* (Keen 1988, 143). The multiple tip-lines of discarded hearth waste (bearing fragments of charcoal, fired clay and heat-affected salt slag residues) intercalated with the filtration waste within each mound's profile suggest a somewhat chaotic surface topography for these salt-making sites as they expanded in size with each campaign.

III. Dating framework
(Figs 4.2–4.4)

The potential for salt-making on the North Marsh having originated in the Anglo-Saxon period was first suggested following the excavation of a saltern at Marsh Lane in 2015 (Clarke and Clarke 2018), where the earliest group of features were radiocarbon dated to cal AD 670–890 (95% confidence; SUERC-65063, 1225 ± 35 BP). The application of radiocarbon assay was extended to the current study where ten radiocarbon dates were determined for a range of features and deposits. Bayesian modelling was subsequently undertaken to provide a better insight

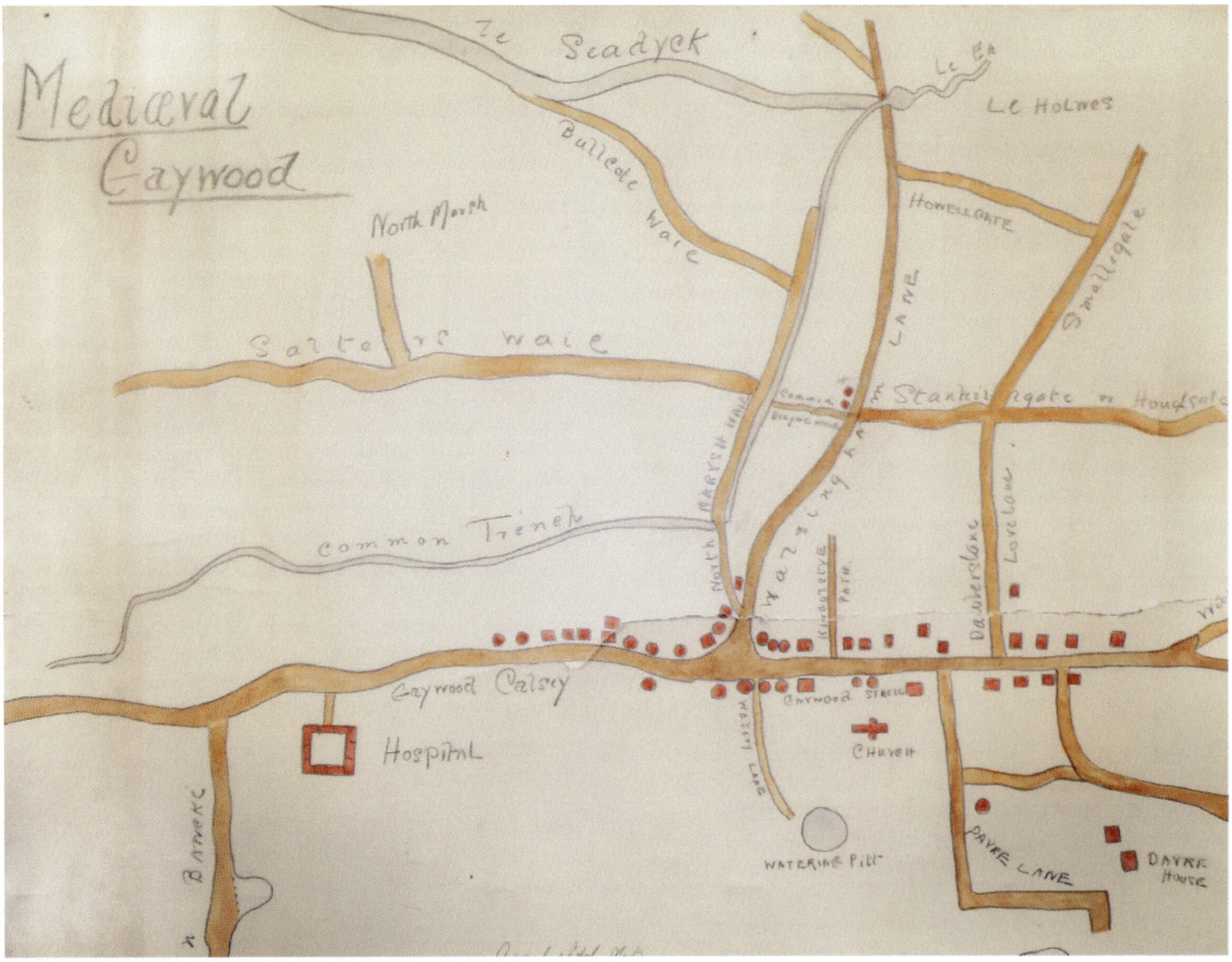

Figure 4.3 A modern (1914) sketch map of Gaywood parish based on the 1487 Gaywood Dragge, showing waies into the North Marsh (NRO, BL 55/1. Reproduced by kind permission of the Norfolk Record Office)

Figure 4.4 Aerial photograph of the North Marsh in 1946 showing *Salters Waie*, *Bullcote Waie* and Marsh Lane (TF62_TF6321_A_RAF_16Apr1946.tif. Reproduced with kind permission of the NHER, © Crown Copyright)

into the chronology of salt-making across the marsh. This chronological modelling, undertaken by Dr Derek Hamilton of SUERC, is provided as a complete report in Appendix 2. In addition, nineteen sherds of pottery were recovered comprising a mixture of Ipswich ware, Thetford-type ware, Grimston Thetford-type ware and Early medieval ware. Sherds in a shelly fabric were also present which have been tentatively identified as Lincoln Kiln-type ware pottery. The combined date range (*c*.650 to *c*.1200) of the small group of pottery recovered from the salterns broadly supports that of the radiocarbon assay. In addition, an archaeomagnetic date of cal AD 870–1050 (95% confidence) was also achieved for the brine boiling hearth uncovered within Saltern 5, part of the (slightly later) *Bullcote Waie* Group (Wilkinson and Batt 2019, 82–91; see below). The sum of dating evidence for the two groups of salterns is organised in Tables 4.2 and 4.7 to provide a dating framework in relation to each sub-phase of activity identified within the vertical profiles of each mound. It must be noted that these sub-phases (I–VI), although based on a secure stratigraphical footing, were an artificial construct to aid the presentation of the great wealth of evidence recovered from the sites during analysis and in the related reports (see Chapter 1 and Table 1.1).

The significant radiocarbon dates achieved by the Marsh Lane excavation have been incorporated into the Bayesian modelling for the current investigation to allow greater chronological and geographical scope in the following discussions into salt-making in the North Marsh at its widest possible extent. The radiocarbon determinations for Marsh Lane suggest that salt-making may have begun between the 7th and 9th centuries (*cal AD 645–865 (68% probability)*) and ceased between the 11th and 13th centuries (*cal AD 1040–1240 (68% probability)*). However, this date range can be refined and the overall span of salt-making probably covered some 400 years (*230–610 years (68% probability)* (see below and Appendix 2). The implications of these dates are fully considered within Chapter 6 of this volume.

Together, this evidence suggests these mounds began to spring up in the North Marsh in the 8th or 9th century, growing with each campaign until the eventual decline of this industry here during the

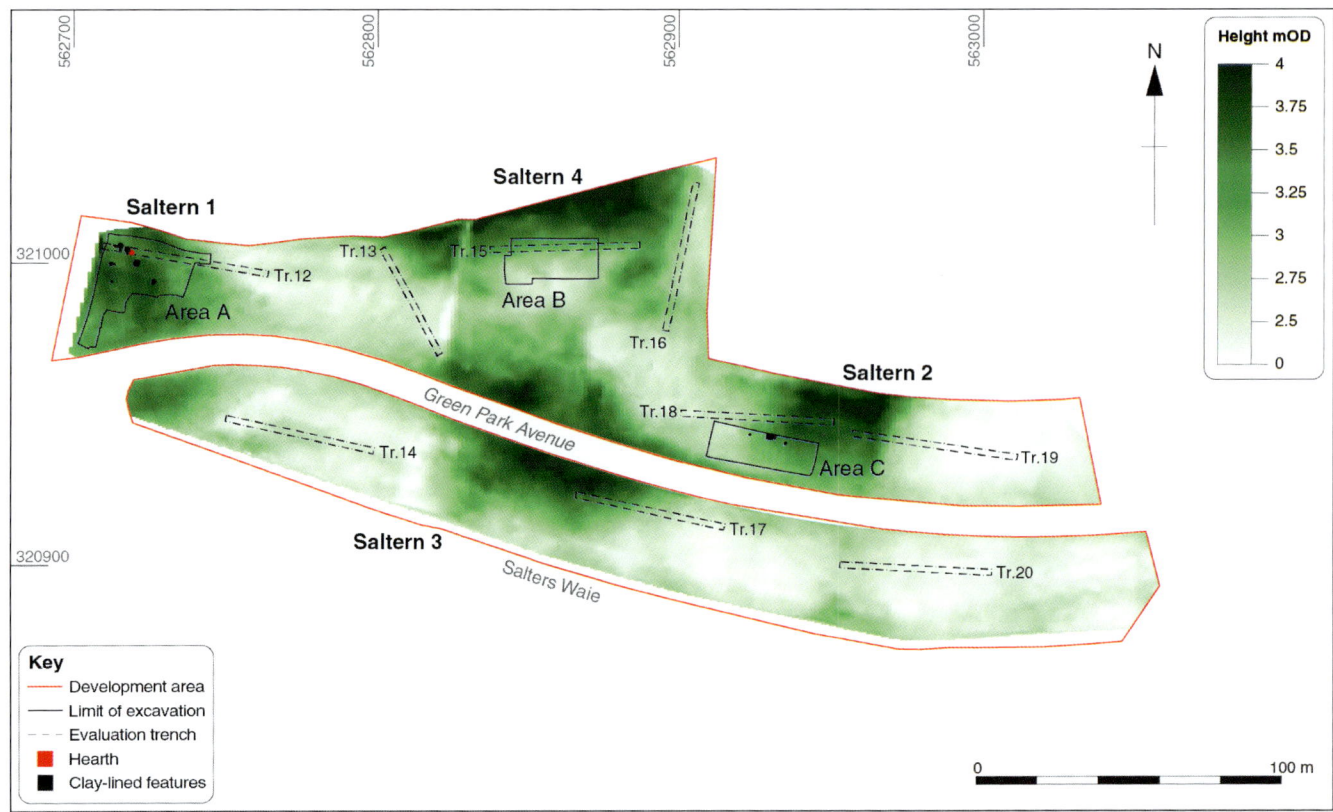

Figure 4.5 Topographical model of the Lynnsport 4 & 5 development site (*Salters Waie* group). Scale 1:2500

12th and 13th centuries. However, considering the changing topography of a mature saltmarsh outlined in Chapter 3, this observation of the data is perhaps an over simplistic and flat view of salt-making on the North Marsh over the course of these several centuries. It is very likely that these salterns were not all in operation at the same time, with preferred locations shifting in relation to the rising or lowering of sea-levels, the spatial penetration of spring tides, the evolving creek patterns and river course, and availability of salt-impregnated muds. Along an idealised flat coastline, the active salt-making zone would be expected to advance uniformly seawards as the landward salterns became marooned within a belt of reclaimed land above the saltmarsh. Nevertheless, the Gaywood river's course through the centre of the saltmarsh would have created a more complex mix of shifting saline and freshwater environments more or less suitable for salt-making.

Therefore, an attempt has been made to link the dating evidence to a direction of travel of the active salt-making zone across the North Marsh during the period in question. Firstly, the sum of the dating evidence recovered from each saltern was plotted on a comparative graph which also incorporated dating from the saltern excavated at Marsh Lane (Fig. 4.2). This comparison strongly suggested that the salterns formed part of two chronologically distinct groups of salt-making. By considering this evidence alongside their spatial layout in relation to historical maps, there appeared to be a link between these groups and ancient trackways which once led into the saltmarsh, namely *Salters Waie*, *Bullcote Waie* and Marsh Lane. These routes can all be traced back cartographically to at least 1487 and are presumably much older (NRO, BL55/1; Figs 4.3 and 4.4). The salterns were therefore attributed to either the *Salters Waie* group (Salterns 1–3) or *Bullcote Waie* group (Salterns 4–12).

The chronological (Bayesian) modelling of radiocarbon dates established that it is highly probable that salt-making at *Salters Waie* began prior to that at *Bullcote Waie* (probabilities >99%) with a 71% probability that salt-making at *Salters Waie* ended prior to its commencement at *Bullcote Waie* (Appendix 2). Consequently, primarily on the basis of the (modelled) date ranges and geographical evidence, the presentation of the results of the excavations into the salterns has been split into two chronological groups with the aim of providing a clearer insight into the evolving technology and environmental setting of the salt-making industry across these four centuries.

IV. Period 1: *Salters Waie* group (*c.* 8th to 10th century)
(Figs 4.5–16)

Outline of works
Although the NNMP survey did not map any saltern mounds within the Lynnsport 4 & 5 development areas, a topographical survey of the site prior to the excavations showed that four distinct mounds lay partly or wholly within these areas, three of which (Salterns 1–3) have been assigned to this earlier group (Fig. 4.5). Following a phase of evaluation trenching that confirmed the presence of salt-making deposits and features within these mounds, subsequent excavation targeted Saltern 1 in Area A (Figs 4.6–7) and Saltern 2 in Area C (Figs 4.8–9).

Chronology

The Mid to Late Anglo-Saxon radiocarbon dates and Thetford-type ware pottery came exclusively from Salterns 1 and 2 (Table 4.2), both of which lay adjacent to the ancient *Salters Waie* (just to the south of the current route of Greenpark Avenue) that once flanked the southern margins of the North Marsh. The marginal situation of these salterns in relation to the saltmarsh mirrors that of the saltern previously excavated at Marsh Lane: a route that once led into the eastern fringes of the North Marsh (see Chapter 1). At both these locations salt-making commenced on the saltmarsh at a height of *c*.2m OD. Sparse pollen and sedimentological evidence from Saltern 2 indicate that it was raised on the upper saltmarsh during a period of possible relative sea level fall. In this light, it may not be a coincidence that the upper end of the radiocarbon date ranges from Salterns 1 and 2, around *c*.AD 1000, corresponds to a period of maximum regression of sea level (see Chapter 3). Together, these strands of evidence, underscored by the Bayesian modelling of the radiocarbon dates (see Appendix 2), suggest salt-making began along *Salters Waie* (and Marsh Lane) during the 8th or 9th century (*cal AD 735–870 (68% probability)*). The modelling, in addition to the absence of definitely post-10th-century pottery, also indicates that salt-making had ceased at Salterns 1 and 2 by the close of the 10th century (*cal AD 835–985 (68% probability)*). The overall span of salt-making at these salterns probably lasted no more than 200 years (*1–215 years (68% probability)*) (Appendix 2).

Overview of pottery
by Sue Anderson

A small group of eight pottery sherds from six Late Saxon vessels was recovered from both salterns: a brine evaporation tank (80) and rake-out pit (83) within Saltern 1 (Fig. 4.6); and a filtration unit (117) and waste deposit (143) within Saltern 2 (Fig. 4.8; see below). The vessels are in two main fabrics, which were probably broadly contemporary with each other. In total, there are seven Thetford-type ware sherds (43g; MNV=5) with a date range of between the late

Saltern	Sub-phase	Height (m OD)	Remains	Dated feature or deposit	Dating technique	Date
1	I	>2	Filtration units complete example 146 (Figs 4.6 and 4.10); *sleeching* and hearth waste	-	-	-
	II	>2.4	Soil 171	-	-	-
	III	>2.5	Heavily truncated brine boiling hearth 34 (Fig. 4.6); hearth rake-out pits; possible clay-lined brine evaporation tanks; incomplete filtration unit; *sleeching* waste and hearth waste	Rake-out pit 83 hearth waste (Fig. 4.6)	Radiocarbon: charred rhizome/tuber fragment	cal AD 700–960 95% confidence SUERC-75156 (1191 ± 31 BP)
					1 x sherd (6g) Thetford-type ware pottery	10th century
					1 x sherd (19g) Late Anglo-Saxon Shelly ware pottery	10th century
				Rake-out pit 128 hearth waste (Fig. 4.6)	Radiocarbon: charcoal of *Corylus avellana* (hazel)	cal AD 770–980 95% confidence SUERC-75162 (1166 ± 31 BP)
				Storage/evaporation tank 80 (Fig. 4.6)	1 x sherd (6g) Thetford-type ware pottery	10th century
	IV	>2.5	Soil 89	Soil (Fig. 4.6)	Radiocarbon: charcoal of *Salix* sp/ *Populus* sp (willow/poplar)	cal AD 770–1000 95% confidence SUERC-75161 (1136 ± 31 BP)
	V	>2.5	*Sleeching* waste	-	-	-
2	I	>2	Soil 142	-	-	-
	II	>2.3	Incomplete filtration unit; *sleeching* waste	*Sleeching* waste 143 (Fig. 4.8, Section 75)	1 x sherd (10g) Thetford-type ware pottery	10th century
	III	>2.6	Soil 144	-	-	-
	IV	>2.6	Filtration units (1 complete example); *sleeching* and hearth waste	Filtration unit 117 (Figs 4.8 and 4.11)	Radiocarbon: charcoal of Maloideae	cal AD 670–890 95% confidence SUERC-75157 (1239 ± 31 BP)
					1 x sherd (4g) Thetford-type ware pottery	10th century
	V	>2.6	*Sleeching* and hearth waste	-	-	-
	VI	>3m	Hearth rake-out pit 47	-	-	-
3	I	>2	*Sleeching* waste	-	-	-

Table 4.2 Dating framework of *Salters Waie* group

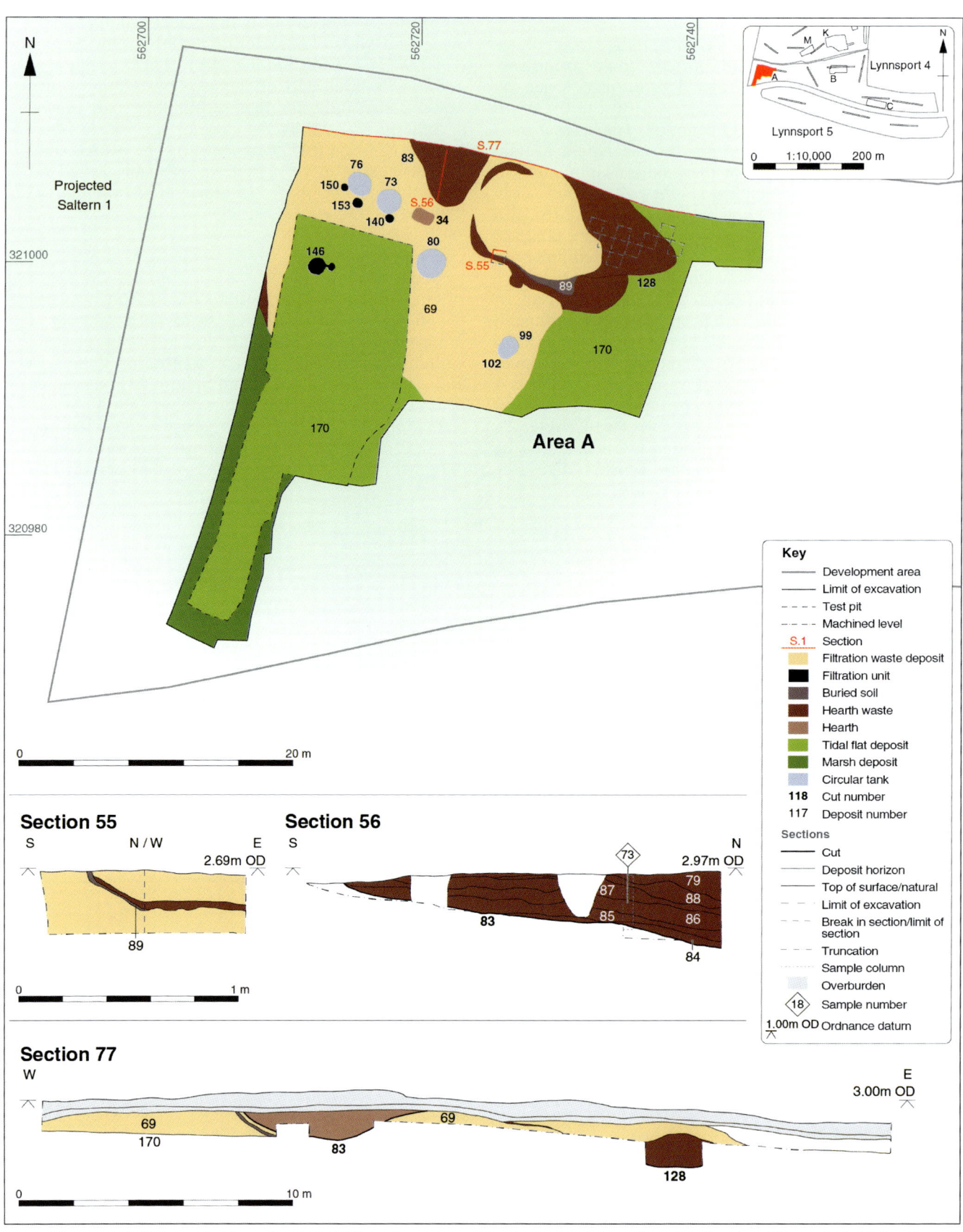

Figure 4.6 Saltern 1: Plan (scale 1:400) and sections (Sections 55–56, scale 1:25; Section 77, scale 1:200) of salt-working features (c.8th to 10th century)

Figure 4.7 Saltern 1: Area A, looking west

9th to 11th century, and a fine shelly ware sherd (19g; MNV=1) which probably represents a Lincoln product of 10th-century date (most likely Lincoln Kiln-type ware; Young *et al.* 2005, 47–62). Only the shelly ware sherd (which came from the basal hearth waste of rake-out pit 83) is a fragment of rim, a rounded wedge type from a jar of 140mm diameter. One Thetford-type ware sherd is decorated with rouletting. None of the Thetford-type ware in this group is of the most local Grimston Thetford-type ware, which appears to have started production in the later 10th or 11th century. Most of the sherds are in the relatively fine, hard fabric typical of Thetford itself, but there are two sherds which are in similar but softer fabrics (both abraded) and these may be from elsewhere, perhaps also from Lincoln given the presence of Lincoln shelly ware.

Salt-making processes

The filtration (sleeching) process

Filtration units
Only two complete clay-lined filtration units were revealed during excavation of the *Salters Waie* group (Fig. 4.6, filtration unit 146 and Fig. 4.8, filtration unit 117), alongside a number of partial examples for which full dimensions were not discernable where just the circular tank elements survived (Table 4.3). Filtration unit 146 was excavated at the very base of Saltern 1 and cut into the underlying saltmarsh deposits at a height of *c*.2m OD (Fig. 4.10), while the second complete example within Saltern 2 (filtration unit 117) cut into an older deposit of discarded waste muds at a height of *c*.2.6m OD (Fig. 4.11).

Charcoal from the lining (118) of the latter filtration unit was radiocarbon dated to AD 670–890 cal (95% confidence SUERC-75157 (1239 ± 31 BP)), although its backfill deposit contained a sherd of Thetford-type ware pottery dated to the late 9th to 10th century.

There appear to be some slight variations in the 'standard' morphology of this class of feature common to both phases of salt-making on the North Marsh. For example, the brine collection tanks or cisterns excavated within both the *Salters Waie* and *Bullcote Waie* groups varied between a rectangular and circular design. The notably more regular and larger construction of the complete filtration unit excavated within Saltern 2 (117) compared with that excavated at the base of Saltern 1 (146) perhaps reflects the relative scale and permanence of each salt-making campaign. Nevertheless, the morphology of these remains generally conforms to the established design of this characteristic salt-making feature excavated on the opposing Lincolnshire coastline of the Wash at Bicker Haven (Healy 1975 and 1999) and Wainfleet St Mary (McAvoy 1994). Although the Lincolnshire examples are clearly later in date, based on the recently excavated sites at Marsh Lane (Clarke and Clarke 2018) and at the current Salterns 1 and 2 within the *Salters Waie* group, this tradition seems to have originated during the Middle to Late Saxon period, at least on the Norfolk side of the Wash.

Plant remains
by Rachel Fosbery
The clay linings identified within the excavated features during the current excavations all utilised the same light to mid blue grey clay that may have been sourced from further inland given the range of seeds, notably

Saltern	Sub-phase	Filtration Unit	Max. Dimensions (m)			Filtration Pit (m)			Tank (m)		Deposits		
			L	W	D	L	W	D	Dia.	D	Lining	Filtration Pit	Collection Tank
1 (Fig. 4.6)	I	140	-	-	-	-	-	-	0.6	0.25	139	-	138
		146	1.96	1.16	0.36	1.2	1.16	0.08	0.8	0.36	147	148	149
		150	-	-	-	-	-	-	0.5	0.15	151	-	152
		153	-	-	-	-	-	-	0.7	0.17	154	-	155
2 (Fig. 4.8)	II	159	-	-	-	-	-	-	0.65	0.48	-	-	160
	IV	117	3.1	1.6	0.6	2.1	1.6	0.2	1.1	0.6	118	119	120
		156	-	-	-	-	-	-	0.6	0.13	157	158	-

Table 4.3 *Salters Waie* filtration unit elements, dimensions and associated deposits

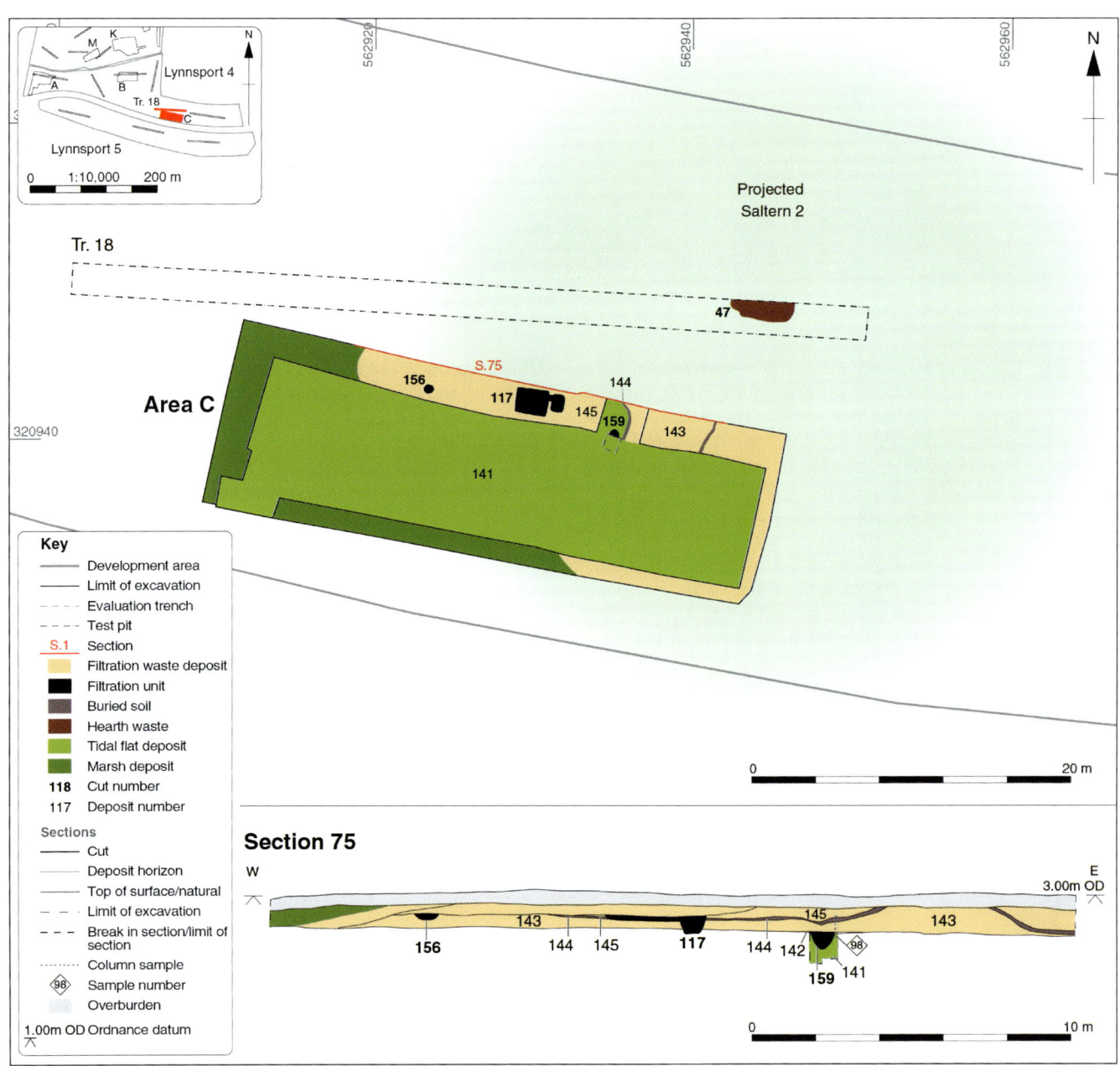

Figure 4.8 Saltern 2: Plan (scale 1:400) and section (scale 1:200) of salt-working features (*c*.8th to 10th century)

Figure 4.9 Saltern 2: Area C, looking west

Lemna (duckweed), recovered from environmental bulk samples. *Lemna* is a freshwater-taxa which can only tolerate low salinity, suggesting that the clay came from elsewhere, although it is possible that its presence here may have resulted from the use of freshwater in the *sleeching* process. Duckweed seeds were not present within any of the *Bullcote Waie* saltern samples (see below).

Circular tanks

Of particular interest was the discovery at Saltern 1 of a set of five (two inter-cutting) shallow sub-circular tanks measuring between 1.6m and 2.15m wide that were found higher up in the sequence of deposits (Fig. 4.6). Each tank was lined with brown clay membranes (not the blue grey clay colour of the filtration unit linings) and cut into the uppermost sequence of filtration waste muds (Fig. 4.12; Table 4.4), and together produced a single sherd of 10th-century Thetford-type ware pottery from the backfill of tank 80 and a small glass object. The latter, a translucent annular bead (*c.*2mm in diameter), was retrieved from a sample of the clay lining of tank 73 and appears to have been made from soda-lime silica. Colourless beads are noted by Guido (1999) as having had a minor revival during the 5th and 6th centuries AD, suggesting that it was residual in this context (Andrews 2017, 61).

These shallow features may represent a type of evaporation tank which was filled with a strongly saline solution that was allowed to evaporate naturally to the required >50‰ concentration of brine (see 'Ostracods' below). Equally, they may represent the base of another type of storage tank which would perhaps have incorporated a barrel-like superstructure similar to the water-tight superstructures suggested for the filtration units (see below).

Cut	Max. Dimensions (m)			Filtration Pit (m)	
	L	W	D	lining	backfill
73	1.7	1.6	0.35	74	75
76	1.6	1.5	0.14	77	78
80	2.25	2.15	0.3	81	82
99	1.7	1.6	0.27	100	101
102	1.6	1.52	0.22	103	104

Table 4.4 *Salters Waie* possible brine evaporation tank inventory (Saltern 1, Sub-phase III)

The brine boiling process

Hearth

A single, heavily truncated hearth (34) was revealed at the very top of the deposit sequence forming Saltern 1, within evaluation Trench 12 (Figs 4.6 and 4.13). This sub-rectangular feature lay on the crest of the saltern at a height of 3m OD. It measured 1.54m long, 0.96m wide by 0.19m deep and comprised just the surviving *in situ* fired clay hearth base. A circular area of more hardened green clay, that represents vitrification due to intense heat within the hearth chamber, was observed on the inner wall and is reminiscent of the inner walls of the double-chambered hearths previously excavated at both the former Queen Mary's Nursing

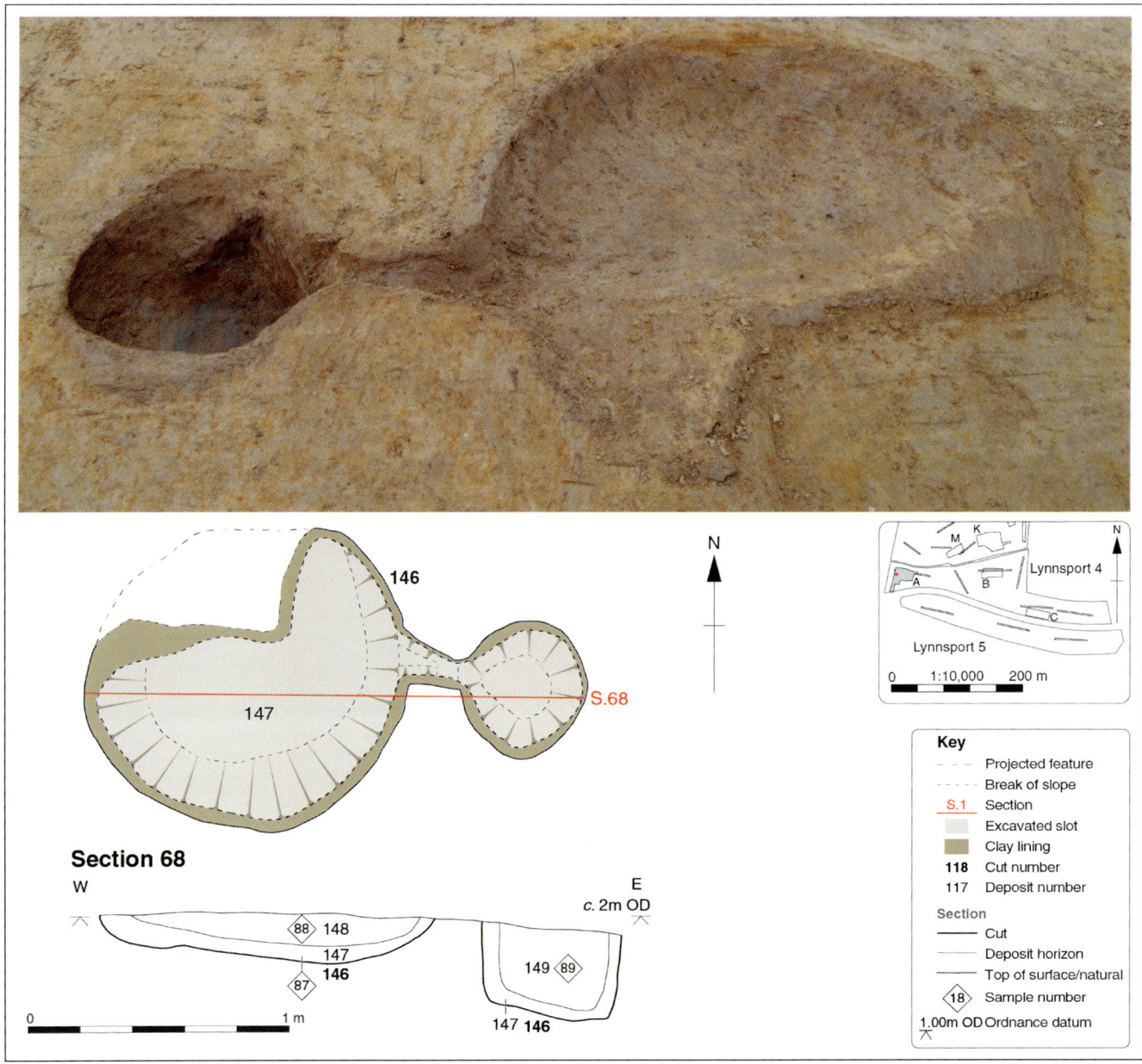

Figure 4.10 Saltern 1: Filtration unit 146. Scale 1:25

Home (Cope-Faulkner 2014) and Marsh Lane, King's Lynn (Clarke and Clarke 2018).

Fired clay fabric
by Ted Levermore
The surviving surface of the hearth base displayed impressions of organic material and some remnant flattened surfaces indicative of the material used in its construction. Fired clay (1283g) recovered from the hearth was attributed to a single silty clay fabric with occasional fine mica and quartz inclusions, rare coarse angular flint or stone inclusions and common elongate organic impressions and voids suggesting burnt out grassy temper. Although the exact source of the clay or the inclusions has not been proven for this assemblage, these are likely to have been naturally occurring in the local clay. The poor sorting of the inclusions suggests minimal paste preparation, although organic matter (chaff?) was probably included in the recipe. It was fired to a mid to dark orange and some fragments were quite friable.

Rake-out pits
Whereas hearth waste observed within the excavations (including at Marsh Lane) was often found 'tipped' as layers of varying thickness over the surface of the mounds, at least a proportion of this waste product within the *Salters Waie* group appeared to have been purposefully raked-out and disposed of within pits. Two large, amorphous pits containing well-stratified sequences of burnt fuel-ash were identified within Saltern 1 (Fig. 4.6; rake-out pits 83 and 128) and a further example within Saltern 2 (Fig. 4.8; rake-out pit 47 in Trench 18). Charcoal excavated from the two pits in Saltern 1 returned comparative radiocarbon determinations centred on the 9th century: pit 83 dated to cal AD 700–960 (95% confidence SUERC-75156 (1191 ± 31 BP)) and pit 128 dated to cal AD 770–980 (95% confidence SUERC-75162 (1166 ± 31 BP)).

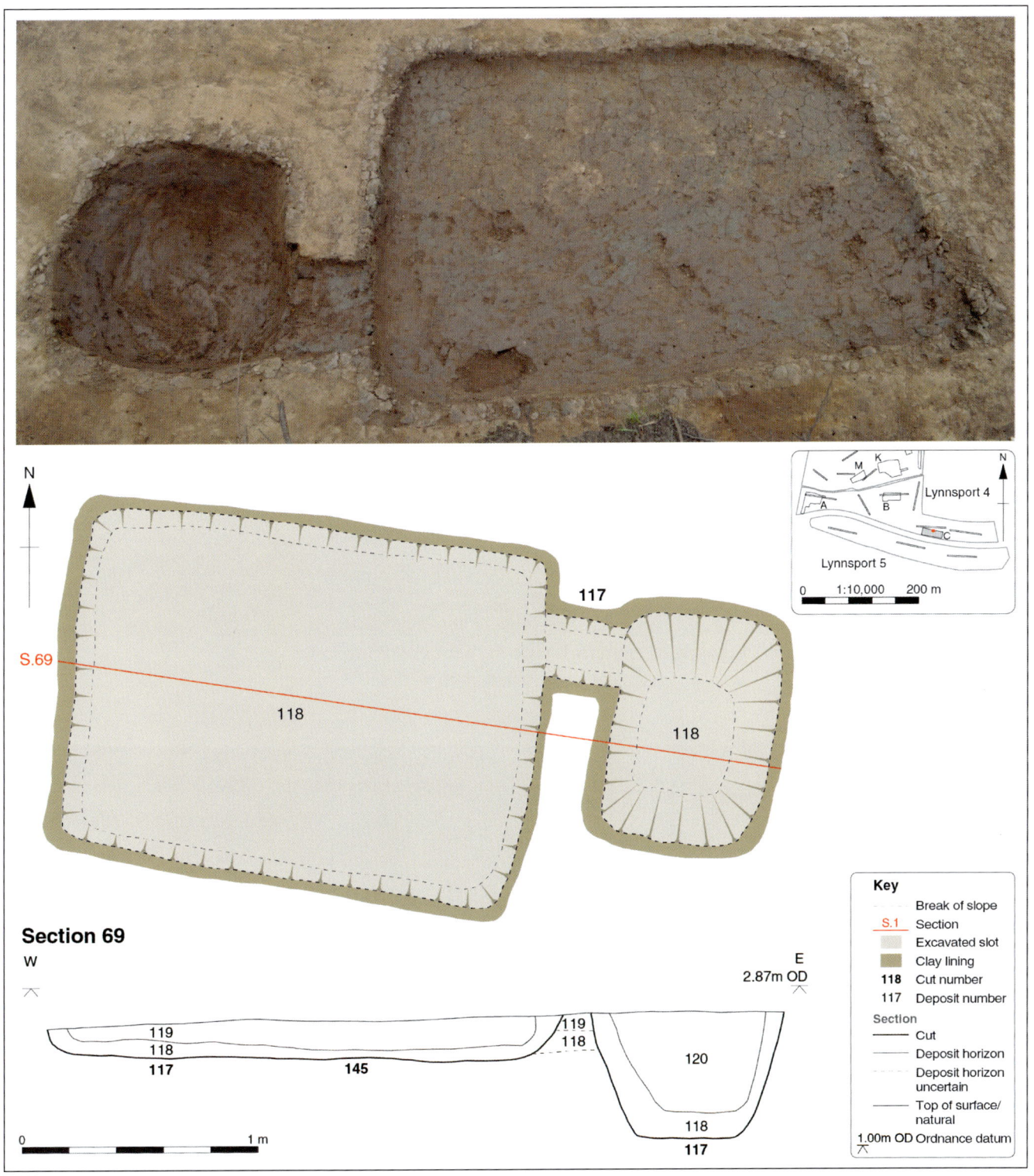

Figure 4.11 Saltern 2: Filtration unit 117. Scale 1:25

Single sherds of Shelly ware and Thetford-type ware pottery (alongside a single incomplete fragment of corroded iron nail with a flattened wedge-shaped head) were also recovered from pit 83. The radiocarbon dating suggests that salt-working continued into the c.10th century at this site.

Located immediately to the north-east of hearth 34, rake-out pit 83 was partly exposed against the northern limit of excavation. It was probably directly associated with the hearth and measured c.6m in diameter and 0.8m deep. The pit contained a series of burnt fuel waste deposits that no doubt reflects the scale and duration of each salt-making campaign (Fig. 4.6, Sections 56 and 77; Fig. 4.14). Bands of relatively clean naturally-laid sand deposits were observed between three distinct tips of brine boiling hearth waste, which potentially represent annual abandonments (see 'Sedimentology' below). These sand deposits were made-up of very thin lenses of material, indicating they were laid down by natural processes rather than being dumps of filtration waste silts. No pollen was found in the ash deposits sampled

Figure 4.12 Saltern 1: Circular tanks, looking south

Figure 4.13 Saltern 1: Hearth 34, looking south-west

Figure 4.14 Saltern 1: Rake-out pit 83, looking west

from a monolith tin sample, making it inconclusive whether peat or wood was the source of fuel for the adjacent hearth. However, the sediment contained soil fungi suggesting that time had elapsed between deposits being dumped. Fragments of baked clay brick-like fragments from this feature are of a type also excavated at the nearby Queen Mary's Nursing Home and Marsh Lane sites (Cope-Faulkner 2014; Clarke and Clarke 2018). The fragments, for which no full dimensions survived, displayed greenish colouration on their surfaces and an orange core made of silty clay with sandy inclusions. Other collected fragments possess indicators of hand forming and flattened surfaces, with one fragment displaying a thumb/finger impression reminiscent of props or spacers to support pans. A proportion also have a mineral crust on the surviving surface, probably derived from salt production.

Rake-out pit 128 was encountered to the east as a large spread of burnt deposits measuring approximately 8m by 4m in plan. A series of test pits was excavated into this area, which revealed a similar sequence of burnt waste tips sandwiched between clean layers of yellow sand (Fig. 4.6, Section 77; Fig. 4.15). This sequence extended down to a height of 1.5m OD; below the level of the natural saltmarsh deposits, indicating that these deposits infilled a cut feature. The fuel-ash continued to be tipped at this location, resulting in a low-lying midden or mound of waste which spilled beyond the edge of the pit cut.

The third rake-out pit (47) was uncovered at a height of 3m OD towards the eastern end of Trench 18, at the crest of Saltern 2 (Fig. 4.16). It measured 3.9m in diameter and was found to be greater than the 1m depth that safe excavation allowed. The backfill consisted of multiple layers of soft dark grey, red and yellow brown fine sandy silt. This burnt, ash-like fill yielded *c*.400g of fired clay displaying organic impressions and flattened surfaces indicative of lining material and 70g of more amorphous fragments, many of which were clearly salt-affected and displayed orange, pink and green hues.

Sedimentology and micromorphology of hearth waste
by Frances Green
A 50cm-long monolith taken across the profile of rake-out pit 83 was logged using Tröels-Smith's (1955) classification scheme (Fig. 4.6, Section 56, Monolith 73; Table 4.5).

The discrete layers with sharp boundaries suggest episodic backfilling of the pit with hearth waste presumably from heating for salt evaporation. The fine lenses of clean sand in most deposits show that during the deposition of hearth waste, sands weathered-in from the pit sides and surrounding areas as a result of rain and especially wind. The general lack of massive sand layers, particularly after the lower 10–15cm of the pit, may suggest the pit was covered between periods of raking out hearth waste. Possibly the discrete layers identified may have resulted from seasonal periods of salt production with the pits covered over during inactivity. Potentially the layers recorded in Monolith 73 may be annual events, accumulating over a period of perhaps five to six years.

Figure 4.15 Saltern 1: Rake-out pit 128, looking west

Figure 4.16 Saltern 2: Excavation of rake-out pit 47, looking west

Depth (cm) from top of monolith. Top of unit	Top of unit m OD	Depth (cm) base of unit	Base of unit m OD	Description	Context	Interpretation
0	2.90	2	2.88	Dark grey 'soil' not *in situ*. Fine sand with humified organic. Gamin3, SH1, Sharp contact with below.	79	Redeposited soil?hearth waste? in pit 83
2	2.88	8	2.82	Dark purple-pink ash with fine sand with frequent charcoal and small lumps of yellow silt. Gamin1, Ash3, charcoal++ Sharp boundary with below	88	Hearth waste dumped in in pit 83
8	2.82	10	2.80	Pale brown with grey brown lenses. Very fine soft sand with grey ash and silt. Gamin3, Ag/ash1 Sharp boundary with below	87	Windblown? sands and ash from hearth waste in pit 83. Lenses indicate reworking and weathering by wind and rain.
10	2.80	21	2.69	Purple-pink ash and lenses of sand and charcoal rich sand. Lenses of clean white sand and black charcoal-rich ash. Gamin2 ash, charcoal, Sharp boundary with below.	87	Hearth waste in pit 83. Lenses of washed-in or windblown sands.
21	2.69	33	2.57	Black charcoal rich sand with small lumps of orange fired clay. Lenses of fine white sands. Gamin3, charcoal. Sharp boundary with below.	86	Small fragments of briquetage or hearth lining from the evaporation pans included in the hearth waste in pit 83. Weathered-in/windblown sands.
33	2.57	35	2.55	Dirty pale brown and orange sand with iron staining. Very fine sand. Soft and friable. Gamin4. Sharp boundary with below.	85	Windblown sands-weathered-in.
35	2.55	40	2.50	Black sand and probably ash with lenses of white sand. Gamin2, Charcoal 2, ash. Sharp boundary with below	85	Hearth waste with some windblown/weathered-in lenses of sand in pit 83.
40	2.50	44	2.46	Mid brown firm silty sand with fine lenses of pale brown sand. Gamin3, Ag1. Sharp boundary with below.	84	Weathered-in filtration waste. The basal fill of the pit.
44	2.46	50	2.40	Pale brown very fine, soft and friable massive structureless sand with Fe staining. Gamin4.		Sediments below base of pit (83). Probably filtration waste (69) or earlier natural sand flat deposits.

Table 4.5 Sedimentology of Monolith 73 taken through hearth waste in rake-out pit 83, after Tröels-Smith (1955)

Evidence for fuel
by Rachel Fosberry and Denise Druce

There is scant evidence of what was used to fuel the open pan brine boiling hearths, which is a common theme on saltern sites of this period. Earlier OA East excavations at Marsh Lane and nearby at Walpole St Peter recovered only a few fragments of charred heather from the hearths and a single seed of bogbean (*Menyanthes trifoliata*), a peat-loving plant, from a clay-lined tank. It was considered most likely that any dried peat used to fire the hearths had decayed to leave only a carbon-rich, black-stained soil (Clarke and Clarke 2018, 13 and 16). The extremely low levels of charcoal recovered from the features directly associated with salt-making at this site suggest that either other forms of fuel, other than wood/charcoal, were used during the activities, or that preservation of wood charcoal at the site was poor. Charcoal samples submitted for identification from hearth waste from Saltern 1 revealed primarily small twig fragments of shrubby taxa such as blackthorn-type (*Prunus* sp., which includes sloe/blackthorn, wild or bird cherry), and hawthorn-type (Maloideae, which includes hawthorn, apple, pear or whitebeam). Other taxa recorded from this saltern include hazel (*Corylus avellana*) and possible heather (Ericaceae). Untransformed seeds are also common in the hearth waste deposits excavated from the *Salter's Waie* group and include brambles (*Rubus* sp.), goosefoots (*Chenopodium* sp.), elderberry (*Sambucus nigra*) and nettles (*Urtica dioica*). These may represent more modern contaminants, or indicate a fairly overgrown, scrubland environment in the vicinity.

Salt-making environment

Filtration unit sediments

Ostracods and other remains (Saltern 1)
by Simon Timberlake

Ostracods are clearly useful as an environmental indicator in the archaeological excavation of saltern sites, especially in terms of confirming their immediate environment and the purpose of the clay-lined filtration units. Numerous ostracods were encountered within Sample 87, from the base and clay lining of filtration unit 146 within Saltern 1. Samples 88 and 89 were also taken from the backfill sediments of the collection tank. Foraminifera and molluscs were also present, and the evidence of these has been used simply to support the information provided by the ostracod analysis. These assemblages are of very low diversity, with most species being euryhaline brackish to freshwater in nature. Both adults and juveniles (carapaces and valves) were identifiable, therefore it seemed possible to determine the likelihood of autochthoneity. Due to the preservation and numbers of ostracods present a much more comprehensive analysis of Sample 87 (both flot and residue fractions) was possible and in all probability this has provided a good indication of the salinity and environment of the filtration unit.

Sample 87
Some 1133 ostracods were counted within a sub-sample (5.98g) of Sample 87 taken from the lining of filtration unit 146, consisting of 1g from a flot weighing 8.69g in addition to 4.98g from the residue of 111.34g. Just over 82% (935) of these ostracods consist of the 'smooth' polymorph form of the brackish to hypersaline tolerant species *Cyprideis torosa* (Jones 1850; Kilyeni and Whittaker 1974); the population of which is made up of 457 adults (238 carapaces and 219 valves, >60% of which were female) and 469 juveniles (225 carapaces and 244 valves, some of which are sexually dimorphic). The above population structure is a good indication of an autochthonous species. In contrast, *Limnocythere inopinata* (Baird 1843) is represented just by juveniles (193, of which 126 are carapaces and 68 are valves). All of these were recovered from the flot fraction, and are likely to be allochthonous, though nevertheless well-preserved and probably therefore proximal to this environment. Just two juvenile valves of the mesohaline ostracod *Loxoconcha elliptica* were recorded alongside two juvenile carapaces of the oligohaline *Candona ?candida*. Large numbers of marine foraminifera were noted, most of which are rotaliines (most likely *Elphidium* sp., a littoral-shelf genus) although certain other forams are also present (*Lagena* sp. etc.). The presence here of small terrestrial gastropods such as *Cochlicopa* sp. probably relates to the surface environment of the saltern mound itself, whilst brackish water snails such as *Hydrobia ventrosa* are more likely to have been associated with the surrounding saltmarsh.

Sample 88
Some 34 ostracods were counted within the total flot (0.83g) from Sample 88, sampled from the backfill sediment (148) of the filtration pit of filtration unit 146. These consist of just 20 'smooth' polymorph *Cyprideis torosa* (one adult valve and nineteen juveniles (most of them carapaces)), four *Limnocythere inopinata* (one adult valve and three juveniles), one *Loxoconcha elliptica* juvenile, four *Candona* sp. juveniles, and five juveniles of *Cypria opthalmica* (another oligohaline species). In some respects the species pattern of this assemblage is similar to Sample 87, although the ostracods are in much lower abundance and not wholly autochthonous, either to the filtration pit brines or to the sediment backfill. Nevertheless the backfill clearly contained some element of the tank fauna. Once again very large numbers of marine rotaliine foraminifera were noted, presumably as foraminiferal tests washed-out from the marine silts. A wide range of terrestrial molluscs was provisionally identified: *Cochlicopa* sp., *Oxychilus* sp., *Columella* sp. and *Vertigo pygmaea* (marshland habitat) alongside large numbers of the saltmarsh species *Hydrobia ventrosa*.

Sample 89
Sample 89 taken from the backfill sediment (149) of the collection tank or cistern of filtration unit 146 contained seventeen ostracods (present within the total flot weighing 0.74g). These comprised ten 'smooth' *Cyprideis torosa* (six adults (two carapaces and four valves) and four juveniles), three *Limnocythere inopinata* juveniles, two *Loxoconcha elliptica* juveniles, one *Loxoconcha rhomboidea* juvenile and one *Candona* sp. juvenile. From the numbers present, population structure and condition of preservation, it would appear that these ostracods are allochthonous to the sediment backfill of the tank, but may have originated within the brackish saltmarsh environment of the saltern. Shallow-water marine foraminifera are similarly abundant, consisting of rotaliines such as *Elphidium* sp., but rarely including others such as *Lagena* sp.

Despite big differences in ostracod abundance and population structures between samples (adults : juveniles + males : females), a certain commonality in species count patterns links the fauna at the base of filtration unit 146 with those of the tidal mud flat deposits (Area A, context 170; Area C, context 141; see also Chapter 3) and waste filtration silts (context 69, see below). It is conceivable also that traces of the faunal pattern of the tidal mud flats may also be seen within the tank itself (Sample 88).

The only certainly autochthonous species to the saltern environment appears to be *Cyprideis torosa*, a brackish to hypersaline-tolerant species of ostracod (Brasier 1980; Frenzl *et al.* 2012; Bloomer *et al.* 2016) found in large numbers upon the basal surface of the filtration tank and thereafter incorporated into its basal clay lining. Clearly this population would have been periodically depleted as the saline water was tapped off, yet these ostracods would quickly have replenished their numbers, with the species living in some sort of balance below the level of the sediment sieve or filter. Indeed, this tank (or others nearby) may well have been the origin of, or at least an important source for, the allochthonous ostracod assemblage(s) which included this same smooth-shelled polymorph of *Cyprideis* sp. encountered as juveniles and occasionally as adult ostracods within the dumped waste filtration silts and the backfill silts found within the tanks and pits. Periodic relining of these tanks may have resulted in the inclusion of the microscopic dead and moulted shells of these creatures into the clay base.

The occurrence of *Cyprideis torosa* within the ostracod assemblage suggests the presence of salt water of variable but moderately high salinity between 7–30‰ (psi). The implication is that the *sleeching* process produced water which was strongly saline, but not concentrated enough to be a proper brine (*i.e.* >50‰). It is possible that this water was then naturally evaporated within another shallow tank (such as the sub-circular examples described above) to produce a brine (>50‰ (psi)) before being boiled dry to crystalline salt within pans on the saltern hearth.

Freshwater may have been used in the *sleeching* process, although this would not make a lot of sense if all the salterns lay within the tidal zone. The only reason might be if this was the preferred method used for maximising the solution / uptake of salt from the silt; this being more efficient perhaps than using salty water which was already 10–30‰ saline.

Filtration (sleeching) waste

The salt-depleted *sleeching* waste tipped onto the salterns was sampled during the excavations for a range of microbotanical assemblages to inform the environmental conditions of the saltmarsh and to confirm whether the *mould* was only gathered from that part of the upper saltmarsh reached by the spring tides, or whether this included muds from the lower saltmarsh or even tidal flat environments.

Ostracods and other remains (Saltern 1)
by Simon Timberlake

Due to the relatively poor recovery of ostracods within a sample taken from the filtration waste tips on Saltern 1 (Fig. 4.6, Section 77, context 69), the same caveats apply to the interpretation of this assemblage as those given for the ostracod assemblage recovered from the unworked silts of the natural saltmarsh outlined in Chapter 3. However, the identified species here are clearly all allochthonous to the sedimentary environment of the saltern and are most likely, therefore, to represent a transported population of ostracods dominated by littoral species. This would confirm a tidal flat origin comparable to the sample taken from the backfill sediment of filtration unit 146.

Sample 109
Just thirteen ostracods were counted, marginally dominated by *Loxoconcha elliptica* (four well-preserved juveniles), with one juvenile *Cyprideis torosa*, two juvenile *Limnocythere inopinata*, three juvenile *Candona* sp., two juvenile *Herpetocypris reptans* (less brackish mesohaline) and a juvenile *Cypria opthalmica*. These are freshwater-brackish species, the ratios of which suggest some degree of commonality in fauna between the tidal mudflats, the waste mound silts, and the material backfilling the filtration units. A similar range of marine foraminifera is present, whilst the presence of terrestrial snails confirms the subsequently emergent and drier conditions of the mound.

Pollen (Saltern 2)
by Frances Green

Pollen in fair condition but at low to very low counts was recovered from a column soil sample (monolith) taken across the profile of one of the filtration waste deposits (143) within Saltern 2 (Fig. 4.8, Section 75, Monolith 98). Two coverslips were counted and the maximum pollen count ranged between twelve and seventy-seven, although spores with environmental significance were found in addition to this in all samples. The low pollen counts are not statistically valid and therefore the following interpretations of landscape are tentative.

Monolith Sample 98
Poaceae is the most important pollen type (*c.*50% total land pollen (tlp)) in the filtration waste. Another important element of this assemblage is plants of disturbed ground *Taraxacum*-type (*c.*30% tlp). Spores of *Polypodium* (polypody) were recorded at low levels. The genus of *Polypodium* ferns include those which grow in a range of habitats including sand dunes. There is a relatively high count of *Lycopdium selago* (*clavatum*) (staghorn clubmoss) (125% tlp+spores) which again lives on acid sand soils and can be abundant in dune-heath succession of sand dunes. A single pollen grain of *Listera* type is significant as this group includes helleborines which are found in a variety of habitats including dunes and dune-slacks. The presence of *Glomus* in this sample is indicative of a bioactive soil. The uppermost sediments contained a similar pollen assemblage to the lower deposits with the importance of Poaceae (*c.*30% tlp) and the dominance of *Taraxacum*-type (*c.*60% tlp) suggesting areas of open grassland with disturbed areas which probably reflect quiescence of saltern accumulation. This upper sample differs slightly as it contains a higher proportion of tree and shrub pollen (10% tlp) mostly *Pinus* (pine) and *Corylus* (hazel). Such changes are indicative of an increasingly developed woody scrubland above the saltmarsh. A relatively high proportion of *Glomus* reflects continued soil development in the upper deposits.

In summary, the salterns appear to have been colonised with plants of the dandelion family and clubmoss, typical of dune slacks where a bioactive soil is established, before having been buried with further accumulations of waste. The pollen assemblage is characterised by low tree pollen (less than 5% of total land pollen (tlp)) and dominated by Poaceae (grasses) and *Taraxacum*-type (dandelion family).

Soil development

Micromorphology and sedimentology (Saltern 2)
by Frances Green

A 50cm-long monolith taken across the profile of Saltern 2 was logged using Tröels-Smith's (1955) classification scheme (Fig. 4.8, Section 75, Monolith 98; Table 4.6).

Above the pre-saltern deposits was a firm, clayey silt with anthropogenic remains (142) representing a ground surface over which silty sands of saltern deposits (filtration waste 143) were dumped. Overlying this was a thin band of grey clayey silt (144), up to 0.1m thick. There was a sharp boundary between them, indicating a hiatus of some sort, possibly an erosive one. This band appeared to drape unconformably over the saltern deposits and has been interpreted as a soil. Its undulating course through the homogenous filtration waste was useful in mapping the evolution of the topography of Saltern 2. There is no doubt that the cessation of deposition of filtration waste material through abandonment of a saltern or a more temporary hiatus in salt-making would ultimately have allowed the upper surfaces of mounds to periodically stabilise to allow soil development.

The salterns may have been abandoned periodically due to flooding by sea-surges or large storms, such as the storm surge recorded on the eastern coast of England in 1099 (Stevenson 1996, 321; Simmons 2015). The severity of impact to salt-making would depend on the season. Salt-making was primarily carried out during the hot dry summer months after the high spring tides had deposited salt-rich *mould* upon the upper reaches of the saltmarsh to be gathered by the salt-workers. For example, the storm of 1099 was in November and although it may have submerged the salterns for a time during the general destruction of coastal settlements, may not have directly impacted production. A thin band of mid grey soil (89) was also observed to slope steeply downwards to the north across Saltern 1 (Fig. 4.6, Section 55). This layer yielded a fragment of charcoal (*Salix* sp./*Populus* sp.) radiocarbon dated to cal AD 770–1000 (95% confidence SUERC-75161 (1136 ± 31 BP)).

Pollen (Saltern 2)
by Frances Green

A pollen assemblage extracted from Monolith 98 taken from band/layer 144 (Fig. 4.8, Section 75) had a strong woodland component.

Depth (cm) from top of monolith. Top of unit	Top of unit m OD	Depth (cm) base of unit	Base of unit m OD	Description	Context	Interpretation
0	2.35	7	2.28	Pale orange brown fine structureless sand with a trace of silt. Firm. Gamin3, Ag1, Sharp contact with below.	145	Saltern 2. Waste filtration sands
7	2.28	8	2.27	Mid-orange sand, soft with no silt, friable. Gamin4. Sharp contact with below.	145	Saltern 2. Waste filtration sands
8	2.27	10	2.25	Mid-grey clay silt with a trace of sand. Moderately firm slightly elastic. Ag2, As2, Gamin+ Sharp boundary with below.	144	Ground surface – 'soil'
10	2.25	13	2.22	Lens of mid-brown firm sandy silt. Gamin3, Ag1. Moderately sharp boundary with below	143	Saltern 2. Waste filtration sands
13	2.22	15	2.20	Lens of super fine sand, not laterally extensive. Gamin4. Gradual boundary with below.	143	Possibly windblown sands- reworking of Saltern 2. Waste filtration sands
15	2.20	35	2.00	Firm, structureless mid-brown, orange, fine sand and silt Gamin3, Ag1. Gradual boundary with below	143	Saltern 2. Waste filtration sands
35	2.00	41	1.95	Firm dark brown structureless clayey silt with some sand, rare fine charcoal. Ag3, Gamin1, As 1. Sharp boundary with below.	142	Ground surface
41	1.95	50	1.85	Fine soft pale brown very fine sand.	141	Sandflats

Table 4.6 Sedimentology of Monolith 98 taken through the profile of Saltern 2, after Tröels-Smith (1955)

Monolith Sample 98
Alnus (alder) dominates the assemblage (c.40%) with a small proportion of *Corylus* (hazel) (c.5% tlp) the suggestion being that this pollen was derived from immediately adjacent to alder carr at the freshwater end of the saltmarsh in a zone away from all tidal influence. Pollen of Poaceae (c.30% tlp) suggests areas of open grassland with disturbed areas supporting *Taraxacum*-type (15% tlp) and *Pteridium* (bracken) (>5% tlp). The grass was likely to have been grazed, as supported by the presence of fungal spores of the Sordariaceae, a family of fungi of which many live on herbivore dung (Innes and Blackford 2003). Damper areas of poor fen are suggested by pollen of *Filipendula* (meadowsweet) and Cyperaceae (sedge). Monolete spores (undifferentiated ferns) were encountered at low levels. No soil mycorrhizal fungi were recorded in this deposit, which may or may not have significance.

The overall impression is of grassland with wetter areas of poor fen at the margins or within a clearing of alder carr. There is, however, an unresolved problem regarding the origin of the sediment and therefore the taphonomy of the pollen. This clayey silt is not the same as the substrate from which it is thought to have developed. Therefore, there is a question as to where the clayey silt came from. Despite the fact that broken (unidentifiable) diatoms were found in this deposit, there was no indication that this layer had any marine or even brackish signal. The diatoms may have been freshwater types or even soil diatoms. The lack of any marine indicators suggests that it may have been deposited by an extreme flood of the River Gaywood. After this layer was deposited the sediments may have been colonised and an immature soil developed but there was no evidence of rooting or any macropedological features. The taphonomy of the pollen from this deposit therefore remains unknown; the pollen represent flora from the site or from the catchment. Contrastingly, the lack of aquatic pollen hints that this was perhaps a soil and the pollen reflects *in situ* vegetation. The presence of *Glomus* (fungus) also suggests a thin soil may have developed in periods of hiatus in the saltern's development. In addition, thin lenses of relatively clean naturally-lain sand deposits were observed in the deposit sequences that may also relate to periods of disuse. Combined, this evidence may be indicative of the seasonal nature of the salt-winning campaigns or may represent episodes of temporary abandonment, possibly due to flooding.

V. Period 2: *Bullcote Waie* group (*c.* late 10th to early 12th century)
(Figs 4.17–41)

Outline of works
The NNMP had previously plotted multiple salterns on the Lynnsport 1 and 3 sites, and within the area of the Greenpark Avenue School development (Figs 1.4 and 4.1). Two of these salterns (NHER 13785 and 2795) lay within the bounds of Lynnsport 1 where evaluation trenching confirmed the presence of saltern NHER 13785 (Saltern 12), which survived as a recognisable earthwork. However, the trench and test pit excavated within the footprint of saltern NHER 2795 only encountered a recent build-up of made ground overlying the natural tidal flat deposits. Salt-making features and deposits comprising a further

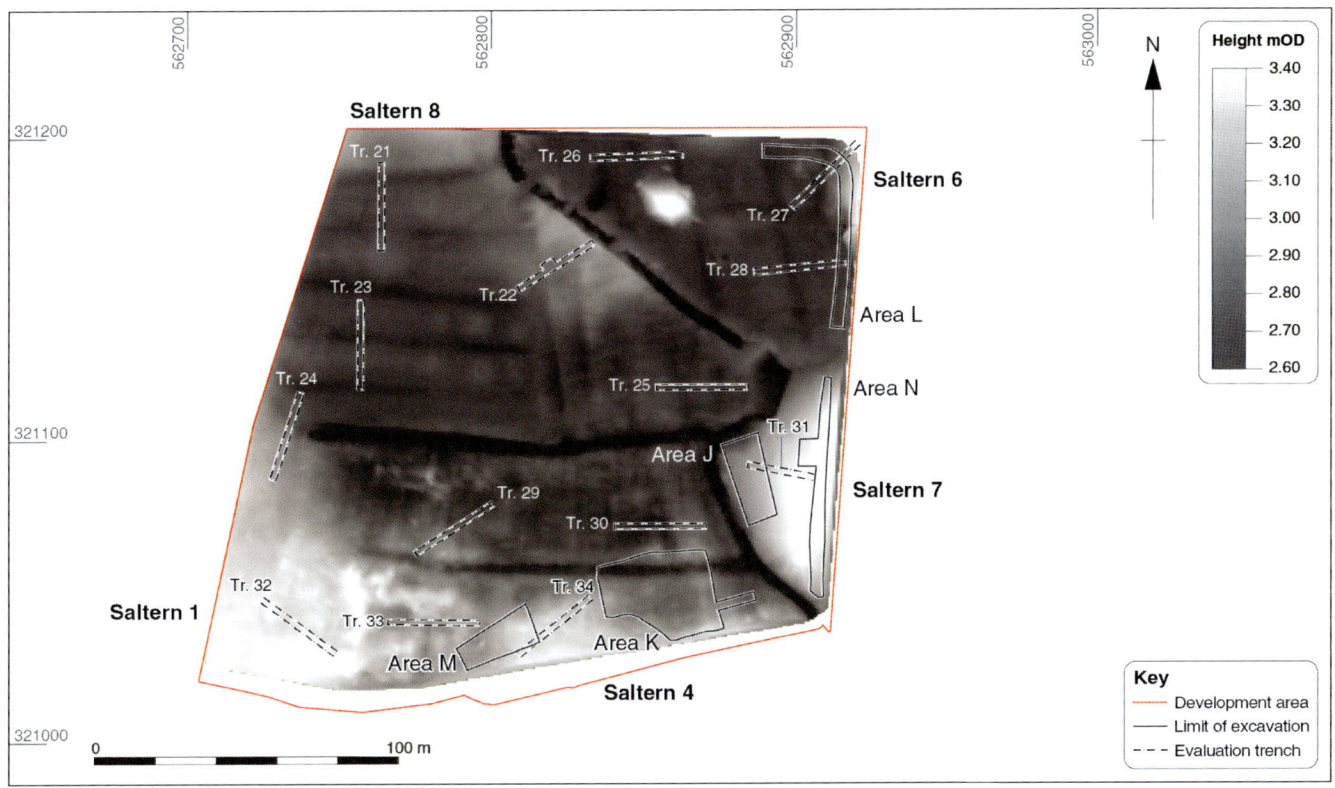

Figure 4.17 Topographical survey of the Greenpark Avenue School development site. Scale 1:2500

two previously unknown saltern mounds (Salterns 10 and 11) were also identified at this stage, located completely within the development area of Lynnsport 1. Within Lynnsport 3 to the south-west, saltern NHER 27910 (Saltern 9) was revealed, which lay partially within the north-western extremity of the site. A further two salterns (NHER 27907 and 27909; Salterns 6 and 8) had been identified by the NNMP to the west of this, the edges of which extended into the northern part of the Greenpark Avenue School investigation area. In addition to Saltern 1 (see above), a topographical survey indicated the presence of three further salterns within the bounds of the site (Salterns 4, 5 and 7), subsequently confirmed by the evaluation trenches (Figs 4.17 and 4.23). The ensuing excavations targeted seven of these mounds (Salterns 4, 5, 6, 9, 10, 11 and 12) which yielded significant groups of *in situ* salt-making remains.

Chronology

In contrast to the *Salters Waie* group, Salterns 4, 5, 9, 11 and 12 yielded radiocarbon dates spanning the 10th to (early) 12th centuries and pottery sherds of a correspondingly later date in both Grimston Thetford-type, ?Lincoln Saxo-Norman and early medieval fabrics (Table 4.7). Consideration of the distribution of these salterns alongside the dating evidence suggests that there may have been an abandonment of the earlier salt-making sites which accompanied a shift of this industry deeper into the saltmarsh (and in greater proximity to the river) during the later 10th century. This part of the North Marsh appears to have remained the focus of salt-making into the early medieval period. Salt-winning commenced at these locations at a lower elevation of between 1.4–1.7m OD. This period coincides with a regression in sea level and a low point around the year *c*.AD 1000 before sea levels began to gradually rise continuously until *c*.1380 (see Chapter 3). This later group of salterns lay close to and on either side of *Bullcote Waie* which led into the central part of the North Marsh, and suggests this route may have been established at this time to provide access for the salt-workers. Together, these strands of evidence alongside the Bayesian modelling of the radiocarbon dates (Appendix 2) suggest salt-making began in the vicinity of *Bullcote Waie* towards the end of the 10th century (*cal AD 970–1020 (68% probability)*). Furthermore, the Bayesian model strongly suggests salt-making probably ceased here during the latter half of the 11th or early/mid-12th century (*cal AD 1040–1165 (68% probability)*). The overall span of salt-making probably covered between *40–185 years (68% probability)*.

Not all 'landward' parts of the saltmarsh were abandoned completely. The saltern at Marsh Lane appears to have been reoccupied after its suspected hiatus across the latter part of the 10th century but with perhaps a greater emphasis on brine boiling than *sleeching* (Clarke and Clarke 2018).

Overview of pottery
by Sue Anderson
A single sherd (22g) of Grimston Thetford-type ware was found in a layer of filtration waste within Saltern 4, which seemingly lay on the transitional ground between the two main groups of salterns. Four sherds (67g; MNV=3) in this fabric were also collected from the backfill of an incomplete filtration unit and *sleeching* waste uncovered within Saltern 12. Filtration waste in the latter saltern also produced three sherds (6g) of Early Medieval ware (MNV=3) to suggest the continuation of activity across the two ceramic

Saltern	Sub-phase	Height (m OD)	Remains	Dated feature or deposit	Dating technique	Date
4	I	>2	Sleeching waste	-	-	-
	II	>2.8	Incomplete filtration units; *sleeching* and hearth waste	Hearth waste 1035 (Fig. 4.23)	Radiocarbon: charcoal of *Calluna vulgaris/Erica* sp (common heather)	900–1030 cal AD 95% confidence SUERC-75162 (1052 ± 26 BP)
				Sleeching waste 816 (Fig. 4.23)	1 x sherd (22g) Grimston Thetford-type ware pottery	Late 10th to 11th
	III	>3.2	Incomplete filtration units; *sleeching* waste	-	-	-
5	I	>1.4-1.7	Soil	-	-	-
	II	>1.4-1.7	*Sleeching* and brine boiling hearth waste	-	-	-
	III	>2	Two unlined pits; *sleeching* and hearth waste	-	-	-
	IV	>3	Open-pan hearth; rake-out pit; incomplete filtration units; *Sleeching* and hearth waste	Hearth 1018 (Figs 4.23 and 4.24)	Archaeomagnetic	870–1050 cal AD 95% confidence 900–1030 cal AD 68% confidence
				Rake-out pit 1011 (Figs 4.23 and 4.24)	Radiocarbon: charcoal of *Calluna vulgaris/Erica* sp (common heather)	1020–1170 cal AD 95% confidence SUERC-87802 (939 ± 26 BP)
				Hearth waste 958 (Fig. 4.23, Section 217)	Radiocarbon: charcoal of *Quercus* sp (oak)	1020–1170 cal AD 95% confidence SUERC-87801 (939 ± 26 BP)
				Hearth waste 964 (Fig. 4.23, Section 217)	3 x sherds (70g) ?Lincoln Saxo-Norman Sandy Ware pottery	Late 10th to 11th century
	V	>3	Incomplete filtration units; *sleeching* waste	-	-	-
6	I	>1.7	*Sleeching* and hearth waste	-	-	-
7	I	>1.7	Incomplete filtration unit; *sleeching* waste	-	-	-
8	I	>1.7	*Sleeching* and hearth waste	-	-	-
9	I	>1.75	Incomplete filtration unit; *sleeching* and hearth waste			
	II	>2.2	*Sleeching* waste	*Sleeching* waste 1068	4 x sherds (19g) early medieval ware pottery	11th to 12th century
10	I	>1.7	*Sleeching* waste	-	-	-
	II	>2.3	Filtration units 3 complete examples: 405, 408 and 414 (Figs 4.18 and 4.19–21) *Sleeching* and hearth waste	-	-	-
11	I	>1.7	Soil 481	Soil (Fig. 4.32, Section 142)	2 x sherds (55g) Ipswich ware pottery	Late 8th to 9th century
	II	>1.7	Incomplete filtration unit; *sleeching* and hearth waste	Hearth waste 676 (Fig. 4.32)	Radiocarbon: charcoal of *Betula* sp (birch)	1020–1160 cal AD 95% confidence SUERC-87794 (965 ± 26 BP)
12	I	>1.7	Soil 654	-	-	-
	II	>1.7	Incomplete filtration unit; *sleeching* and hearth waste	-	-	-
	III	>2.2	Possible soil or flood deposit 653	-	-	-

Saltern	Sub-phase	Height (m OD)	Remains	Dated feature or deposit	Dating technique	Date
	IV	>2.8	Clay-lined features; *Sleeching* and hearth waste; Post-holes and gully	Group of possible brine storage tanks 451, 453 and 457 (Fig. 4.22)	Radiocarbon: charcoal of *Quercus* sp (oak)	990–1160 cal AD 95% confidence SUERC-87796 (984 ± 26 BP)
					1 x sherd (17g) Grimston Thetford-type ware pottery	11th century
				Filtration unit 457 (Fig. 4.22)	Radiocarbon: charcoal of Maloideae	900–1040 cal AD 95% confidence SUERC-87795 (1045 ± 26 BP)
				Sleeching waste 460	3 x sherds (21g) Grimston Thetford-type ware and early medieval ware pottery	11th to 12th century
	V	>3	*Sleeching* and hearth waste	-	-	-

Table 4.7 Dating framework of *Bullcote Waie* group

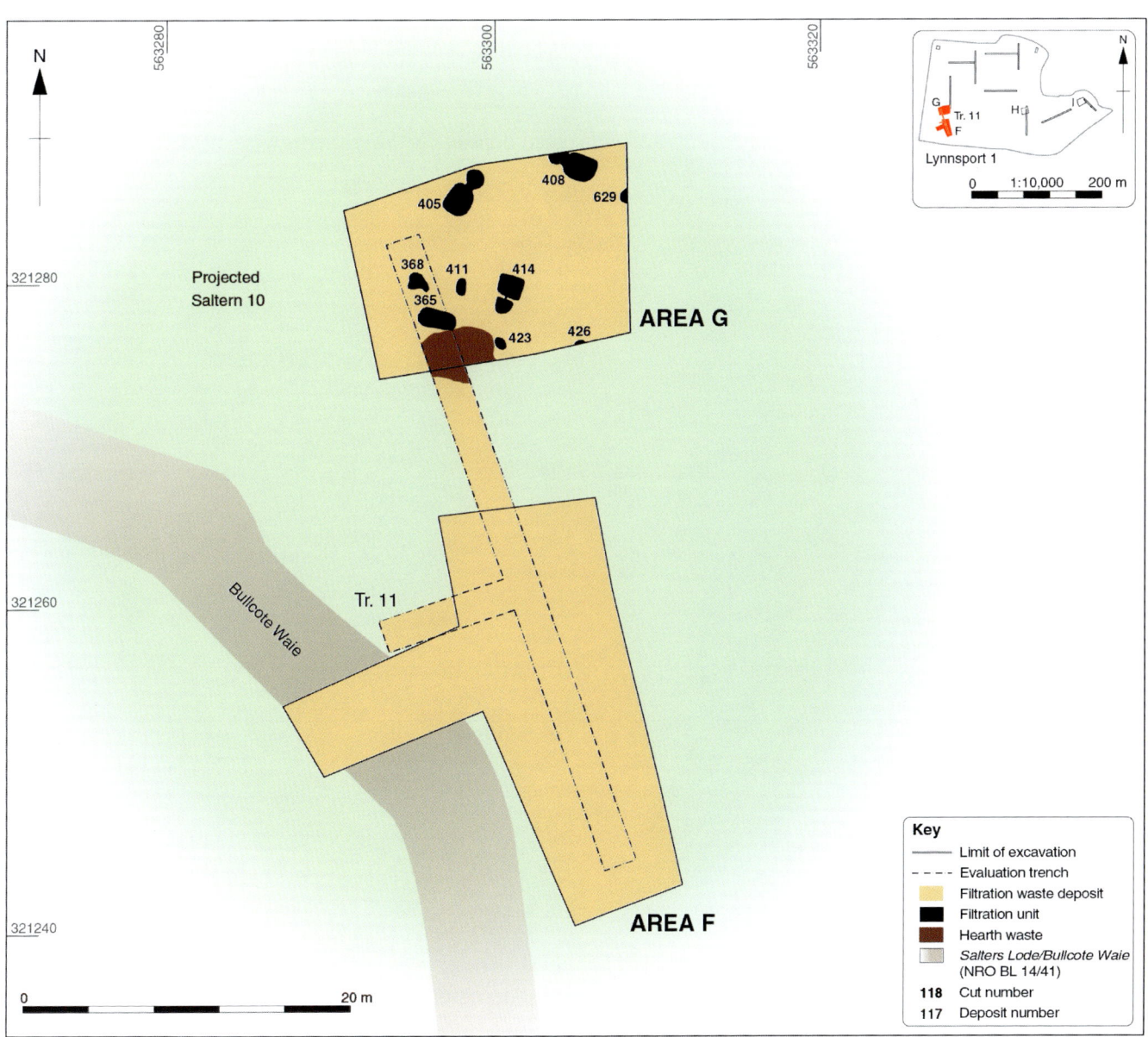

Figure 4.18 Saltern 10: Plan of salt-working features (*c*. late 10th to early 12th century). Scale 1:400

Saltern	Sub-phase	Filtration unit	Filtration pit (m)			Tank (m)		Deposits		
			L	W	D	Dia.	D	Lining	Filtration pit	Collection tank
4 (Fig. 4.23)	II	803	-	1.6	0.4	-	-	804	805	-
		808	-	1.7	0.15	-	-	806	807	-
	III	923	-	-	-	0.4	0.25	924	-	925
		926	-	1.25	0.5	-	-	927	928	-
5 (Fig. 4.23)	IV	892	-	-	-	0.9	0.16	893	-	894
		895	-	2	0.5	-	-	896	897	-
		900	-	-	-	1.5	0.5	901	-	902
		942	3	-	0.9	-	-	941	943/944	-
		945	2.3	-	0.7	-	-	946	947	-
		948	2	-	0.6	-	-	949	950	-
		951	2	-	0.7	-	-	952	953/954/955	-
	V	872	2.76	>1.9	0.55	-	-	874	873	-
		875	>2	-	0.19	-	-	876	877/878	-
		879	-	-	-	1.25	0.5	880	-	881
7 (Fig. 4.23)	I	221	2	1.9	0.35	-	-	222	223	-
9	I	1050	1.3	0.7	0.21			1052	1053/1054/1055	-
		1070	-	-	-	0.42	0.14	1071	-	1072
		1074	-	-	-	0.5	0.14	1075	-	1076

Table 4.8 Filtration unit elements, dimensions and associated deposits within salterns west of *Bullcote Waie*

Saltern	Sub-phase	Filtration unit	Max. dimensions (m)			Filtration pit (m)			Tank (m)		Deposits		
			L	W	D	L	W	D	Dia.	D	Lining	Filtration pit	Collection tank
10 (Fig. 4.18)	II	365	-	-	-	1.86	1.05	0.15	-	-	366	367	-
		368	-	-	-	1	1	0.05	-	-	369	370	-
		374	-	-	-	-	-	-	0.65	0.18	375	-	-
		405	3.1	1.58	0.48	1.9	1.58	0.25	1.5	0.48	513	514–5/521	517–20/522
		408	3	1.58	0.73	1.9	1.58	0.15	1.1	0.73	509	512	510/632–3
		411	-	-	-	-	-	-	0.93	0.11	412	-	413
		414	2.4	1.5	0.28	1.3	1.5	0.15	1	0.28	415	418/420/422	416
		423	-	-	-	-	-	-	0.78	0.16	424	-	425
		426	-	-	-	-	-	-	0.5	0.1	427	-	428
		629	-	-	-	-	-	-	0.93	-	630	-	631
11 (Fig. 4.32)	II	463	-	1.2	0.2	-	-	-	-	-	464	465	-
12 (Fig. 4.22)	II	662	-	-	-	3.4	1.48	0.7	-	-	663	664/666/669–71	-
	IV	451	-	-	-	2.5	1.3	0.57	-	-	505	452/466–71	-
		453	-	-	-	2.5	0.9	0.74	-	-	456	454/455	-
		457	-	-	-	2.3	1.25	0.66	-	-	458	459–62/494–6/498	-
		489	-	-	-	-	-	-	1.1	0.6	490	-	491

Table 4.9 Filtration unit elements, dimensions and associated deposits within salterns east of *Bullcote Waie*

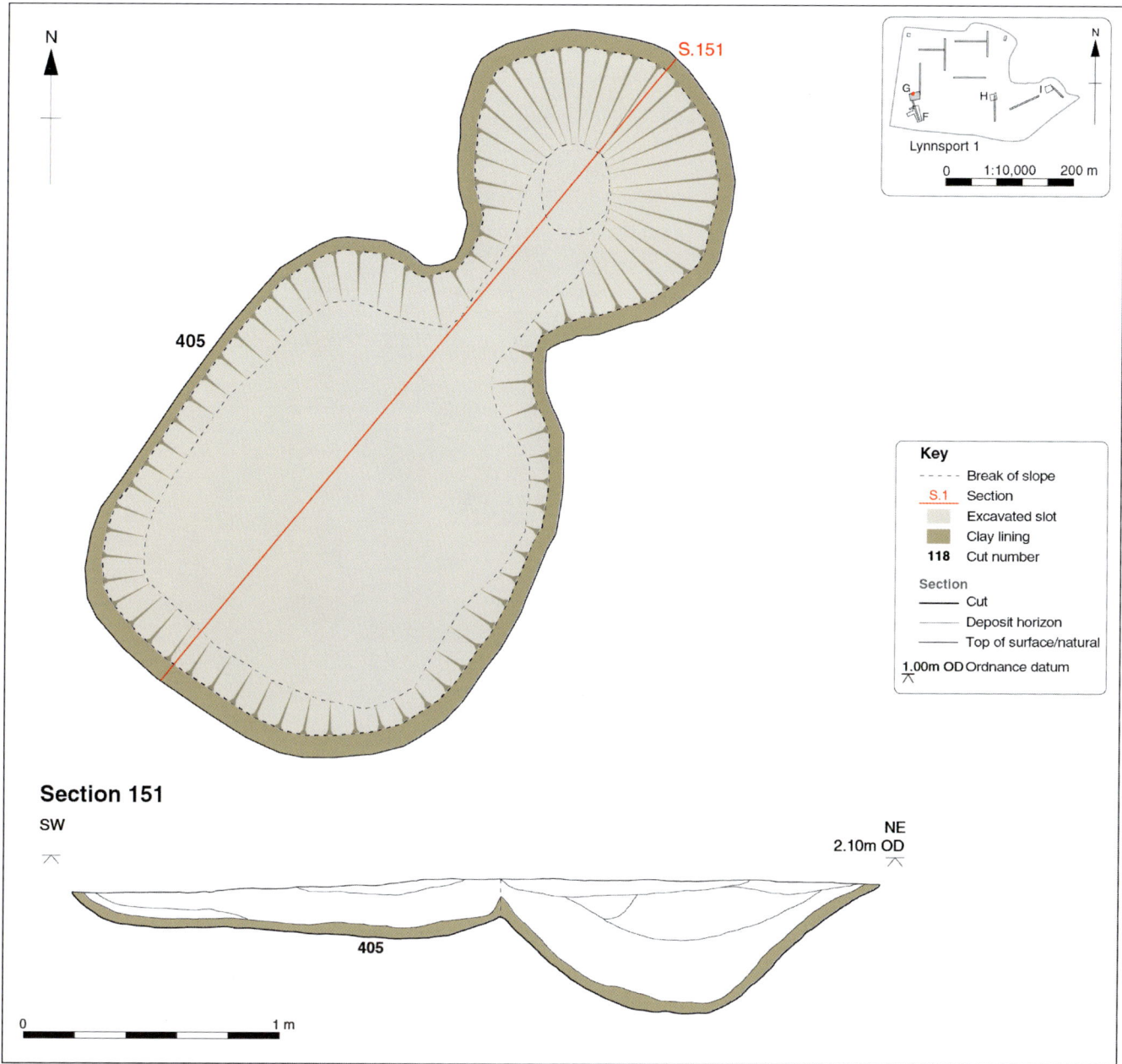

Figure 4.19 Saltern 10: Filtration unit 405. Scale 1:25

periods (11th to 12th century), although in reality both pottery fabrics were in use in the 11th century in this area. The early medieval sherds are from the thin-walled vessel types also identified at nearby Castle Acre (*e.g.* Milligan 1982). Three sherds (70g; MNV=1) of a possible Lincoln Saxo-Norman Sandy ware jar were found in hearth waste from Saltern 5 and are likely to date to between the late 10th to 11th century.

Salt-making processes

The filtration (sleeching) process

Filtration units
Many examples of incomplete filtration units were excavated within each of the *Bullcote Waie* salterns (Tables 4.8 and 4.9). This is taken to indicate their clay-linings either eroded quickly when not in use or were perhaps recycled for later constructions as each successive working area was gradually engulfed by tips of salt-depleted mud (see Clarke and Clarke 2018). It was this process which caused each saltern to rise up out of the marshland. These incomplete examples consisted of both the concave bases of collection tanks and flat bases of the larger filtration pits. If this scenario of recycling the clay-linings is correct, the bases of these features would seemingly have been the most difficult elements to recover.

Three complete filtration units were excavated during the investigation of Saltern 10 (Table 4.9; Fig. 4.18). These features followed the same arrangement in morphology as the earlier complete examples excavated at *Salters Waie* (Figs 4.19 and 4.20; Table 4.9). The remains of twelve circular turves (0.25 x 0.3 x 0.05m) were arranged on the base of a further filtration unit, 414 (Fig. 4.21). Similar 'fossilised' turf layers have also been uncovered at the base of

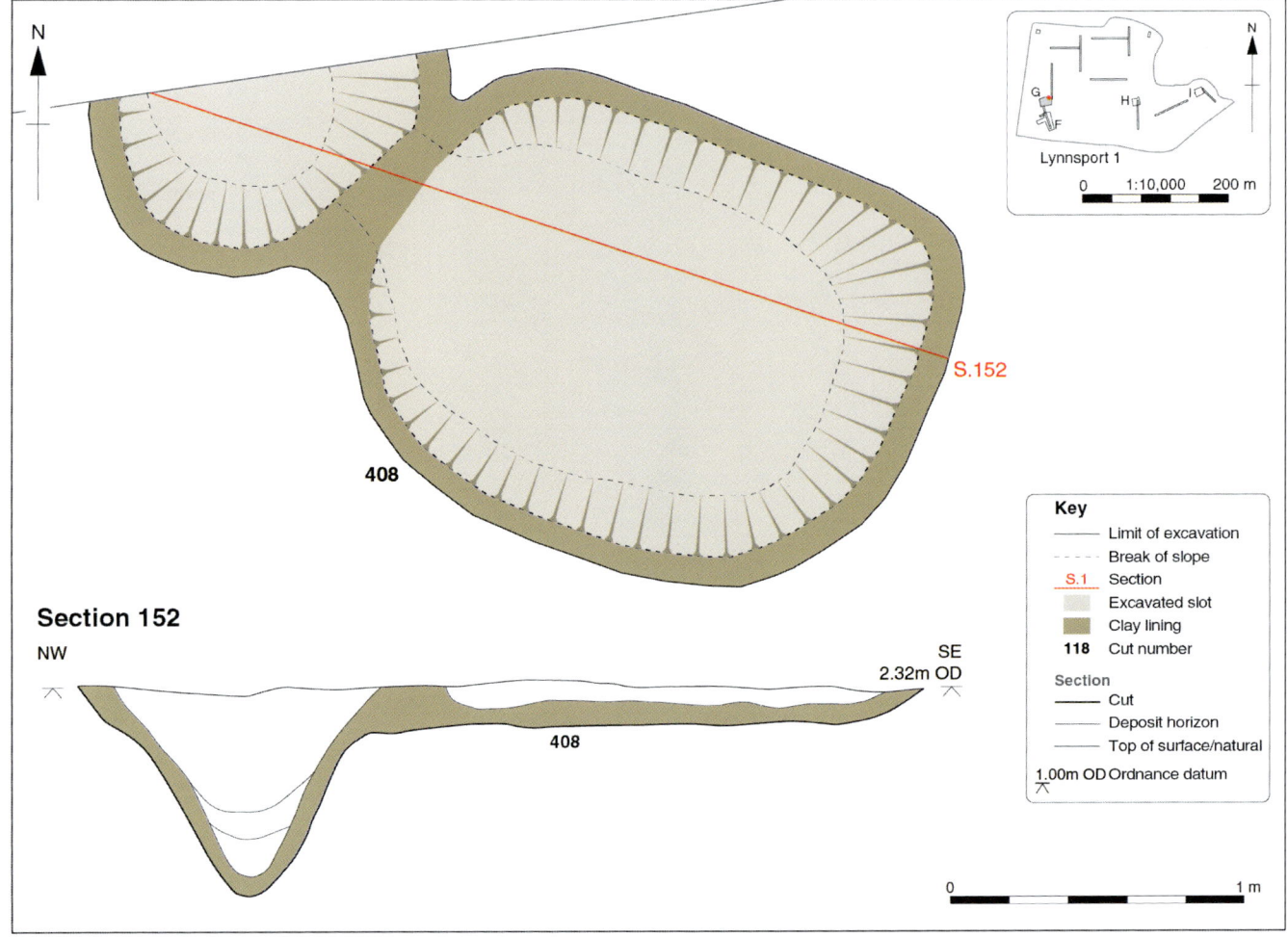

Figure 4.20 Saltern 10: Filtration unit 408. Scale 1:25

filtration units at Wainfleet St Mary, Lincolnshire (McAvoy 1994, fig. 5) and from one of the few complete examples of filtration units excavated nearby at Marsh Lane (Clarke and Clarke 2018, fig. 3). Their absence within the two remaining complete filtration tanks suggests that such turves were usually recycled along with the wooden box superstructures placed above the filtration pits.

Unlined features
Eight unlined sub-circular pits with U-shaped profiles were revealed within Saltern 5 (Table 4.7). These pits ranged between *c*.1–6m in diameter by *c*.0.1–0.5m deep. Each pit was infilled by sterile *sleeching* waste sediment. Of unknown function, these pits may represent partially excavated filtration units which were never lined or used.

Sub-rectangular tanks
A group of three relatively deep sub-rectangular and flat based clay-lined features excavated in Saltern 12 (Table 4.9; tanks 451, 453 and 457; Fig. 4.22) are reminiscent of a deeper clay-lined rectangular feature excavated at Marsh Lane (2.1m in length x 0.85m wide x 0.3m deep) interpreted as a tank for the storage of the concentrated brine produced in the adjacent filtration units (Clarke 2016, 4).

The brine boiling process

Salt-cotes
At least some of the brine-boiling hearths are presumed to have been housed within purpose-built shelters — salt-houses known in medieval times as salt-cotes — to protect this volatile activity from any adverse weather (see Discussion below). Amongst the many, mostly extinct, saltern mounds mentioned by name in the Gaywood Dragge survey of 1487 (NRO, BL/MA 2/2), the examples of *Bulecote*, *Turncoults*, and *Hashecoates* probably best illustrate the former presence of such structures upon them.

The upper parts of each of the salterns were commonly found to have been disturbed by roots or modern truncation so that shallow structural remains are less likely to have survived on these sites. Five sub-circular post-hole-like features (472, 474, 499, 501 and 503) and a gully (492) were observed at the top of the deposit sequence at Saltern 12 which may represent some type of associated post-built structure (Fig. 4.22). These features were also notable for not having been lined with clay. The linear gully extended for 1.4m into the excavation from the south-west before terminating. It measured 0.2m wide x 0.25m deep with vertical sides and a flat base, reminiscent of the square-cut profile of a beamslot. To the east of the gully, the post-holes measured between 0.3–0.5m in diameter and 0.1–0.35m deep. Three closely-set post-

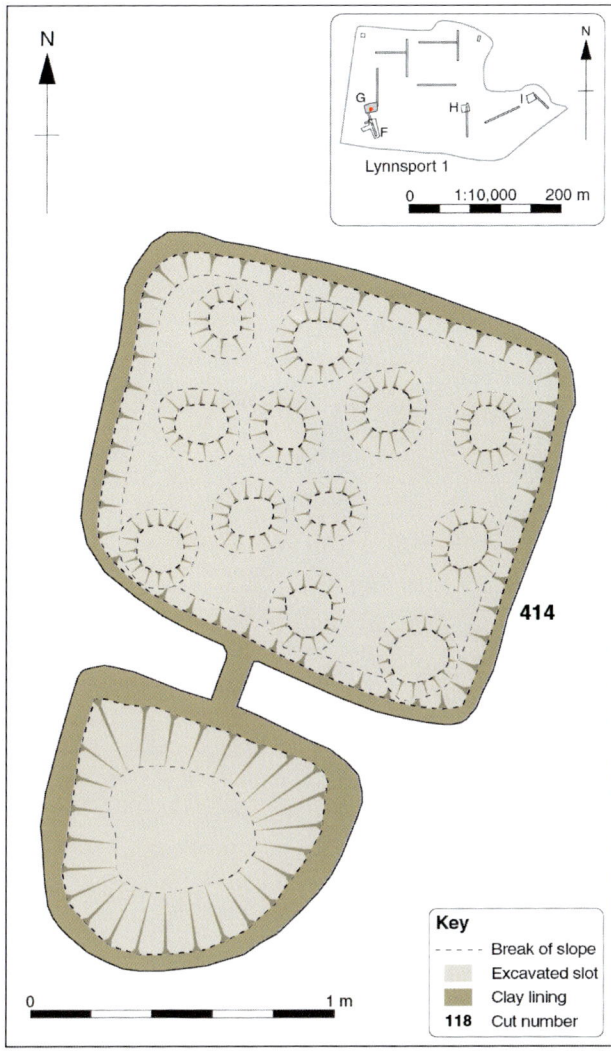

Figure 4.21 Saltern 10: Remnants of *in situ* turves in filtration unit 414. Scale 1:25

holes forming a 4m-long line aligned north-north-east to south-south-west may have denoted a wall. However, any firm interpretation for the presence of a structure is hampered by the lack of excavated examples with which to compare this evidence. Few finds were recovered, with just a single unidentifiable sherd (1g) of pottery and two fragments (17g) of iron smithing slag found within the gully. As only relatively small areas were excavated, it is quite possible that the remains of structures survive outside the limits of excavation (and the development). It is equally possible that modern truncation and disturbance by the dense vegetation observed across the upper profiles of many of the salterns had removed any evidence for these. If these structures were closely allied to the preferred locations of open-pan hearths on the crests of salterns, then any associated features would similarly be most at risk from later activity.

Hearth and hearth waste pit
An *in situ* hearth (1018) was discovered near to the crest of Saltern 5, immediately below the subsoil truncation level at *c*.3.2m OD (Figs 4.26–9). The hearth lay within the north-eastern end of a sub-rectangular pit (1010) that measured *c*.9m in length and 7m wide by 0.5m deep. Both the hearth and pit were orientated towards the prevailing south-westerly wind direction. The hearth's fired clay construction comprised a square feature (3m in length) with elements of the superstructure and base remaining *in situ*, surviving to a height of 0.5m. The superstructure extended up from the base as a central rectangular column. Further elements of this superstructure also extended around the north-western, north-eastern and south-eastern sides. This construction resulted in two similar-sized chambers either side of the central column which were open to the south-west. Each chamber was similarly backfilled with dark brownish grey ash-like silt. The pit was backfilled around the hearth with brownish yellow sandy silt. A spread of burnt deposits extended to the south-west, beneath which lay a pit (1011) backfilled with a stratified sequence of waste products that probably represents an associated rake-out pit excavated to receive the hearth's waste.

Historical sources (see Section VI) describe brine boiling being carried out using lead pans (see below) placed over clay-built hearths, such as the one discovered in Saltern 5. This distinctive double-chambered hearth arrangement first came to light in King's Lynn when a single example, dated by archaeomagnetic means to *c*.AD 1245, was excavated at the former Queen Mary's Nursing Home (Cope-Faulkner 2014). Two further early medieval examples (*c*.AD 1066–1250) were later excavated by OA East at the Marsh Lane saltern (Clarke and Clarke 2018). A secure archaeomagnetic date of AD 870–1050 (95% confidence) was determined for the current hearth which pushes the origin of this form back to at least the Late Anglo-Saxon period (Wilkinson and Batt 2019, 82–91). A slightly narrower date range of AD 900–1030 was also suggested (at 68% confidence). These date ranges relate to the last time the hearth was heated above *c*.400°C, and therefore potentially identifies the end of this phase of salt-making on Saltern 5.

Briquetage: brick supports for lead pans (Saltern 5)
by Simon Timberlake
Fourteen fragments (1,780g) belonging to at least nine fired clay brick supports designed for lead pans were recovered from a layer of hearth waste (context 920, Fig. 4.23, Section 217) present within Saltern 5. Similar examples of these supports excavated nearby include that of a single soft fired brick found within the upper mound sequence (*c*.12th to mid-13th century) of the saltern excavated at Marsh Lane (Clarke and Clarke 2018). Possible pedestals were also recovered from the 12th- to 13th-century saltern site at the former Queen Mary's Nursing Home (Cope-Faulkner 2014). Further afield, soft silt brick supports were found *in situ* within the hearth excavated at Wainfleet St Mary, Lincolnshire (McAvoy 1994), with additional examples of hand-made bricks found at Walpole St Peter, Norfolk (Clarke 2009).

All but two of the pieces are composed of a fine grained soft pink quartz silty fabric with a small amount of mica, occasional soft/clay laminae, and moderate amounts of fine-grained and finely-broken up plant material such as thin grass or algal material. The latter were identified as flattened burnt-out voids present within very thin layers. The remaining

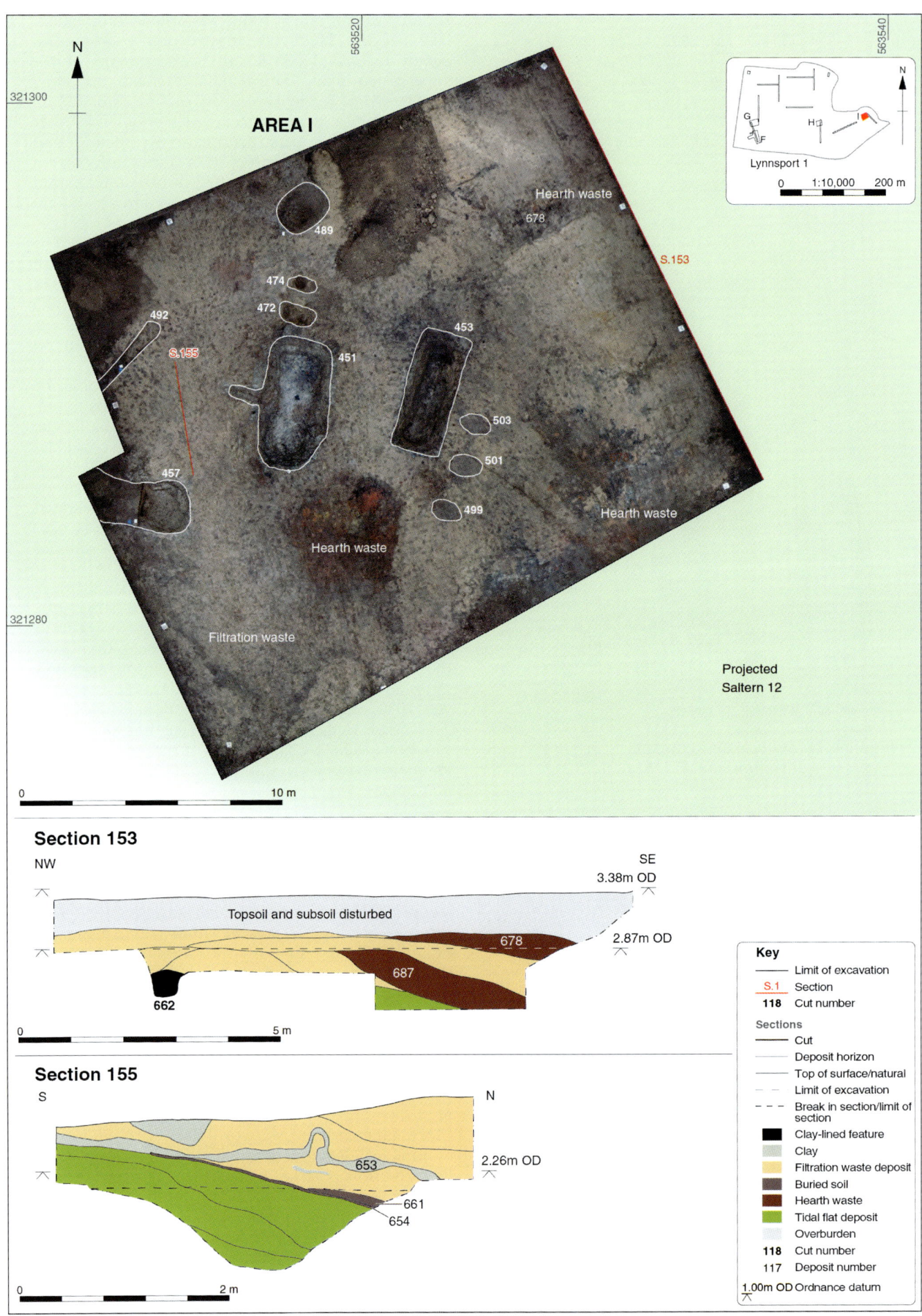

Figure 4.22 Saltern 12: Photogrammetry plan (scale 1:200) and sections (Section 153, scale 1:100; Section 155, scale 1:50) of salt-working features (*c.* late 10th to early 12th century)

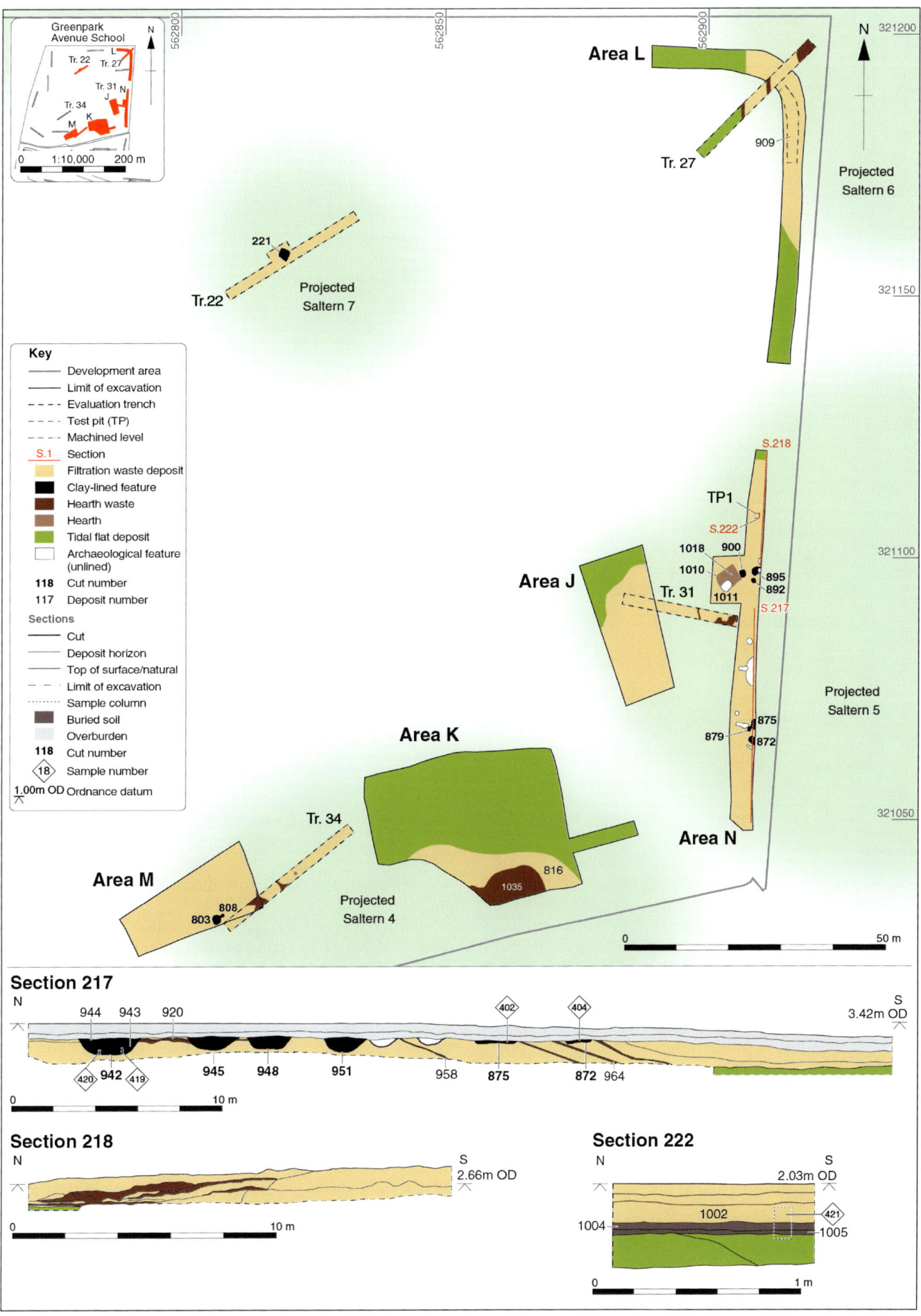

Figure 4.23 Plan of Salterns 4–7 (scale 1:1000) and sections (Section 217, scale 1:250; Section 218, scale 1:200 and Section 222, scale 1:25) of salt-working features within Saltern 5 (*c.* late 10th to early 12th century)

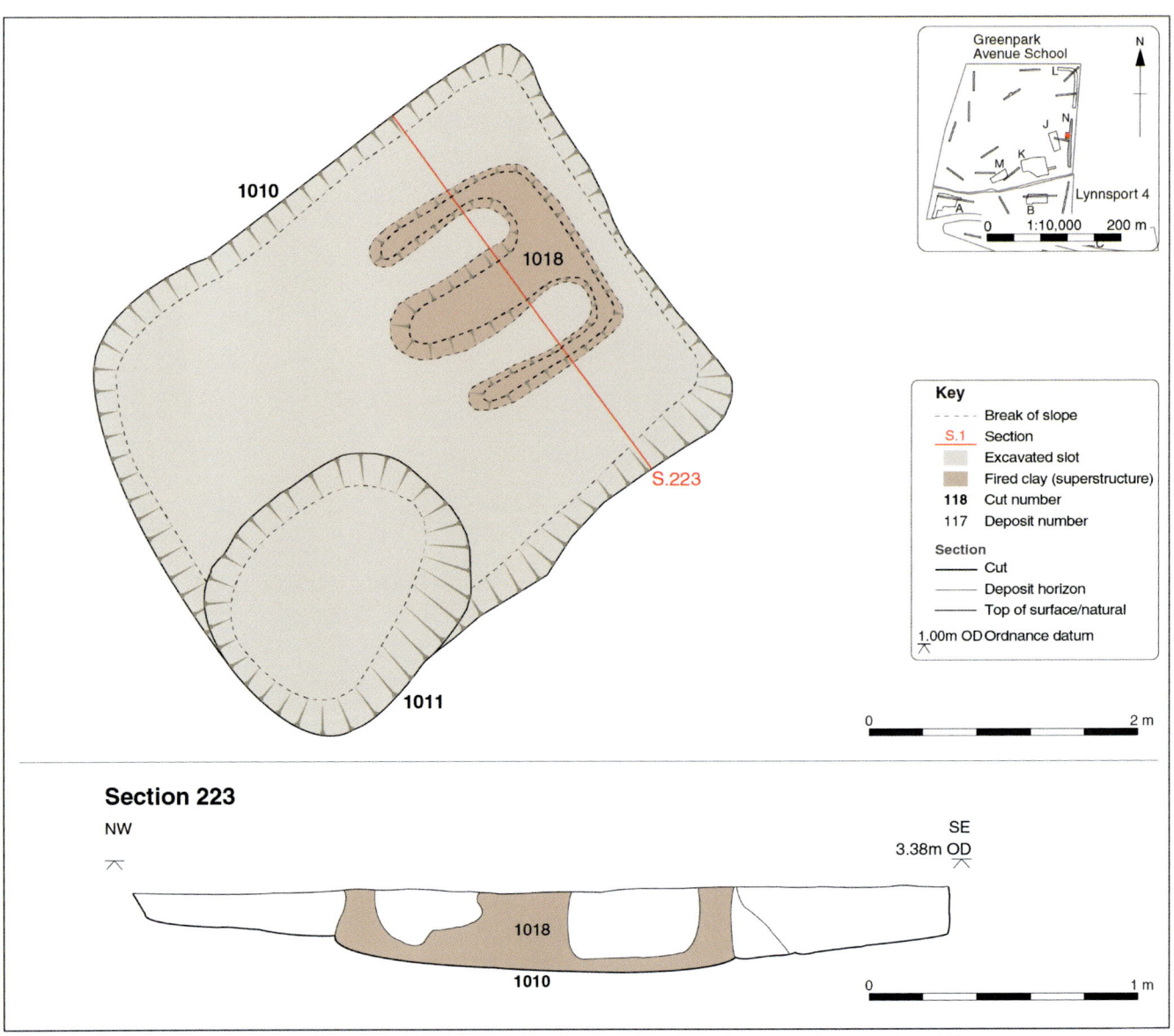

Figure 4.24 Saltern 5: Hearth 1018 plan (scale 1:50) and section (scale 1:25)

two pieces are much harder and 'biscuit-like' with increased amounts of burnt-out organic material.

For the most part these bricks are narrow and rectangular, with approximately half of them having traces of chamfered ends (Figs 4.27–28). No complete examples were seen, the fabric of these being soft and brittle, and easily worn away by physical abrasion and water. The best preserved of these rectangular bricks measures 140mm long x 50mm wide x 60mm thick (Fig. 4.28). Another example of one of the chamfered (or perhaps dome topped) bricks measures 160mm x 70mm wide x 60mm thick. The narrowest brick, however, is only around 100mm long x 40mm wide x 55mm thick. Another square (but incompletely preserved) domed brick measures 30mm long x 35mm thick x 75mm wide across the arched section (Fig. 4.29).

The mode of manufacture of these bricks is clearly evident from the occasionally clean knife cuts associated with the shaping (forming) of the squarish sides. In addition, the flat tops of some of these are marked with a light diagonal hachured line engraving, the lines being parallel and about 20mm apart (Fig. 4.28).

Thin layers of a hackly/ bubbly yellowish-green salt slag were found accreting to the top and occasionally front faces of over 70% of the pieces examined (Fig. 4.27). Examination of the contact of the slag with the brick showed clear evidence of a fused surface, suggesting that this phenomenon related to spillage of the brine through boiling, then the vitrification of these spills upon those sides of the bricks most exposed to the flames and heat of the furnace.

As implied above, both the form and type of salt slag coatings on these bricks suggests that they were constructed and used (probably as unbonded bricks) to support the heavy lead or ceramic boiling pans which sat a short distance (as little as 6cm) above the top of the clay-lined hearths. A reasonable assumption is that the domed and chamfered bricks helped to support the sloping sides of the pans, although the exact arrangement of them cannot be determined from the displaced fragments which survive. What does seem clear is that the various sizes of bricks found at Saltern 5 (all of them slightly different) were not

Figure 4.25 Saltern 5: Overhead view of hearth 1018. Scale 1:40

that dissimilar to those found at Marsh Lane, most of which were dated by associated pottery as Late Anglo-Saxon. The majority of the latter were also narrow and rectangular; the Marsh Lane bricks ranging from 160 x 70 x 90mm to 90 x 60 x 35mm or 60 x 60 x 40mm in size. Analysis of both the brick fabric and local sediment type suggests that all of these bricks could have been made on site; either from the more clay-rich parts of the sub-mound silts or from the dumped (ex-sleeched) silts themselves (Timberlake and Haylock 2016, 6; table 13).

The use of these hand-made brick supports for the boiling pans appears to be the favoured method of mounting these pans upon the salt hearths across the entire medieval period, as was suggested by the excavation of later 15th-/16th-century coastal salterns at Wainfleet St Mary on the Lincolnshire coast (where bricks were actually found *in situ*). At the latter site a series of 15th-century *sleeching* mounds, filtration tanks and pan boiling hearths were excavated; the pans in this case had been removed, but a series of lead off-cuts from these (or from others) remained alongside

Figure 4.26 Saltern 5: Excavation of hearth 1018

Figure 4.27 Briquetage: brick pan supports with residues of accreted salt slag showing suggested original outlines and profiles. Scale 1:2

the arrangement of brick supports (McAvoy 1994, 142). The use of bricks during the medieval/post-medieval period is similarly confirmed by historical sources, notably both Brownrigg (1748) and Duncan (1812):

'the brine being thus prepared they boil it with turf fires in small leaden pans...' (Brownrigg 1748, 137)
'These pans....made of lead...are placed on bricks about 20 inches from the ground...to admit a line of peats beneath them. The pans are commonly about 4 feet long, 3 feet broad, and 5 inches deep...' (Duncan 1812).

Evidence for the lead pans — in the form of small 'repairs' and offcuts — utilised to boil the concentrated brine in the open pan method of salt-making has been found on a number of excavated saltern sites in Norfolk (Clarke 2009; Cope-Faulkner 2014, 80) and Lincolnshire (McAvoy 1994, 142). At Marsh Lane, evidence for lead pans took the form of lead contamination present within the chemical

Figure 4.28 Briquetage: brick pan supports with chamfered ends showing suggested original outlines and profiles. Scale 1:2

Figure 4.29 Briquetage: square brick with domed top. Scale 1:3

make-up of slags (see below) and the brick supports (Timberlake and Haylock 2016; Clarke and Clarke 2018, 15). The latter were related to the earliest phase of salt-working, radiocarbon dated to around AD 800, suggesting an early use of lead pans that evidently pre-dated the medieval period. At the current site, a deposit of hearth waste in Saltern 1 (Trench 32; see above) yielded a small piece of lead which may have been a metal drip, perhaps from the repair of a pan.

Salt slag (Saltern 5)
by Simon Timberlake

Some 24 pieces (*c*.6kg) of salt-making slag composed of fragments of hearth cakes (hearth bottoms) made of vitrified saline silicate with a thin flint-tempered clay and silt lining attached to the underside were recovered from the hearth waste (context 920; Fig. 4.23, Section 217) of Saltern 5. The very irregular tops to these (consisting of a spatter surface) and the sharp edges of the fragments all suggest that these are most likely to have been formed close to where they were found.

By matching individual pieces of these slag cakes, it was possible to calculate a minimum of ten discarded hearth bases from two different (or one subsequently modified) hearth of between 180mm and 220mm diameter (Fig. 4.30). The imprint of the tongs used to remove these cakes (or perhaps the blast holes from the use of a tuyère) can be seen within parts of the formerly molten surfaces. Inclusions of flint-tempered clay hearth wall and a heat-reddened silt layer are present on the top and inside of this variably vitrified, alternating dense/porous slag. The denser re-melted layers of slag are represented in this case by a greenish-yellow to light green glass (vitrification). However, there are clearly considerable amounts of salt still present within the porous groundmass of this

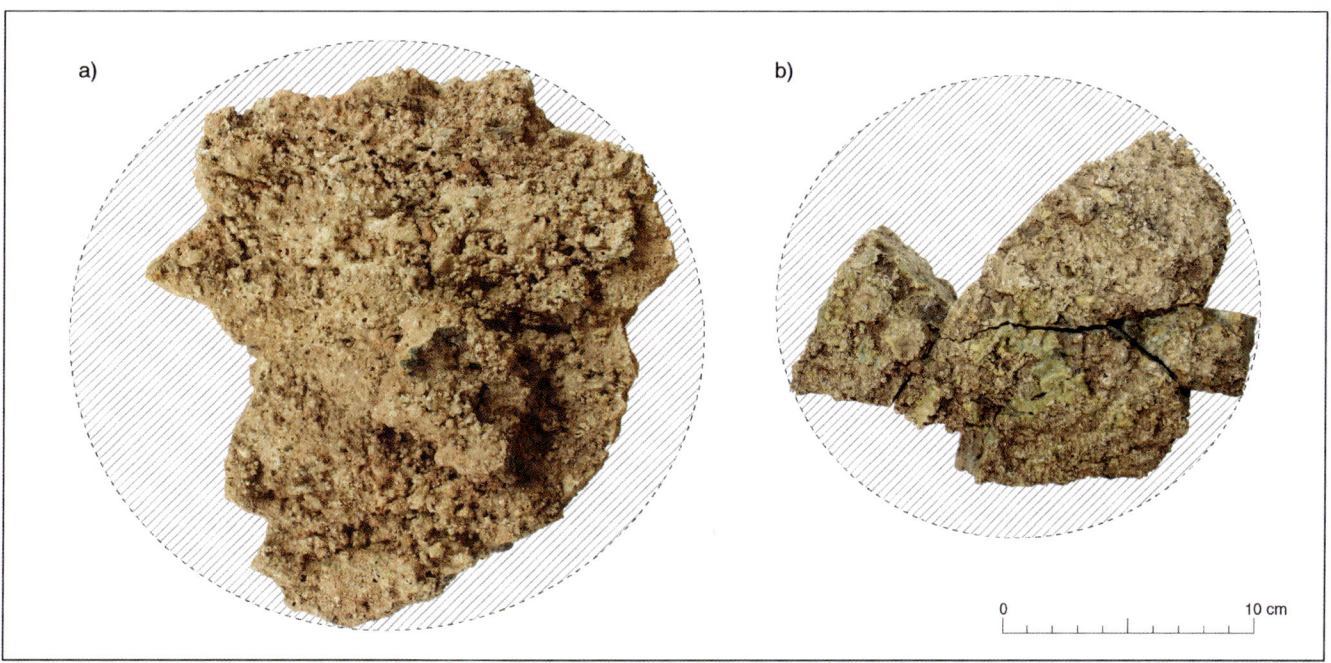

Figure 4.30 a) A salt-making slag cake of *c*.220mm diameter and b) Refitting pieces of a cake of *c*.180mm diameter. Scale 1:3

slag. More rarely inclusions of dark grey-black peat ash and animal bone were noted.

As anticipated, both the salt slag and small amount of iron slag (see below) analysed from this site are similar in form to those described from Marsh Lane (Timberlake and Haylock 2016, 65–81; Clarke and Clarke 2020, 15). Interestingly, the size(s) of the ten slag cakes identified within the assemblage from Saltern 5 correspond well with the estimated size(s) of the salt slag cakes and iron smithing hearth bases from Marsh Lane. This would seem to suggest that it may have been the general practice to boil these salt pans over shallow round pit-like clay-lined hearths of around 220mm diameter, although the presence of smaller cakes than this might indicate the use of other still smaller hearths (thus potentially smaller salt pans). The latter hearths may have been constructed as such, or alternatively were rebuilt as re-modified examples.

Whatever the actual situation, it is important to recognise how a salt slag cake (or hearth bottom) is formed. As with smithing hearth bases formed during ironworking, the salt slag cakes form and grow as a result of the re-melting of waste material. This would invariably have included the 'boiled-over' salt crystal and/or skimmed off waste 'salt bitters' accidentally dropped into the fire, fragments of the silicate-rich fired clay, the *sleeching* silt, fuel ash, and the collapsed clay wall lining of the hearth. All of the latter will have fallen into the base of the fire and become fused together as the temperature of the hearth increased and the process intensified. Frequently this would have been accidental – given that the sea winds would have made it difficult to control the temperature of the fire. Salt slag is an agglomerate of all these components; in some places this would have re-melted to form a pale cream grey to yellowish-green coloured glass, yet in others it would have been porous and cindery. The presence here of what might be air blast holes within the side or base of the slag cakes would appear to suggest the use of a tuyère and bellows to raise the temperature of the fire, but not necessarily (as in the case of blacksmithing) in the form of a continuous and vigorous air blast. Such a set-up would help to explain why these hearths appear to have been used interchangeably between salt-making and iron smithing: the latter most probably an occasional event associated with the re-forging of the iron tools and perhaps the making of horseshoes and other equipment necessary for the operation of the salterns and for the haulage of silt, fuel and salt.

Metalworking
by Simon Timberlake
Evidence for the secondary use of these salt hearths for iron smithing was recovered from a deposit of filtration waste excavated in Saltern 6 (Fig. 4.23, context 909). This included three refitting lumps (Fig. 4.31; total dimensions 190 x 130 x 90mm; 486g) of vitrified clay as part of a large diameter (possibly 200–250mm) iron smithing hearth. The fragile low-density slag in this case appears to be relatively low in iron, yet it is still magnetic, with a distinct rusty surface discolouration. The association of these pieces and the lack of abrasion suggests that this hearth is most likely to have been *in situ* within a feature (or group of features) close to where it was found. An examination of the form and surface of the cindery slag revealed the presence of blast holes from a tuyère tip, and the sort of oxidation patina with which it might be associated. The formation of these light gaseous slags may be interpreted as being the result of the melting of the hearth lining and the slumping of this mass across the air inlet, the air blast having then become ineffective until this had been broken and snapped-off from the end of the tuyère pipe, most probably using iron tongs. The possible imprint of the tongs can be seen upon several of the pieces.

Figure 4.31 Three refitting pieces of vitrified clay melted in front of the tuyere hole of an iron-smithing (re-used saltern) hearth. Scale 1:3

Eight pieces of iron slag (129g) and 54 pieces of more cindery contaminated salt slag/iron slag (213g) linked to iron smithing were also recovered from the neighbouring Salterns 10–12. This suggests that most if not all of the brine-boiling hearths could have been used on occasions for metalworking. All of the pieces of iron slag are unweathered, with few signs of breakage or abrasion to suggest transport and re-deposition. At least two of these samples consist of pieces of iron smithing slag; the largest piece (92 x 50 x 40mm; 91g), recovered from a layer of filtration waste within Saltern 10, being a fragment of iron-rich vitrified hearth lining (VHL) which includes some fused and melted hammerscale, slag drips and the traces of a blowhole of *c.*22mm diameter covering the tuyère pipe (Bayley *et al.* 2001). The smaller piece of slag (3g) came from the sediment infill of clay-lined tank 457 in Saltern 12 (Fig. 4.22). This small fragment of solid slag drip may also have originated from the end of a clay or metal tuyère. The unequal magnetisation of the largest VHL fragment (213g) recovered from layer 687 of the hearth waste within Saltern 12 (Fig. 4.22, Section 153) most likely reflects its heterogenous composition with re-melted inclusions of hammerscale.

Evidence for fuel
by Rachel Fosberry and Denise Druce
An informative assemblage was recovered from hearth waste excavated from a group of deposits tipped across the upper profile of Saltern 11 (Fig. 4.32, context 676; Fig. 4.33). Plant remains include a single charred barley (*Hordeum vulgare*) grain and seeds of wetland plants such as sedges (*Carex* spp.), Great Fen sedge (*Cladium*

Figure 4.32 Saltern 11: Photogrammetry plan (scale 1:100) and section (scale 1:25) of salt-working features (*c.* late 10th to early 12th century)

Figure 4.33 Saltern 11: Section through hearth waste 676

mariscus), rushes (*Juncus* spp.), cleavers (*Galium aparine*) and a grass (Poaceae) seed. Several of the charred seeds were too poorly preserved for accurate identification. These include several small seeds that are possibly of heather (*Erica/Calluna* sp.) and charred flowers that are also likely to be heather. Charcoal was identified as mainly oak (*Quercus* sp.) and heather with occasional fragments of holly (*Ilex aquifolium*), alder/hazel (*Alnus/Corylus* sp.), elm (*Ulmus* sp.) and apple/pear/cherry-type (Maloideae). A fragment of birch (*Betula* sp.) charcoal was radiocarbon dated to cal AD 1020–1160 (95% confidence; SUERC-87794). Some of the charcoal is vitrified through repeated exposure to high temperatures. The identification of heather and charred stems (rhizomes) from Saltern 11 may be an indication of their use as fuel, possibly as peat, in addition to wood.

An environmental sample of hearth waste taken from the upper profile of Saltern 12 also includes peat along with seeds of spike rush (*Eleocharis* sp.), bramble and elder, foraminifera and charcoal of coniferous wood and oak. This sample also produced occasional seeds in an untransformed state (not carbonised) and must therefore have either been waterlogged or resistant to decay. Taxa include elder (*Sambucus nigra*) and bramble (*Rubus* sp.) and sedges, which all produce woody seeds that are more likely to survive, particularly in salt-rich deposits. Charcoal preservation was notably better at Saltern 12 than within the other excavated salt-making sites. Charred stems/rhizomes of heather (indicative of peat) and oak fragments were commonly identified and are therefore considered the most likely fuel sources for brine-boiling here. Furthermore, charcoal of holly, alder/hazel, elm and fruit trees is also present, suggesting these may also have been utilised as fuel. Even allowing for the low levels of charcoal from the salterns, it is noticeable that the assemblages comprise small roundwood or twig fragments, rather than mature wood. This suggests *ad hoc* collection of what may have been locally available rather than wood sourced from managed woodland. However, the very limited dataset means that any interpretation is extremely tentative, especially given the possibility of re-working.

Of note is the identification of a small (45mm) preserved but partly incinerated lump of peat with its fibrous structure clearly visible, which was found within a dump of hearth waste tipped onto Saltern 12. The assemblage of vitrified/fused hearth lining (see above) includes fragments of both heat-reddened but unfused reddish silt with traces throughout of peat ash. Indeed, dark, peat-like stains were also observed in other burnt deposits common to all of the salterns, further suggesting its use as a fuel source (see Section VI).

Salt-making environment

Filtration unit sediments

Ostracods (Saltern 5)
by Simon Timberlake
Two samples were taken from the backfill sediment present within the clay-lined tanks of filtration units 872 (Sample 404) and 875 (Sample 402) from Saltern 5 and another two sub-samples from monolith tins (Samples 419 and 420) from across the sediment profile infilling the north and south sides of the clay-lined tank 942 (Fig. 4.23, Section 217). Ostracods in

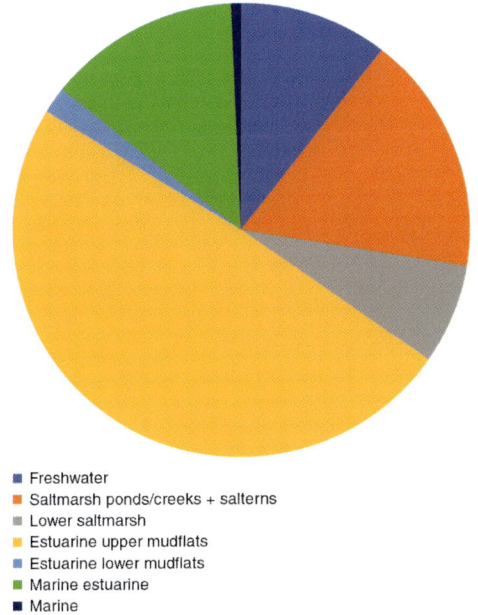
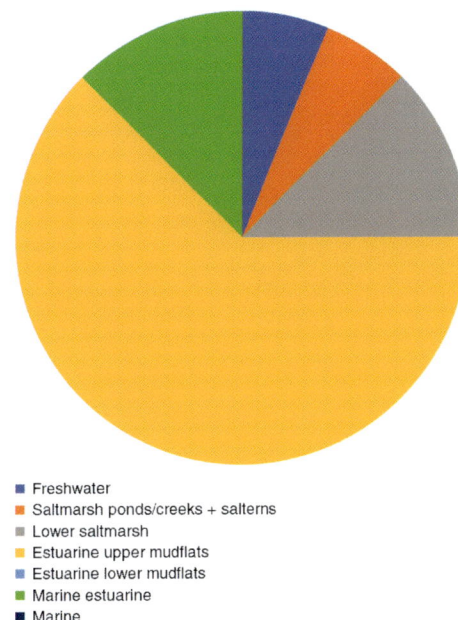

Figure 4.34 Habitat preferences of ostracods from Samples 402 and 404, clay-lined tanks 872 and 875, Saltern 5

Figure 4.35 Habitat preferences of ostracods from Samples 419 and 420, clay-lined tank 942, Saltern 5

moderate amounts are present within Samples 402 and 404, but by contrast they are rare and poorly diverse within the sampled sediments from tank 942. Most of the ostracods were found within the smaller sized flot fractions (0.5–0.25mm and <0.25mm).

Sample 402
A total of 306 ostracods were counted within Sample 402 (fill 878 of filtration unit 875; identified from a sample consisting of 7.91g of sieve residue made up of 1.15g (2mm–1mm), 1.53g (1mm–0.5mm), 4.06g (0.5–0.25mm) and 1.17g (<0.25mm) fractions (NB no ostracods were found within the largest-sized fraction 2mm–1mm)). The minimum number of individuals (MNI) based upon the population structure (as determined by numbers of instar moults valves/carapaces present) is estimated as 199, with an ostracod density per sample of 45 individuals per gramme of sediment. Some 8% (twenty-four) of these ostracods consist of the brackish water (lower saltmarsh) species *Loxoconcha elliptica*, 15% (forty-six) of them *Cytheromorpha fuscata* (a species of the saltmarsh creeks) and up to 55% (168) of them *Leptocythere* sp. Most of the latter consist of *Leptocythere lacertosa* (another saltmarsh/estuarine upper mudflat species). These show a good population structure composed of similar numbers of both adult and juvenile carapaces and left and right valves – indicating a high degree of autochthoneity. *Loxoconcha rhomboidea* (a species typical of the estuarine lower mudflats) make up just 0.3% of the total (*i.e.* one individual). Truly freshwater species such as *Candona candida* (ten) and *Darwinula stevensoni* (ten) make up another 7% of the ostracods, while the various estuarine/ marine species *Xestoleberis* sp. (thirty-four), *Semicytherura angulata* (five), *Semicytherura nigrescens* (one) and *Cythereis fischeri* (five) make up another 13% of these. Finally, the clearly allocthonous fully-marine species *Hemicytherura cellulosa* (one) and *Cytheropteron nodosa* (two) (both of them present as slightly less well-preserved individuals) form the remaining balance of *c*.1%. Molluscs were also noted within the samples, including large numbers of *Valvata piscinalis* (freshwater snail), *Hydrobia* sp. (a brackish water snail), *Columnella edentula* (a terrestrial marshland snail), *Bithynia tentaculina* (a freshwater snail), *Pisidium* sp. (a freshwater bivalve) and *Ceciloides acicula* (a terrestrial sub-ground dwelling snail). Fragments of echinoid spine and fish teeth almost certainly represent washed-in marine allochems.

Sample 404
Some 121 ostracods were counted within Sample 404 (fill 873 of filtration unit 872; identified from a sample consisting of 7.11g of sieve residue made up of 1.32g (2mm–1mm), 1.58g (1mm–0.5mm), 3.58g (0.5–0.25mm) and 0.63g (<0.25mm) fractions (NB no ostracods were found within the largest-sized fraction 2mm–1mm)). The minimum number of individuals (MNI) based upon the population structure of instar moults valves/carapaces is estimated as 102, with an ostracod density per sample of 21 individuals per gramme of sediment. Twenty-six (21%) of these consist of the 'smooth' polymorph form of the brackish to hypersaline-tolerant species *Cyprideis torosa* (*cf.* variant *C. littoralis*) that inhabits the saltmarsh ponds (pans) or creeks. Another 31% (thirty-eight) of these consist of the brackish water species *Leptocythere lacertosa* typical of the estuarine upper mudflats, and *Loxoconcha elliptica* (an ostracod characteristic of the Lower Saltmarsh) a further 5% (six individuals). *Loxoconcha rhomboidea* (a species typical of the estuarine lower mudflats) makes up just 2% (seven individuals). Truly freshwater species such as *Candona candida* (six) and *Cypridopsis vidua* (ten) (a species which is often associated with the stonewort *Chara*) make up 20% of the ostracod total. Meanwhile the estuarine/ marine species *Xestoleberis* sp. (twelve) and *Semicytherura sella* (two) make up a further 13%. More clearly allocthonous in this situation is the marine species *Cytheropteron nodosa* (six) at around 5%. A number of molluscs were also noted in the samples including the small shells of *Bithynia tentaculina* (a freshwater snail), *Vertigo antivertigo* (a terrestrial marshland snail) and *Ceciloides acicula* (a terrestrial sub-ground dwelling snail).

Monolith Samples 419 and 420
Just three ostracods (MNI=2) were recorded from Monolith Sample 419 (contexts 941 of filtration unit 942; at a density of two ostracods per gramme (just 1.86g of residue from the >0.25mm fraction was examined). These consist of a single left valve (juv.) of *Cyprideis torosa* (*cf. C. littoralis*) and a left and a right valve of *Leptocythere lacertosa*; both of these being brackish-water species. From the overlying context 943 associated with the same sample from the north end of this clay-lined tank came another five brackish water ostracods (MNI=2) which were recovered from just 2.61g of residue (this represents a similar ostracod density of two individuals per gramme of sediment). The latter consists of three *Leptocythere lacertosa* (two adult and a juvenile valve) plus two valves of *Loxoconcha elliptica*. From the southern Monolith Sample 420 taken from the same feature came a further four ostracods recovered from the lowermost clay lining 941 (these are *Leptocythere lacertosa* (three), the freshwater ostracod *Candona candida* (one)) in addition to another four ostracods from the upper fill 943. The latter includes the brackish water *Leptocythere lacertosa* (two) and the two estuarine-marine species *Cythereis fischeri* (one) and *Semicytherura angulata* (one).

Despite big differences in ostracod abundance and population structures (adults : juveniles + males

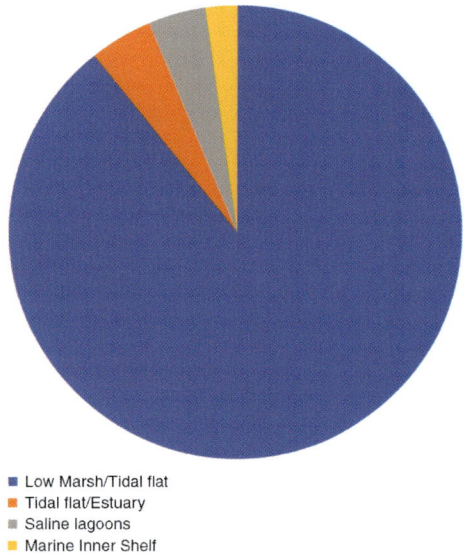
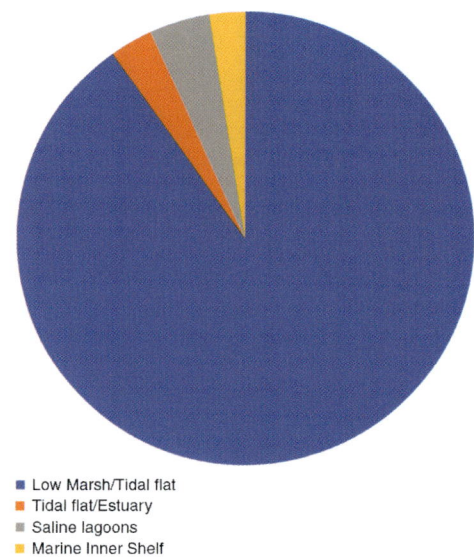

Figure 4.36 Habitat preferences of foraminifera from Samples 402 and 404, clay-lined tanks 872 and 875, Saltern 5

Figure 4.37 Habitat preferences of foraminifera from Samples 419 and 420, clay-lined tank 942, Saltern 5

: females) between the (relatively) ostracod-rich samples taken from the sediment backfilled into tanks 872 and 875 and the monolith samples taken from the interior of tank 942, there exists a certain degree of commonality in the species recorded. This may suggest a similar origin for all of the sediments seen (Figs 4.34–5). In all cases these were dominated by brackish-water saltmarsh species which appear to be autochthonous to the silts and also perhaps to a source within the zone of the estuarine upper mudflats and lower saltmarsh.

By far the most numerous ostracod species present within the waste silts is *Leptocythere lacertosa*, whilst the 'smooth shell' polymorph of *C. torosa* (var. *C.littoralis*) which is autochthonous to parts of the saltmarsh creek environment does not appear to be endemic to the saltern itself, nor to the filtration units sampled. It is possible therefore that some of these tanks may have already been cleaned out and backfilled, or perhaps they were never used for filtration or for brine accumulation in the first place. This then should be compared with the autochthonous ostracod population found within filtration unit 146 sampled at Saltern 1 in the *Salters Waie* group (see above). A few allochthonous marine ostracods were encountered within the clay-lined tank infill sediments alongside a small number of freshwater ostracods such as *Candona candida*, *Darwinula stevensoni* and *Cypridopsis vidua*. The latter would appear to confirm the presence of freshwater bodies such as ponds or tanks within the vicinity, some of which may have supplied water required for the *sleeching* process.

Foraminifera (Saltern 5)
by Simon Timberlake
Due to the abundance of forams present within the samples from the filtration units from Saltern 5 (see above), counting for foraminifera was only undertaken for the 0.25–0.5mm size fraction; the size range which contained most of the better-preserved tests (see Appendix 3 for methodology). Fortunately, the results obtained are believed to be representative of the types and abundance(s) present. The examination involved a whole count of this fraction wherever was practically possible, but if not then a carefully measured fraction of the sediment was counted and the final numbers for the whole sample estimated accordingly. The cut-off point in terms of the volume/weight of sediment which could realistically be looked at (in total) was 2g (as with the ostracods).

Samples 402, 404, 419 and 420
Very large numbers of foraminifera are typical in these samples, particularly in the cases of Samples 402 and 404 from the clay-lined tanks 872 and 875. These contain more than 8000 forams each (more than 1700 individuals in total). In all four samples (two of which (419 and 420 from filtration unit 942) included another two sub-samples) the benthic rotaliine forams *Elphidium* (which includes *E. williamsoni*) and *Hayesina* are the dominant genera; with *Hayesina* being the more numerous of the two in all cases (a high proportion of these are confirmed as being *H. germanica*). The Discorbacean rotaliines *Cibicides* and *Discorbis* and *Planorbulina* are the next most abundant genera, followed by the Rotaliacean *Ammonia* (*cf. Ammonia becarra*), the Miliolinid *Miliolina subrotunda*, the Nodosariacids (*Lagena spicatula* and *Lagena clavellate*), *Trochammina*, *Lenticulina* and ?*Globorotalia* (a rarer planktonic foram). Foraminifera are more abundant within the upper layer (941) than the lower layer (943) of filtration unit 942 that was sampled in each of the two monoliths (Samples 419 and 420); the upper infill horizon having consistently larger numbers of the rotaliine forams *Elphidium* and *Hayesina*.

The pie charts indicate the proportional habitat preferences of the various foraminifera genera/species identified within the four different samples taken from the waste silts (Figs 4.36–37). Foraminifera are present in very large numbers within sediment infills of the clay-lined tanks. All the assemblages examined are dominated by the benthic rotaliine foraminifera *Elphidium* and *Hayesina,* the latter being the most numerous of the two genera. Both of these are typical genera/species of the Low Marsh and Tidal Mudflats (consisting of 85% of the habitats represented by the foraminifera in each case). This similarity in foraminiferal assemblages between samples supports the idea that these clay-lined tanks were infilled with washed-in or backfilled waste silts from the saltern mound, or alternatively that a very similar source

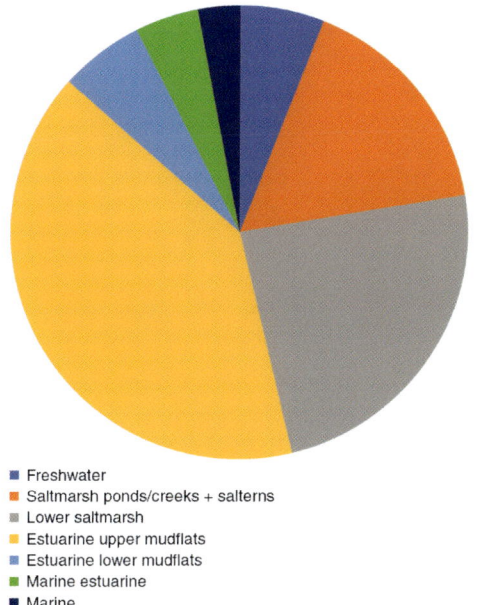
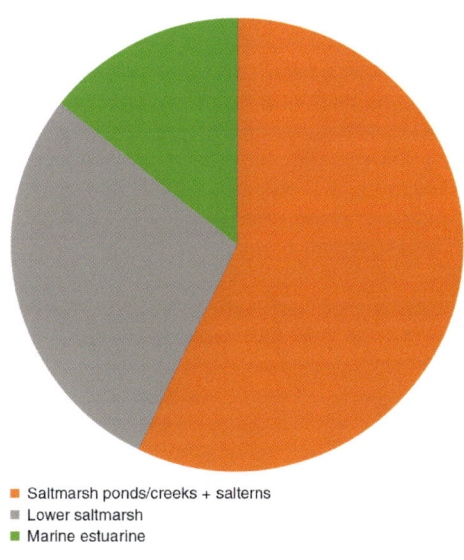

Figure 4.38 Habitat preferences of ostracods from Samples 302 and 303, filtration unit 414 and clay-lined tank 423, Saltern 10

Figure 4.39 Habitat preferences of ostracods from Sample 307, clay-lined tank 463, Saltern 11

(or zone) of the saltmarsh/estuarine mudflat biotope had been exploited over time. The foraminiferal evidence supports that of the ostracods; confirming the hypothesis that the silts used in *sleeching* were collected primarily from the lower saltmarsh/upper tidal mudflats zone of the tidal creeks which lay closest to the salterns.

Ostracods (Salterns 10 and 11)
by Simon Timberlake
A small number of ostracods were identified within Samples 302, 303 and 307 taken from the sediment infills of an intact filtration unit and clay-lined tank (features 414 and 423 respectively; Figs 4.21 and 4.18) excavated within Saltern 10, and a clay-lined tank (463) excavated within Saltern 11 (Fig. 4.32). The evidence suggests that the source of the silts used in the *sleeching* process came from an area of the lower saltmarsh/upper estuarine mudflats and saltmarsh creeks close by. Foraminifera are also present in moderately large amounts; in this case dominated by the benthic foraminifera genera *Elphidium* (various species) and *Hayesina*. Both are typical genera/species of the Low Marsh (saltmarsh) and Tidal Mudflats (between 75–90% certainty of association). Much smaller numbers of estuarine, saline lagoonal and marine (inner shelf) forams are present, some of these clearly allocthonous (washed-in).

Samples 302, 303 and 307
Just a few species of ostracods were identified which are moderately autochthonous to the saltmarsh/mudflat origins of the *sleech* (Figs 4.38–4.39). Brackish water ostracods including *Cyprideis torosa* (var. *C.littoralis*), *Cytheromorpha fuscata*, *Leptocythere lacertosa* and *Loxoconcha elliptica* and *L. rhomboidea* were identified alongside smaller numbers of estuarine-marine ostracods (*Semicytherura angulata*) and non-marine freshwater species such as *Candona candida* and *Cypridopsis vidua*. The latter species confirms the presence of a body of freshwater within the vicinity of the salterns which probably relates to the River Gaywood, the former course of which lay along the northern boundary of the Lynnsport 1 development site which encompasses these salterns.

The habitat preferences for the various ostracod species recovered reveal a distinct (60%+) positive association with saltmarsh ponds and creeks and the lower saltmarsh biotope (*c*.25%) present within Sample 307 (Fig. 4.39), and to species common to the estuarine upper mudflats (45%), lower saltmarsh (20%) and the saltmarsh ponds and creek (10%) biotopes present within Samples 302 and 303 (Fig. 4.38). However, if the species incidence is weighted according to their probable degrees of autochthoneity with respect to the silts there is a much greater likelihood that both sets of data are quite similar. In this case, the results appear to indicate predominantly autochthonous species associated with the lower saltmarsh: with tidal creeks and the estuarine mudflats. In all probability it is the tidal mudflats which are key to the source of these silts.

Possibly the most significant species present within this 'processing silt' assemblage are the following: *Leptocythere lacertosa*, *Cytheromorpha fuscata* and *Loxoconcha elliptica*. *Leptocythere lacertosa* is a euryhaline and slightly eurythermal species which prefers a sandy/muddy substrate at water depths of little more than 1m, typical perhaps of an estuary saltmarsh environment, in particular to the upper mudflats zone (Rosenfeld 1977; Smith *et al*. 2012, 152–3; Smith 2013, 68 fig. 3.12). *Cytheromorpha fuscata* is a chloride-dependent species more properly tolerant of marine-brackish water which is occasionally also found in inland lakes where brine seepages occur (Neale and Delorme 1985, cited in Thorp and Covich 2001, 821). However, this is often found alongside *L. lacertosa* and *C. torosa*. *Loxoconcha elliptica* is an ostracod of the lower saltmarsh biotope, commonly inhabiting salt ponds and sea-grass communities within the muddy substrates of tidal estuary mudflats (Horne and Boomer 2000; Athersuch *et al*. 1989; Smith 2013, fig. 3.12).

Smith (2013, fig. 3.12) noted the occurrence of *Semicytherura angulata* and other *Semicytherura*

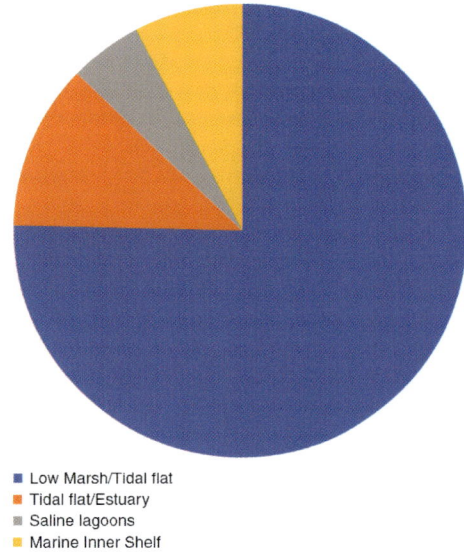
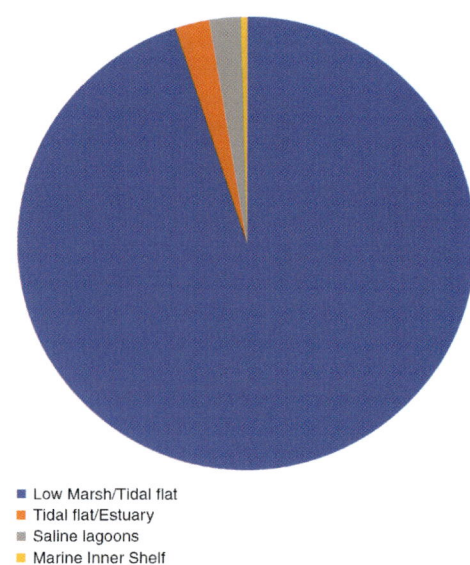

Figure 4.40 Habitat preferences of foraminifera from Samples 302 and 303, filtration unit 414 and clay-lined tank 423, Saltern 10

Figure 4.41 Habitat preferences of foraminifera from Sample 307, clay-lined tank 463, Saltern 11

species within the brackish water tidal-marine environments of the Late Pleistocene – Holocene roddon network which links the Flag Fen basin of Whittlesey (North Cambridgeshire) with the Wash and North Sea coastline. These species she considered typical of the marine/estuarine environment, therefore marginally allocthonous to the zone of saltmarsh/mudflats, although their inclusion within the latter sediments does not appear to be uncommon. Similarly, a small percentage of fully allocthonous shallow-water marine shelf species such as *Neocytherideis* sp., *Xestoleberis* and *Cytheropteron* is also to be expected within the active tidal zone. This matches the partially allocthonous composition of the foraminifera population identified within the same samples.

Foraminifera (Salterns 10 and 11)
by Simon Timberlake
Large numbers of forams were also recorded from Samples 302, 303 and 307 removed from the sediment infill of the intact filtration unit and clay-lined tank (features 414 and 423 respectively) in Saltern 10 and the clay-lined tank (463) excavated in Saltern 11.

Samples 302, 303 and 307
In all three samples the benthic rotaliine genera *Elphidium* and *Hayesina* are dominant, the only exception to this being Sample 302 with very high numbers of *Elphidium* (281) but low numbers of *Hayesina* sp. (eight). Only within Sample 307 (the saltern waste silts) was Hayesina almost 1.5 times more abundant than *Elphidium* (730 individuals compared to 472). The Discorbacean rotaliines *Cibicides* and *Discorbis* are the next most abundant genera, followed by the Rotaliacean *Ammonia* (*cf. Ammonia becarra*), *Trochammina*, *Planorbulina*, the Miliolinid *Miliolina subrotunda*, *Ceratobulimina* and the Nodosariacid *Lagena spicatula*. There is some, but probably little, significant variation in the foraminiferal abundances between samples, although the different proportions of these may have some significance, perhaps suggesting slightly different locations for the extraction of the silts which were then dumped within the saltern waste heaps, backfilled, or otherwise concentrated within the filtration tank(s).

The pie charts shown in Figs 4.40 and 4.41 indicate the proportional habitat preferences of the various foraminifera genera/species identified within the three different samples. Given that most of the forams have not been identified to species level, this should only be considered as an indication of the sort of habitats suggested and a likely environment based upon the current evidence known (*i.e.* the probability of this being determined by the proportionate numbers of similar-known species). By comparing the percentage preferential habitats represented by the foraminifera derived from the backfill sediment from the filtration unit in Saltern 10 with those from the backfill of the clay-lined tank in Saltern 11, a broadly similar picture emerges of a common source dominated by foraminifera typical of a low saltmarsh/tidal flat environment: 75% in the case of Samples 302 and 303 associated with Saltern 10 and 90% in the case of Sample 307 from Saltern 11.

Filtration (sleeching) waste

Plant remains and pollen
by Rachel Fosberry
Soil samples taken from the waste *sleeching* deposits within Saltern 11 produced the most frequent charred seeds indicative of wetland species such as sedges (*Carex* spp.), Great Fen sedge (*Cladium mariscus*), rushes (*Juncus* spp.), in addition to cleavers (*Galium aparine*) and grass (*Poaceae*). Waste tipped from the *Bullcote Waie* group was also sub-sampled for pollen. Although some pollen was preserved, unfortunately, none of the sub-samples contained sufficient counts to allow interpretation. This is largely attributed to the lithology from which the sub-samples were taken, which — as evident with the *Salters Waie* group — was insufficiently organic.

Micromorphology
by Charles French
Test Pit 1 was excavated into the base of the *sleeching* waste deposits at the northern end of Saltern 5 (Fig. 4.23, Section 222). The micromorphology of the transitional layer at the base of the saltern is

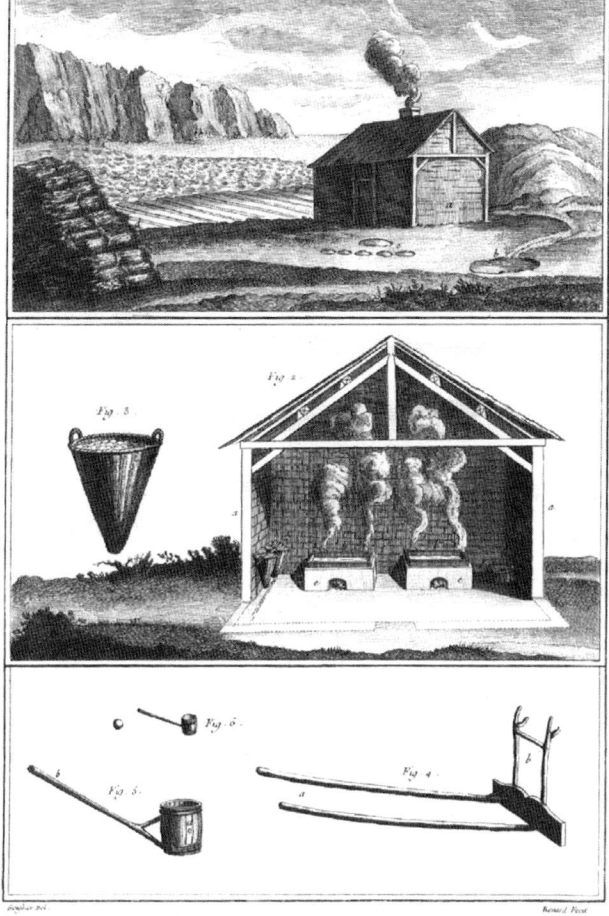

Figure 4.42 A French salicole (l'Encyclopédie Planches tome VI, Travail du Sel – Saunerie de Normandie, Plate I, Paris 1768)

presented in Chapter 3. The soil block sub-sampled from Monolith 421 across this horizon also allowed for a micromorphological description of the lowest filtration waste silts layer of the mound (context 1002).

The sequence is composed of either laminae of very fine to fine sand or silty clay crusts with greater to lesser impregnation with amorphous iron oxides. These sediments have a swirled and convoluted aspect suggestive of erosive impact and mixing processes.

Detailed micromorphological descriptions:
Fabric unit 3 (context 1002): poorly sorted, swirled/convoluted aspects; 70% very fine to fine quartz sand with 25–30% dusty clay with moderate amorphous sesquioxide staining, reddish brown/pale brown (CPL/PPL); a few fragments of brown silty clay crusts, <2mm.

Soil development
Overlying the natural tidal silts at the base of Saltern 12 was a 0.02m-thick layer that consisted of dark brown sandy silt with charcoal inclusions, which was in turn overlain by a 0.08m-thick deposit of white-blue-grey sand (Fig. 4.22, Section 155, contexts 654 and 661). These deposits are thought to represent an early buried soil, a pre-existing land surface in the saltmarsh upon which salt production commenced. They tipped steeply downward to the north-west

between 2.4–1.9m OD towards the possible former course of the River Gaywood.

No thin bands of material like those within the mounds of the *Salters Waie* group indicative of buried soils (periods of inactivity) or clean naturally lain deposits were observed in any of the mounds within the *Bullcote Waie* group (Salterns 4–12). This is perhaps suggestive of a more intensive salt-making regime during this postulated later phase of activity on the saltmarsh.

VI. Discussion
(Figs 4.42–4.44)

The 'moies'
Besides the waste heaps (*hoggas*) which constituted the salterns, there was no surviving trace of the heaps of salt-rich *mould* gathered from the nearby coastal strikes or *grevas*. Their morphology is described on the French coast of the 18th century where '…pressed there as much as possible, it is raised to form a peak which resembles a truncated cone. This supply of sand then takes the name of *moie*' (Regnouf de Vains 1840, cited in Edeine 1970, 104), a term utilised within this report to describe mounds of salt-encrusted *mould*. A large rake drawn by a horse or oxen was documented as still being used for gathering salt-rich sands as late as the mid-19th century on the Normandy coast where it was known as a '*haveau*' (Carpentier *et al.* 2012, 51; see also example shown on Fig. 4.42) whilst a contemporary implement on the Solway Firth was called a 'hap' (Duncan 1812, cited in Holden and Hudson 1981, 124). Following this, they would 'hitch a small dumper [tip-cart] which they call *banneau*, one or two beasts, usually one or two oxen, which are driven between the furrows; four people, two in front and two behind, pick up or load the sand from the furrows into the dumper, and a fifth one leads it to the big heap, which is the main deposit of the saltworks or salterns' (Diderot *et al.* 1765, 549; see Appendix 4).

Salt-cotes
A salt-cote — Old English *sealtærn* [salthouse] (Keen 1988, 137; see also Robertson 1939, 16–17 and 46–47) — has been described in the context of coastal salt-making in Norman England as having been clad in clay or cob with a timber roof covered with thatch or reed (Keen 1988, 143). This type of shelter for open-pan hearths is equivalent to the French 'salicole' of the channel coast where the sand-washing tradition for the extraction of salt continued into the modern period (Diderot *et al.* 1768, plate I; reproduced as Fig. 4.42). These salt-cotes also provided a sheltered place for the drying of the salt: depicted as hanging from the roof in conical baskets (see Fig. 4.42; Holden and Hudson 1981, 126). The slight remains of an earth-fast post and beamslot structure upon Saltern 12 are reminiscent of the post-holes postulated to represent a simple shelter for the hearth excavated at Queen Mary's Nursing Home, King's Lynn (Cope-Faulkner 2014, 75). *Ad hoc* shelters may also have been surface laid or constructed with very shallow foundations that have not survived into the archaeological record. At Bicker Haven, Lincolnshire, the small (2.74 x 2.13m) rectangular structure excavated there consisted of

the remains of mud walls resting on a surface-laid turf foundation with only scant evidence for post-holes (Healey 1999, 90). Hallam (1960, 98) described a Lincolnshire salt-cote as 'having mud walls, a timbered roof covered with reed thatch secured by rush ropes and possessed wooden doors and windows' (Holden and Hudson 1981, 125). Structural evidence, in the form of two post-hole-like features and a short section of possible beamslot, was also uncovered during the excavation of a c.13th- to 16th-century saltern in the Adur Valley at Millfields Caravan Park, Bramber, West Sussex. This possible rectilinear salt-cote was suggested to have been timber-framed with mud-brick or wattle-and-daub walls laid upon shallow chalk and flint cobble foundations and perhaps with a tiled roof and timber door (Ridgeway 2000, 149; fig. 5). Although of uncertain date, the outline of a rectangular structure was recorded in the centre of a 'mound' during excavations further east on the Hampshire coast facing the Solent at Pennington Marshes, south of Lymington. It measured 9.4m long x 4.9m wide externally with remains of 1m-thick clay walls surviving to a height of 0.3m (Powell 2009, 20).

Open pan hearths
The central role of brine boiling in the salt-making process is perhaps at odds with the lack of evidence for *in situ* hearths excavated on the North Marsh salterns. The remains of a single truncated hearth (1018, Fig. 4.24) were excavated within Saltern 5 of the *Bullcote Waie* group. A patch of clay excavated on the crest of Saltern 1 within Trench 12 probably represents a further almost entirely truncated example belonging to the *Salters Waie* group. However, the dense concentrations of hearth waste recorded by photogrammetry within Saltern 11 (Fig. 4.32, 676) and Saltern 12 (Fig. 4.22, 678) are indicative of further hearth sites which have either suffered complete truncation or lay immediately adjacent to the excavation areas. The small rectangular patch of occasionally highly fired red clay shown within the excavation of Saltern 12 (Fig. 4.22) appears to be the best candidate for a truncated hearth site.

In terms of construction, the c.3m-square hearth (1018) of probable late 10th/early 11th-century date within Saltern 5 is clearly of the same design as the 'double chambered' configuration of the c.12th- to mid-13th-century hearths previously excavated at both the former Queen Mary's Nursing Home (c.2.4m square; Cope-Faulkner 2014, fig. 6) and Marsh Lane (1.6m in width; Clarke and Clarke 2018, fig. 6); proving this configuration originated prior to the Norman Conquest. The structural advantage of this design may have been to allow the continued heating of a pan as each alternate chamber was swept clean of its accumulating fuel-ash. The resulting central column would also allow further support for the lead pans placed above. The overall tendency for a rectangular shape for this type of hearth is perhaps indicative of rectangular lead pans of similar dimensions. The same conclusion was also given by McAvoy (1994, 146) for the rectangular remains (c.2.5 x 0.8m) of a single late 15th-/early 16th-century hearth excavated at Wainfleet St Mary. The four 14th-century Bicker Haven hearths were similarly of rectangular design (c.1.4 x c.0.5m) further supporting this conclusion (Healey 1999, fig. 59). Where sand-washing was still practiced on the Normandy coast of France until the first half of the 19th century (Carpentier *et al*. 2012, 27), rectangular lead boiling pans are described as 'about three feet long, two wide and five or six inches in deep' (c.0.9 x c.0.6 x c.0.15m), and which were placed into a square of four to form one 'saline' (Musset 1956, 193). Perhaps the best proof of the use of lead pans in the present context was the geochemical analysis on salt slags excavated from Marsh Lane which yielded small but detectable levels of lead (see Timberlake and Haycock 2016, 65–81; Clarke and Clarke 2020, 15). In addition to the 'double chambered' open-pan hearths for brine boiling, the recovery of broadly circular slag cakes suggests the presence of smaller pit-like ancillary hearths up to around 220mm diameter. The discovery of tuyère holes in these cakes indicates their use in iron smithing as well as brine boiling. These circular hearth bases are similar to examples found at Marsh Lane.

Well-formed brick supports reminiscent of those soft fired bricks found at Marsh Lane and the former Queen Mary's Nursing Home were also found at Saltern 5, which must have been an essential part of the hearth design. Handmade *ad hoc* clay wedges or such supports for pans have also been found at the Marsh Lane and Wainfleet St Mary sites which probably also served the same purpose. Interestingly, the purpose of supports is illustrated by modern studies into sand-washing and brine boiling techniques employed in salt-making at Djègbadji on the present-day coastline of Benin, West Africa (Paquet 2018, reproduced on Fig. 4.43). A group of open pan hearths can be seen placed outdoors which display a strikingly similar, if somewhat larger, design to those excavated at King's Lynn. Hearths of a more rounded design are also shown inside what appears to be a salt-cote, boiling salt pans that are placed upon clay wedges. Space was clearly required between the pan and the hearth to provide a through draft of air to burn the fuel, maintain the chamber's temperature and draw the heat through to the pan. This set-up would also provide a mechanism to regulate the rate of boiling within the pan. Salt crystalised out of the brine in different forms depending on the level of heat (faster boiling gave finer crystals) and could then be graded for different purposes/consumers.

Brine boiling was necessarily a careful process. Whilst the solution was boiled the salt crystals, which sank to the bottom as they grew larger, were drawn to one side and regularly scooped out. It was essential that the pan did not boil dry and contaminate the pure salt with other unpalatable salts known as bittern or bitters (such as magnesium carbonate/sulphate/chloride and calcium sulphate) which were equally not suitable for use in the preservation of meat or fish (Holden and Hudson 1981, 126). Bitters formed either as pan scale on the surface of the container (requiring regular cleaning of the pans) or as scum on the surface of the solution, which had to be skimmed and discarded. The skimming of bitter salts and other impurities from the solution probably contributed (along with boiling spatter) to the formation of salt slags observed caked onto the recovered fragments of hearth superstructures. Healey references Bridbury's explanation (1955, 8–9) of the early crystalisation of the salts calcium carbonate and calcium sulphate, of

a) Brine boiling on open-pan hearths

b) The use of fired clay wedges or spacers

c) Leaching basket

Figure 4.43 Salt production in modern day Djègbadji, Benin a) Brine boiling on open-pan hearths, and b) The use of fired clay wedges or spacers (© Paquet 2018) c) Leaching basket (© Adounkpè *et al*. 2021)

which the scale or scum could be removed (Healey 1999, 98). An 18th-century observation of this process on the coast of Normandy describes the removal of bitters: '…we remove the scum that it throws away; and as it decreases, we fill [the pans] with other water that we continue to skim. When it thickens, it is stirred continuously with a large stick curved at one end' (Musset 1956, 193). As a footnote to this separation of unwanted salts, there is an interesting description by Dr Gidon on how a physiochemical phenomenon resulting from the action of sea in laying down the salt facilitated the elimination of a large part of the deliquescent (easily dissolved) salts prior to its gathering up: '…when the coastal sands dry up under the action of the sun, the efflorescent salts of sea water, and in particular sodium chloride, tend to rise towards the surface, then to exceed it, constituting above this surface a crystalline layer which shines in the sun. On the contrary, deliquescent salts tend to be retained, below the surface, in the wet layers which tend to become saturated with magnesian salts' (Gidon 1939, cited in Edeine 1970, 98).

Large lumps of the more highly fired and consolidated parts of broken up hearths were found scattered across most of the salterns to suggest they may have been deliberately destroyed after each salt-winning campaign, perhaps to discourage any opportunistic and unsanctioned use of a site after its abandonment. Similar evidence has been found on Romano-British salt-working sites, where it was thought that the open features such as pits and ditches may have been filled in at the end of each season to stop injury to animals which pastured on the marsh (Tom Lane pers. comm.). It is likely, given the value of this commodity, that the right of access to the North Marsh to produce salt was controlled by the manorial lord. The *in situ* hearth discovered within Saltern 5 may therefore be viewed as a very fortunate survival. There was probably also a practical reason for moving hearths to more favorable locations as waste material produced by the filtration process threatened to engulf each site. Equally, the greater number of incomplete filtration units encountered by these excavations may be attributed to opportunistic recycling of their clay to line or mend tanks on later filtration sites or may even represent deliberate sabotage of illicit salt-making activities. Salt-making sites would probably have shifted annually and perhaps even seasonally. Filtration units, hearths and other infrastructure would have been fragile to the vagaries of the weather and more violent episodes of storms and flooding, especially when sites were not maintained outside of the salt-making season.

The make-up of each mound suggests a lesser volume of fuel-ash was produced by brine boiling than salt-leached sands were produced through the *sleeching* process. Where the highest concentrations of waste ash occurred within Salterns 1 and 2, these were tipped into hollows in the mound's topography, which in places may have been accentuated into deeper 'rake-out' pits. No pits of this morphology were excavated at the broadly contemporary sites identified at the former Queen Mary's Nursing Home or Marsh Lane. Many 'pits with burnt infill' were however present at the 15th/16th-century site excavated at Wainfleet St Mary (McAvoy 1994, fig. 3). Overall, the distribution of *sleeching* and brine boiling remains suggests these activities were mutually inclusive, which perhaps best reflects the *ad hoc* seasonal nature of these processes. The safest location for the more volatile brine-boiling process appears to have been upon the more elevated parts of a saltern. It could be assumed that such locations would also benefit from the prevailing wind to aid the burning of fuel. The entrance to the hearth chambers excavated within Saltern 5 did indeed face into the prevailing wind. However, this orientation is not replicated in any of the other hearths excavated at King's Lynn: the former Queen Mary's Nursing Home example lay on a north–south axis; and the two Marsh Lane double-chambered hearths on an east–west axis (Cope-Faulkner 2014, fig. 6; Clarke and Clarke 2018, figs 5 and 6). The group of four hearths excavated by Healey at Bicker Haven, Lincolnshire also had flues facing north or south (1999, fig. 59). The fact that these hearths do not respect the prevailing wind may be taken as circumstantial evidence for them having been sheltered from the weather by a salt-cote.

The identification of tuyère holes within the vitrified salt slag debris demonstrates that higher temperatures were sometimes achieved through the means of bellows, which suggests some temperature control was needed and/or at least some of the hearths were at times employed in the mending of iron tools. Most of the evidence for this activity came from four of the salterns within the *Bullcote Waie* group (Saltern 6, and Salterns 10–12). There was no evidence for pan repair except one small drip of lead recovered from Trench 32 excavated into Saltern 1. Referring to the destructive effect of brine boiling on the lead pans, Keen quotes a useful description of 19th-century brine boiling on the Normandy coast whereby 'the vats overflow onto the fire, or when their rims break down, there is a flat stone on which the rims are put back into place. An iron poker is used for breaking the blisters on the bottom of the vats, which form when the lead starts to melt' (Keen 1987, 27 quoting Le Héricher 1845, 342–3).

Fuel
A close link between the supply of fuel and saltworks is clearly evident in Anglo-Saxon charters for other parts of the country (Owen 1980, 144). A 9th-century charter of the grant of a *sealtern* at Faversham, Kent included a wood which belonged to it (Robertson 1939, 17 no. X). South of the saltern-endowed religious house at Lyminge, Kent listed by Blair (2005, 258, n.58) lay the coastal settlement of *Salteode* (Saltwood); clearly associated and no doubt having provided timber for salt production (Powell-Smith 2011). There is also documentary evidence for salterns on the northern coasts of Normandy having been supplied with wood or 'joncs-marins' – sea rushes (Musset 1956, 193). A further example is of a 12th-century bequest of salterns to the monastery of Saint-Étienne de Caen that included permission to take all the necessary wood from the neighbouring forest (Carpentier 2010, 7). Documentary reference to the use of peat as a fuel at similar types of saltern sites during the medieval to post-medieval periods comes from Brownrigg (1748, 137): 'the brine being thus prepared they boil it with turf fires in small leaden pans...'. Darby (1940, 40) also mentions a close association between salterns and turbaries in the medieval fenland. Overall, the impression is of gathering fuel from whatever resources lay closest to hand. In this regard, the saltmarshes of Gaywood and those of Wootton to the north, were probably closely linked with the substantial belt of woodland that still extends across these parishes today upon the coarse sandy soils (see Chapter 3; Fig. 3.9). The southern portion of Reffley Wood lies within Gaywood parish. Woodland was probably managed to maintain a constant supply of fuel using the technique of coppicing: cutting the wood on a rotation to encourage the new growth of underwood every few years (Dyer 2002, 25). The rich peaty soils on the floor of the river valley between Gaywood Bridge and Bawsey would have provided an easily available source of turf and possibly peat. The British Geological Survey map of King's Lynn also delineates an extensive tract of peat within the upper reaches of the Middleton Stop Drain valley, south of Mintlyn. It was possible to import peat by cart from nearby turbaries (Went 2011, 3–4) and there are records of salterns in Lincolnshire that had associated rights of turbary (Hallam 1960, 92; Hall and Coles 1994, 143–5).

The fragment of peat found at Saltern 12 (see above) is a small but significant find as it helps to confirm that locally cut peat was one of the fuel sources utilised for salt production on the North Marsh. Other plant remains (notably charcoal) recovered from the salterns indicate that locally available wood and other plants, such as oak, hazel/alder, holly, rushes and grasses were collected, probably on an *ad hoc* basis.

Filtration units and clay-lined tanks
Both the ostracod and foraminiferal evidence corroborate the historical narrative that the muds used in the *sleeching* process were collected from the lower saltmarsh/upper tidal mudflats zone. The five complete examples of filtration units uncovered within both the *Salters Waie* group (Salterns 1 and 2) and the *Bullcote Waie* group (Saltern 10) are of the same design as the broadly contemporary Mid to Late Anglo-Saxon and early medieval examples excavated at the former Queen Mary's Nursing Home and Marsh Lane sites (Cope-Faulkner 2014, fig. 4; Clarke and Clarke 2018, fig. 3). Comparing these sites, a filtration tank could range between *c*.1.2m square to a more rectangular form up to *c*.2.1m long by 1.6m wide. A brine collection tank varied between a sub-square and a sub-circular form measuring between *c*.0.5–1.2m in diameter by *c*.0.4–0.65m deep. The remains of the turf layer at the base of filtration unit 414 is a further indicator of the longevity and conservative character of a salt-making method which persisted essentially unchanged between *c*.AD 750–1250 on the North Marsh. The late 15th/early 16th-century filtration units excavated at Wainfleet St Mary in Lincolnshire incorporated filtration tanks which measured *c*.3m long by *c*.1.5m wide with circular brine collection tanks that measured *c*.1m in diameter by *c*.1.5m deep. However, even these larger-scale examples conform to a configuration first utilised perhaps 800 years earlier. This is even more remarkable when considering that this method of construction persisted in use in some places to be described by Brownrigg and Duncan in the 18th and 19th centuries.

There was no evidence, in the form of impressions in the clay or otherwise, for the superstructures which must have retained the *sleech* as each batch was washed of its salt. A filtration pit merely represents the impermeable floor of a mostly removable watertight construction placed above it (Fig. 4.44). Traces of the latter have only been found at Wainfleet St Mary which indicate they were timber-framed boxes (McAvoy 1994, 140). Descriptions of the sand-washing process still being practiced on the Normandy coast until the early 19th century probably provides the best possible reconstruction for these elements. Regnouf de Vains (1840) describes: 'Next to this sand heap [the *moie*] a clay floor is formed, beaten with a *pilon* [pestle] to compact it strongly and make it waterproof. Its plane is inclined to conduct the water in the prepared reservoirs. On this area we establish a floor on joists, which we cover with a layer of *glu* [pitch], on which we put the sides of a square box, formed of boards with a width of 23 centimetres and a length of 3 metres. This large box (called a pit) thus prepared, is then filled with sand taken from the *moie* and is trodden there as much as possible with bare feet; then water is poured into it….and the water gradually filtrates through the sand, becomes saturated with salt contained in the sand, continues through *noes* [pipes], which flows into barrels….and soon after, this salted water (called *brune*) is subjected to boiling' (cited in Edeine 1970, 104). The morphology of these late French tanks is clearly more in keeping with the larger scale 15th/16th-century rectangular examples excavated at Wainfleet St Mary, which also utilised an inclined base to aid drainage to the reservoir (McAvoy 1994, fig. 5). Filtration units of this late date are described as usually being loaded twice a day with water taking between four and six hours to pass through depending on how well pressed the sand was within the tank (Diderot and d'Alembert 1778, in Edeine 1970, 107). The more rounded form of the much earlier Anglo-Saxon filtration pit excavated in Saltern 1 (filtration unit 146; Fig. 4.10) may have been the result of truncation, although it remains a possibility that a barrel-type superstructure may also have been employed at this early date. Remarkably similar filtration units have been documented at present-day salterns at Djègbadji, Benin — alongside the aforementioned brine boiling hearths — where leaching baskets are constructed of woven mangrove wood sealed with clay (Adounkpè *et al.* 2021, fig. 3(b), reproduced on Fig. 4.43). The use of basket-and-clay-lined superstructures may explain the more rounded and sub-square tank bases excavated on Gaywood's North Marsh. As the most rounded and rectangular examples of filtration units were excavated in Salterns 1 and 2 within the *Salters Waie* group (see Figs 4.10–11), these forms were probably not mutually exclusive, and suggests their design could vary depending on what materials were available at the start of each salt-winning campaign.

The fossilised clods of turf or peat found at the base of filtration unit 414 within Saltern 10 (Fig. 4.21) represent a rare survival of the filtration medium necessary to filter salt particles from the washed sand. According to Dr Gidon it was necessary to wash the sands with fresh water (Gidon 1939 in Edeine 1970, 98). However, an 18th-century French source alludes to the possible use of saltwater for sand-washing whereby 'Near the large heap [the *moie*] is the *quin*, reservoir, or tank from which the salt workers draw out the water to wash the sand; this water of the *quin* is replenished by the tide which brings back the saltwater during the high tides, covering the shores and filling the *quin*' (Diderot and Alembert 1765, 549; see Appendix 4). Within the British context, the use of either salt or freshwater was considered possible for the salterns found at Bicker Haven on the Wash (Healey 1999, 98) and at the Adur Valley, Sussex (Holden and Hudson 1981, 124). However, both these sites were located upon rivers (as were those of the French Channel coast) suggesting that the ease of access to riverine freshwater was a major factor in salt-making sites within all of these contexts, gravitating towards coastal river estuaries. Indeed, based on the historical references and archaeological sites collated for this study, there appears to be a link between the preferred 'marshy river' locations of the Channel coast for salt-making and the Lym- toponym which denotes this specific environment or topography (for example: Lyminge, Kent in Blair 2005, 258, no. 58; Lyme, Dorset in Keen 1987, 25; and Lymington, Hampshire in Powell 2009); names reminiscent of the Lena-/Lyn of the Wash. Brackish groundwater may also have been brought up from wells as was found at Wainfleet St Mary (McAvoy 1994, 141) although there was no evidence for their presence within the current investigation areas. Many of the salterns of the North Marsh (including Salterns 10–12) were placed near to the meandering course of the Gaywood river. It is also possible the salterns were sited near to artificial freshwater conduits. There is historical evidence that water management on a large scale was possible by the local inhabitants. The lower reaches of the River Gaywood were dammed and several mills stood on the North Marsh, the first probably dating to 1101 (Neville 2014). The growing town of Lynn derived its freshwater supply from the River Gaywood. By controlling a system of stone 'cloughs' (or clowzes – the Latin *clusi*/*clusum* – to shut in or out) it was possible to exclude saltwater from the fleets when the tide rose. In *c*.1307 a basin of freshwater (called an *incusae*) was constructed in the Newland north of the Purfleet as a reserve for emergencies (Hillen 1907, 793).

Four of the rectangular clay-lined tanks within sub-phase IV of Saltern 5 and three examples within sub-phase IV of Saltern 12 were notably deeper examples, being between 0.57–0.9m in depth. Interpreted as 'incomplete' filtration units, these features may in fact represent the kind of rectangular brine storage tank of similar dimensions to that excavated at Marsh Lane (Clarke and Clarke 2018). However, that tank's lining was discoloured purple due to long contact with the concentrated brine, something which was not evident on the current sites. On balance, the simpler interpretation is that some filtration pits were excavated to a greater depth with perhaps less substantial timber framed box superstructures. The ambiguous nature of some of the 'incomplete' tanks may otherwise be explained through unknown practical necessities of a salt-making sites such as the opportunistic storage of rainwater, for example.

Of particular interest was the discovery of a set of five shallow circular tanks, between 1.6–2.15m in diameter, lined with brown clay membranes, and cut

Figure 4.44 Reconstruction sketch of a salter's working area

into the uppermost sequence of filtration waste muds of Saltern 1. Currently no parallels have been found for these features. The brown clay is at odds with the blue grey clay found lining features across the rest of the salterns. It is possible these features represent the base of a series of small *Moies*, batches/mounds of unprocessed *sleech* awaiting filtration. Keen translates a French description of 19th-century salt-making in the Bay of Mont-Saint-Michel whereby 'The sand heaps consist of two parts: sand washed and set aside, and virgin sand. The virgin sand is heaped up on a floor of clay, pressed with wooden spades, and often covered by a clay layer' (Keen 1987, 27 quoting Le Héricher 1845, 342–3).

Considering the small size of each excavation area in relation to the saltern mounds it has been difficult to establish any formal planning in the layout of the working areas upon each of the salterns. The overall impression is of an *ad hoc* arrangement of filtration units with no evidence for a dominant alignment of features or orientation, either in respect to each other or nearby natural features such as creeks (Fig. 4.44). There is certainly no evidence for the level of spatial organisation seen at the 15th/16th-century site excavated at Wainfleet St Mary, Lincolnshire. On that site, filtration units were generally grouped into pairs with the collection tanks adjacent to each other and the filtration pits extending in opposite directions, on a broadly north-to-south axis. These pairs, along with single examples, were themselves chained into alignments of filtration units set between *c.*15–25m apart which extended between linear heaps of filtration waste. Slight variations in the alignment of these chains were influenced by the surrounding creek network (McAvoy 1994, 145; fig. 10). This highly organised set-up for the salters working at Wainfleet St Mary is described by McAvoy (1994, 160–61) as possibly having been a late medieval/early post-medieval development. Only a single heavily truncated hearth was uncovered on that site, suggesting that these features were placed between the chains of filtration units. The excavation of a *c.*14th-century saltern mound at Quadring, Lincolnshire uncovered better evidence for the arrangement of hearths, with four hearths arranged into two pairs placed side by side. Each of these pairs lay approximately 7m apart on a shared east-to-west alignment with their flues extending in opposing directions, apparently without regard to the prevailing wind direction (Healey 1999, fig. 59).

A portable industry

Although the potential for preservation of organic remains in marshlands is high, the almost complete lack of organic archaeological remains within the salterns is characteristic of 'dryland' deposits. The intermittent and shifting nature of salt-working sites is possibly also reflected in the paucity of evidence for structures and the array of equipment usually associated with fixed places of work. When a salt-winning campaign had ended, all of the salt-drying baskets and any pots were probably carted back to the village along with the timber framed wooden box or basket of the filtration unit, tools and of course the valuable lead pans. The odd pot evidently broke and become part of an extremely low-level scatter of sherds across the mounds and any worn out baskets or other organic items left behind would no doubt have rotted away. An interesting example of what may have been found if better preservation conditions had allowed is provided by the investigation of a group of coastal salterns demolished in 1955 near Seasalter, Kent. Two pits lined with wickerwork were exposed as the clearance of those earthworks progressed, with mats (each hurdle measuring 5' by 3'6") woven from twigs and surfaced with reeds and paths laid with broken sticks observed to have provided firm platforms for the workers (Thompson 1956). Fragments of wooden implements were also found such as a rake, hoe, bowl and mallet (Thompson 1956, figs 4 and 5). The odd insight into other activities carried out by the salt-workers was provided by the evidence for the mending of ironwork and perhaps even the opportunistic production of implements periodically on the hearths of the *Bullcote Waie* group. It may be of significance that no metalworking debris related to iron smithing was recovered from Salterns 1 and 2 which comprised the *Salters Waie* group. Environmental evidence including plant remains, pollen, ostracods and foraminifera, predominantly relates to the natural saltmarsh and its surroundings, while the scant mammal and fish bones recovered provide little insight into the diet of the salt-workers as they carried out their tasks.

Chapter 5. Salt-making in the Historical Narrative of Lynn

'The champion part [North and West Norfolk] is of another nature consistinge wholy in effect of Corne and sheepe, w[hi]ch by perticular course of husbandry there used, doe maynetayne each other...Those parts of the Coast of Norf[olk] havinge divers ports and Havens use much trade and commerce with New Castle for Salt and Coales both summer and winter and sayle about 60 or 70 Shipps yearelye to Iseland [returning with cod or herring], and provide their Salt from Newcastle for yt voyage, and usuallye carrye great quantities of barly and Mault to Newcastle...'

(Description of Norfolk by Sir Henry Spelman in 1631 to the Privy Council, reproduced from Smith 2012, 19)

I. Domesday, charters and cartularies
by Nick Holder
(Fig. 5.1)

There were two powerful lords in medieval Lynn and its immediate hinterland: the bishop of Norwich and the prior of Holy Trinity Priory, Norwich. These two religious lords were linked (Holy Trinity was a monastic cathedral) but they remained separate lords, both in their ecclesiastical and their secular powers. For Lynn and the adjacent village of Gaywood, the bishop was always more important than the prior.

According to Domesday Book (and the important draft that survives for East Anglia, the 'Little Domesday'), the lord of the manor of Gaywood in the 1060s was Bishop Almer and, twenty years later in 1086, the lord and bishop was William de Beaufeu (Powell-Smith 2011, Gaywood; Editions Alecto 1986, f. 191). In the 1090s the new bishop, Herbert de Losinga, exercised an even stronger influence on the locality. Having established a new Benedictine monastic cathedral in Norwich, Holy Trinity Priory, de Losinga then founded a new town at Lynn. He has been described as an 'episcopal imperialist', founding and building a bishop's empire in this part of East Anglia (Harper-Bill 2004). De Losinga granted some of his manorial income from both Lynn and Gaywood to the new priory, including the church of St Margaret Lynn, and income from the town fairs (Dugdale et al. 1846, vol. 4, 462 (see Appendix 5 in this volume) White 1893; Page 1906, 317–18). In the early 13th century a later prior gave most of this back to the bishop, in exchange for the manors of Sedgeford and Cressingham (NRO, BL/O J3/70; Fig. 5.1).

Gaywood remained one of the seventeen Norfolk manors under the direct jurisdiction of the bishop, and the manor duly appears in the financial accounts of successive bishops (Rutledge 1993, 90). In 1428–9 he received £43 13s 9d in rent from his Gaywood tenants; a century later in 1533–4 his local bailiff William Donne collected the slightly smaller sum of £35 16s 5d (NRO, DN/EST 15/1; 15/7). The accounts also reveal the bishop's investment in his lands. In 1428–9 he spent £4 0s 1½d in the consolidation or reclamation of marginal land: the costs of digging or embanking (*fossatum*) and enclosing or hedging (*sep[iens]*; note the uncertain expansion of the medieval abbreviation).

From an early date the bishop's Gaywood estate included salterns. There were 30 in 1066, reduced to 21 by 1086 (Editions Alecto 1986, f. 191). Salt manufacture was probably one of the economic factors that encouraged Bishop de Losinga to found the new town of Lynn in the 1090s: at least two salterns were swallowed up by the expanding new town, their presence indicated in the early place-names Dowshill and Rondshill (Clarke and Carter

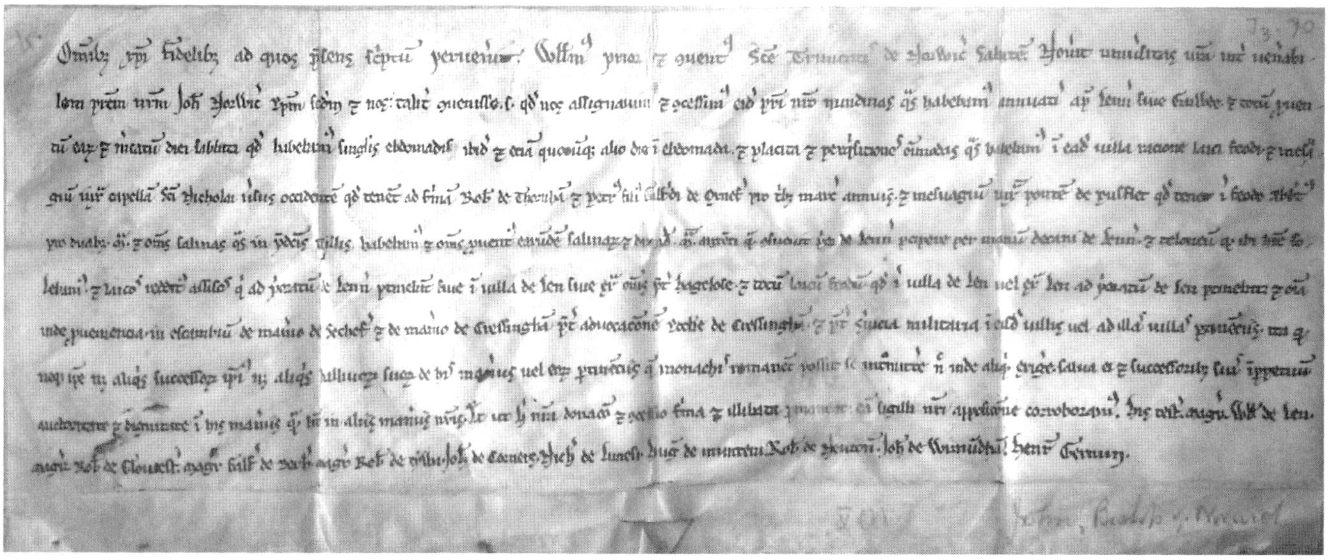

Figure 5.1 Assignment from William, prior of Holy Trinity, Norwich to John, bishop of Norwich, 1200–1214 (NRO, BL/O/J3/70. Reproduced by kind permission of the Norfolk Record Office)

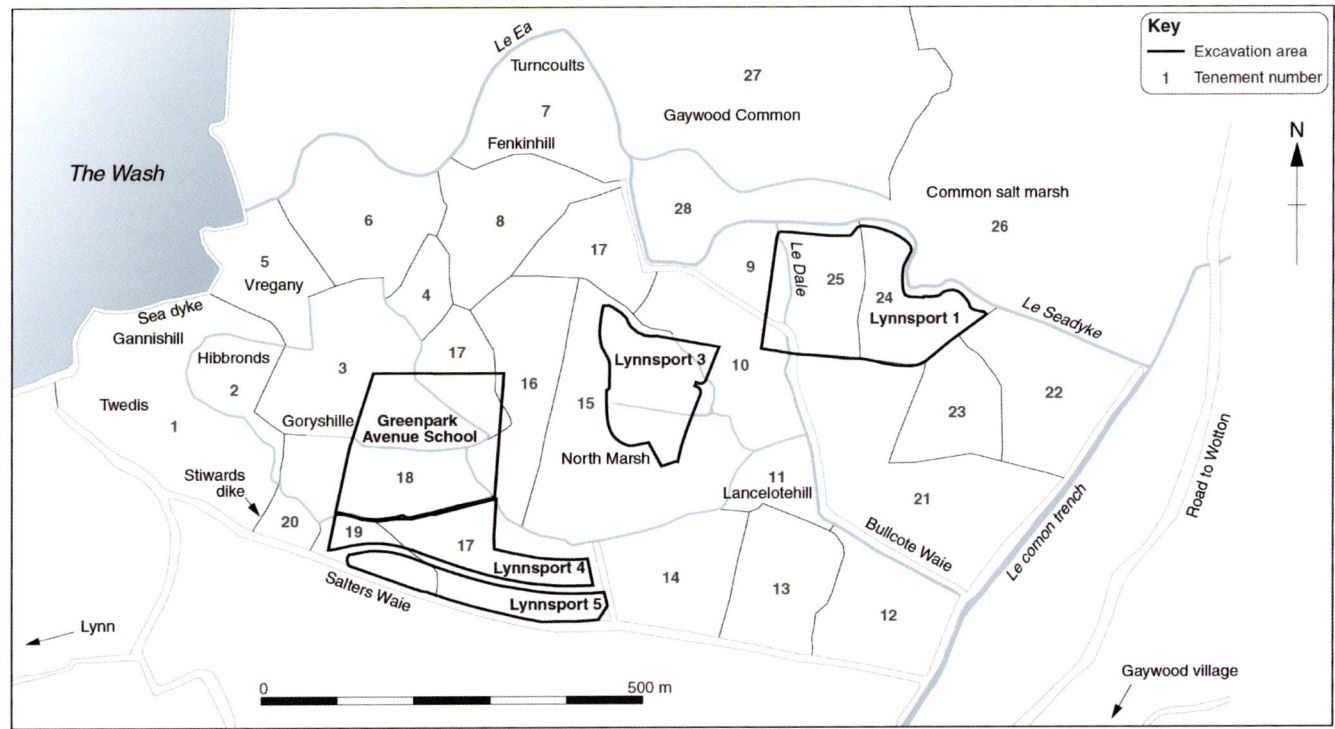

Figure 5.2 Reconstructed map of the land holdings given on the Gaywood Dragge survey of 1487 (based on NRO, BL/MA 2/1); see Table 5.1 for details of Tenements 1 to 28

1977, 411–12, fig. 186). Bishop de Losinga's grant to the new priory of St Margaret Lynn (a dependent cell of Holy Trinity Priory, Norwich) in *c*.1100 included several salt-works in Gaywood (Dugdale *et al*. 1846, vol. 4, 462; see Appendix 5). When the prior of Holy Trinity exchanged land and rents with the bishop of Norwich in the early 13th century, these included 'all the salterns in the same townships [of Lynn and Gaywood]' (NRO, BL/O J3/70).

In addition to the bishop, there were three institutional landlords in Gaywood. Holy Trinity Priory, Norwich, continued to hold some tenements from the bishop (although, as has been discussed, they exchanged most of their Gaywood land in the early 13th century). The priory of St Margaret functioned as a parish church for Lynn (as well as a cell of Holy Trinity Priory, Norwich) and their Gaywood lands appear in their account rolls (Saunders 1930, 146). In 1498–9, for example, they received £4 3s in normal rents and 14s 5d in rents of assize (the latter term indicating the older fixed rents that had largely replaced obligations of feudal service to the lord; NRO, DCN/2/1/77). Thirdly, the small hospital of St Mary Magdalene Gaywood had some fields; no financial accounts of the hospital appear to survive but their holdings are noted in a survey of 1487 (Bradfer-Lawrence 1932, 155, 157–60, 176). All three institutions rented their land to sub-tenants, receiving rents and paying small sums to the bishop.

Gaywood also had a local secular lord, the earl of Arundel, who held Castle Rising four miles to the north and who held land in the north of Gaywood beyond the River Ea (see below), which probably equates to the tidal reaches of the River Gaywood through the North Marsh. In the early 13th century Bishop William de Raley made a legal agreement concerning this land with Hugh d'Aubigny, the fifth earl (NRO, BL/MA 2/1, f. 11v).

II. The 'Gaywood Dragge' of 1487: survey of a fossilised salt-making landscape
by Nick Holder
(Fig. 5.2)

The bishop of Norwich commissioned a very detailed written survey of his Gaywood estate in the late 15th century (Bradfer-Lawrence 1932). The document, written in English rather than Latin, survives as six sheets of paper folded to form a booklet of 12 folios (NRO, BL/MA 2/1). The date of the survey is given as the second year of the reign of Henry VII and the sixth year of the episcopacy of James Goldwell, bishop of Norwich. Unfortunately these dates do not quite match: the second regnal year of Henry VII is August 1486–7 while the sixth episcopal year of James is July 1477–8. It is possible that the sixth year is an error for 16th ('vi' for 'xvi' in an earlier draft?): this might suggest that the survey was carried out in 1487. The surveyor was the bishop's bailiff John Wicks: he and the Gaywood man John Dowdy walked around the roads and field-paths of the manor describing each holding in turn (NRO, BL/MA 2/1, f. 11v).

Concentrating on the study area of the Lynnsport and Greenpark Avenue development sites, it is possible to retrace Wicks' and Dowdy's footprints and define 28 land-holdings between the lane called *Salters Waie* (Way) in the south and Gaywood Common in the north (Table 5.1). Additional property exchange documents have been identified in King's Lynn Borough Archives and the Norfolk Record Office and these can be used to give a more detailed history of six properties (Tenement 6: Table 5.2; Tenement 7:

Tenement no. on Fig. 5.2	Institutional landlord?	Tenant	Description	Size	Rent
1		Thomas Geben	'a certaine hill of pasture called Twedis otherwise Daies and another hill called Gannishill'	15 acres	2s and 3 combs of salt
2	St Margaret's Priory, Lynn	formerly John Curts	called 'Hibbronds otherwise Hashecoates'		¼ [comb] of salt
3		Edmund Bawsey (formerly Andrew Swanton)	includes 'le Nattocks' (mounds)	8 acres	5 bushels [1¼ combs] of salt
4		formerly Robert Tydde	pasture	2 acres	
5		John Barker of Lynn, butcher	pasture and pond ('pasture with a Water in the same'), an acre called Vregany	4+1 acres	free tenant
6	St Mary Magdalene Hospital, Gaywood		pasture with two parcels, one of which has a house	7 acres	
7		Edmund Bawsey (formerly Andrew Swanton)	pasture, including Fenkinhill and Turncoults	5 roods	free tenant
8		Edmund Bawsey	pasture	4 acres	free tenant
9	St Margaret's Priory, Lynn		pasture	3 acres	
10		Elizabeth, widow of Thomas Constantine	meadow	6 acres	6s 8d
11	St Margaret's Priory, Lynn	Richard Willis	land called 'Lancelotehill'	2 acres	
12		John Fisher	pasture	6 acres	6s
13		John Ashly		4 acres	free tenant
14		John Fisher	pasture	4 acres	4s
15		Elizabeth, widow of Thomas Constantine	a close in North Marsh	18 acres	18s
16		formerly Sir Edmund Wickton	pasture	6 acres	
17	St Margaret's Priory, Lynn			16 acres	
18		widow of Edmund Pepper	pasture	5 acres	free tenant
19		widow of Edmund Pepper	pasture	4 acres	4s
20		John Tego [burgess and draper of Lynn] (formerly John Oldmedell, smith)	pasture	2 acres	2d
21		Elizabeth, widow of Thomas Constantine	pasture	12 acres	20s
22		Elizabeth, widow of Thomas Constantine	pasture	5 acres	5s
23		John Wyks (formerly Robert Kirkby)		3 acres	3s
24		Elizabeth, widow of Thomas Constantine	pasture	3 acres	free tenant
25		Edmund Bawsey	pasture	3 acres	3s
26		common	the 'Comon Salt Marrish' of Gaywood		common
27		common	'Gaywood Comon'		common
28		demesne land of the bishop	saltmarsh 'enclosed with le Ea [stream]'		demesne

Table 5.1 Landholdings in the study area in *c*.1487; the bishop of Norwich was the manorial lord for all these tenements (source: NRO, BL/MA 2/1, ff. 4v–6)

Date	Tenant	Notes	Reference
1487		tenant not stated	NRO, BL/MA 2/1, f. 4v; Bradfer-Lawrence 1932, 163
before 1534	William Potter, fishmonger	3 acres in Gaywood marsh, with a fish-drying shed, and a former saltern with 'sandhyll groves nattokkes'	KLBA, KL/C 56/16
1534	Thomas Myller the elder, merchant	described as merchant of Lynn in his will of 1548	KLBA, KL/C 56/16; TNA, PROB 11/32/274
1543	Robert Gervys of Lynn	perhaps the Robert Gervis described as mayor of Lynn in 1567	KLBA, KL/C 56/16; TNA, E 40/13024

Table 5.2 Documented tenants of Tenement 6, held by St Mary Magdalene Hospital, Gaywood (for location, see Fig. 5.2)

Date	Tenant	Notes	Reference
before 1330	John de Glynton rector of church of Hevingham	3 roods of salt meadow (probably = the Turnecole property)	NRO, DCN 44/42/10 (Fig. 5.3)
1330	John Page de Wymondham,		NRO, DCN 44/42/10 (Fig. 5.3
1487–97	Edmund Bawsey	5 roods of pasture, including Fenkinhill and Turncoults	NRO, BL/MA 2/1, f. 4; Bradfer-Lawrence 1932, 163
1497	James Walter of Lynn, chaplain	'5 roods called Turnecole', with salterns, pasture and nattocks	KLBA, KL/C 50/643
before 1507	John Burmond of Geywood	'anciently called Turnecoule'	KLBA, KL/C 50/644
1507	Walter Curson, William Worlesse and Richard Abell, burgesses [of Lynn]		KLBA, KL/C 50/644

Table 5.3 Documented tenants of Tenement 7, known as Turnecole (for location, see Fig. 5.2)

Date	Tenant	Notes	Reference
1295	Isabella, widow of John Curteys de Gaywood	saltern in Gaywood marsh	NRO, DCN 44/42/7
1487	Elizabeth, widow of Thomas Constantine	6 acres of meadow	NRO, BL/MA 2/1, f. 5; Bradfer-Lawrence 1932, 164

Table 5.4 Documented tenants of Tenement 10 (for location, see Fig. 5.2)

Date	Tenant	Notes	Reference
before 1460	Robert Hunt, burgess of Lynn	4 acres of arable land	KLBA, KL/C 50/654
1460	William Philpott, John Tracy and Thomas Caldecott		KLBA, KL/C 50/654
before 1479	Henry Baxter	4 acres	KLBA, KL/C 50/658
1479	John Baker, butcher Robert Wareyn, grocer, William Yates, fishmonger, burgesses of Lynn, and William Langham of Lynn, barber		KLBA, KL/C 50/658
1487	sub-tenant: widow of Edmund Pepper	5 acres of pasture	NRO, BL/MA 2/1, f. 5; Bradfer-Lawrence 1932, 164
before 1527	Richard Bewshere of Lynn, merchant	5 acres in Gaywood marsh	KLBA, KL/C 50/661
1527	Alice Genyns	Alice Genyns, widow of Robert Genyns, merchant, is described as executrix of the will of Richard Bewsher, merchant in 1515	KLBA, KL/C 50/661; KL/C 50/660
1540	mayor and burgesses of Lynn		KLBA, KL/C 50/662

Table 5.5 Documented tenants of Tenement 18 (for location, see Fig. 5.2)

Date	Tenant	Notes	Reference
before 1460	Andrew Scarlett, son and heir of William Scarlett, late of Lynn, tilemaker	'piece of land called Upgongeacre' in Gaywood marsh	KLBA, KL/C 50/653
1460–64	William Philpott and John Tracy, burgesses, and Thomas Caldecott of Lynn		KLBA, KL/C 50/653
1464	William Pilton and John Braibroke, burgesses, and John Smyth of Lynn, chaplain	Upgongeacre	KLBA, KL/C 50/655
before 1479	Henry Baxter	Upgongacre	KLBA, KL/C 50/658
1479	John Baker, butcher Robert Wareyn, grocer, William Yates, fishmonger, burgesses of Lynn, and William Langham of Lynn, barber		KLBA, KL/C 50/658
1487	sub-tenant: widow of Edmund Pepper	4 acres	NRO, BL/MA 2/1, f. 5; Bradfer-Lawrence 1932, 164

Table 5.6 Documented tenants of Tenement 19, known as Upgongacre (for location, see Fig. 5.2)

Date	Tenant	Notes	Reference
before 1285/6	John, son of John de Merlou of Lynn	7 acres in Gaywood marsh	KLBA, KL/C 50/639
1285/6	Alexander Lomb of Lynn	6d annual rent reserved (to bishop of Norwich)	KLBA, KL/C 50/639 and /640
1290	John Sturiun, innkeeper, of Lynn		KLBA, KL/C 50/640
before 1465	Richard Godewyn, burgess, and Richard Collyng of Myntelyng, chaplain,	2½ acres in the north marsh of Gaywood	KLBA, KL/C 50/636
1465–1480	John Oldemedewe of Lenn		KLBA, KL/C 50/636
1480	John Tigo, draper, John Bilney, glover, and Richard Tigo, tailor, burgesses	John Tego was described as burgess and draper of Lynn in his will of 1498	KLBA, KL/C 50/637; TNA, PROB/11/11/409
1487	John Tego	2 acres of pasture	NRO, BL/MA 2/1, f. 5; Bradfer-Lawrence 1932, 164

Table 5.7 Documented tenants of Tenement 20 (for location, see Fig. 5.2)

Table 5.3; Tenement 10: Table 5.4; Tenement 18: Table 5.5; Tenement 19: Table 5.6; Tenement 20: Table 5.7). The next stage was to examine in detail the late 15th-century manorial survey, particularly the route taken by the surveyors and their descriptions of properties and abutments: by applying this topographic information to the Gaywood enclosure map of 1810, it is possible to reconstruct probable boundaries for these 28 properties (Fig. 5.2). Table 5.8 collates the documentary references with the topographic and excavated evidence for the identified salterns within each tenement.

By the time of the 1487 survey, only three of the 28 tenements were still paying rents in salt (nos 1 to 3 on Table 5.1): this was now a predominantly pastoral landscape.

The Lynnsport and Greenpark Avenue development sites in the 15th century
(Fig. 5.2)

Lynnsport 1: Tenements 24 and 25:
According to the medieval survey of c.1487, the area of Lynnsport 1 was used for pasture by the late 15th century. Tenement 24 was a three-acre field held by Elizabeth, widow of Thomas Constantine while, immediately to the west, Tenement 25 was a three-acre field rented from the bishop of Norwich by Edmund Bawsey, who paid 3s annual rent (Fig. 5.2, Table 5.1; NRO, BL/MA 2/1, ff. 5v–6; Bradfer-Lawrence 1932, 166).

Lynnsport 3: Tenement 15:
The area of Lynnsport 3 lay in the North Marsh of Gaywood. The land had probably been part of the holding of St Margaret's Priory, Lynn: in 1295 the land was described, in an abutment description, as the prior's land (NRO, DCN 44/42/7). By the time of the manorial survey of c.1487 the pasture of the North Marsh had been enclosed into several fields, the largest of which was the 18-acre Tenement 15, which was held by Elizabeth, widow of Thomas Constantine (Fig. 5.2; Table 5.1; NRO, BL/MA 2/1, f. 5; Bradfer-Lawrence 1932, 164).

Lynnsport 4 & 5: Tenements 17, 19:
The documentary evidence suggests that the area of Lynnsport 4 & 5 was primarily used for pasture in

Tenement	Topographical evidence for salterns. NHER ref. no. (see Fig. 1.3)	Historical Reference	Evidence	The Excavations NHER Event no. (see Fig. 1.3)	Excavated saltern no.
1		NRO, BL/MA 2/1, f. 4v	hill or mound called 'Twedis otherwise Daies'; another hill or mound called Gannishill in 1487		-
3	NHERs 27906-7; MNFs 42722-3	KLBA, KL/C 50/658; NRO, BL/MA 2/1, f. 4v	saltern earthworks on aerial photo; hill or mound called Goryshille in 1479; 'le Nattocks' (mounds) in 1487	ENF143325 (eval.); ENF145594 (ex.)	7 and 8
5	NHER 27907		saltern earthworks on aerial photo		
6	MNF 5524	KLBA, KL/C 56/16	former saltern described in 1534		
7	NHER 27886; MNF 42706; MNF 5542	NRO, BL/MA 2/1, f. 5; KLBA, KL/C 50/643	archaeological observation of ash and briquetage deposits from saltworking; saltern earthworks on aerial photo; hill or mound called Fenkinhill in 1487; 'salterns, pasturage and nattokes [mounds]' in 1497		
9	NHER 27895		saltern earthwork on aerial photo		
10	NHER 27911; MNF 42727	NRO, DCN 44/42/7	saltern in 1295		
11		NRO, BL/MA 2/1, f. 5	hill or mound called 'Lancelotehill' in 1487		
14					
15	NHER 27910; MNF 42726			ENF138254 (eval.); ENF145065 (ex.)	9
16	NHER 27909; MNF 42725		saltern earthworks on aerial photo	ENF143325 (eval.); ENF145594 (ex.)	5
17				ENF143325 (eval.); ENF145594 (ex.) ENF139746 (eval.); ENF141949 (ex.)	2, 3, 4 and 6
18				ENF143325 (eval.); ENF145594 (ex.)	1 and 4
19				ENF139746 (eval.); ENF141949 (ex.)	1
24	NHER 2795; NHER 13785			ENF139745 (eval.); ENF145343 (ex.)	11 and 12 (NHER 2795 proved to be made ground only)
25				ENF139745 (eval.); ENF145343 (ex.)	10
26	NHER 27912		saltern earthwork on aerial photo		
27	NHER 27899 (Marsh Lane saltern), 27900, 27902, 38265		saltern earthworks and cropmarks on aerial photos	Marsh Lane ENF135847 (WB) ENF137497 (eval.); ENF137496 (ex.); Clarke and Clarke (2018)	

Table 5.8 Summary of documentary and archaeological evidence for the salterns in the study area

the medieval period. Tenement 17 was part of the St Margaret Lynn's pasture in the North Marsh of Gaywood. Further west there was a property known as Upgongacre, Tenement 19, which lay immediately north of *Salters Waie* (Fig. 5.2; Table 5.6). The 15th-century owners of this property (strictly the tenants in fee) can be traced thanks to the later acquisition of the property by the Corporation of Lynn, who retained the earlier deeds in the borough archive (Table 5.6). It is noticeable that the owners named in three medieval deeds are groups of men, probably trustees holding the property in trust on behalf of an organisation such as a religious guild of Lynn.

Greenpark Avenue School: Tenements 3, 17, 18:
The documentary evidence suggests that the area of Greenpark Avenue School was primarily used for pasture in the medieval period. The four-acre field of Tenement 18 seems to have been used for arable as well as pastoral agriculture, some of whose late 15th- and early 16th-century owners and tenants can be traced (Table 5.5). Like Upgongacre (Tenement 19), this tenement was acquired by the Corporation of Lynn. Further north lay Tenement 3, which by 1460 included *Gorishille*, probably a former saltern mound (KLBA, KL/C 50/654).

The social structure of the manor
The 1487 survey reveals a social hierarchy with the lord of the manor, the bishop, at the top and the local religious houses of St Margaret and St Mary Magdalene occupying the next rung. These religious houses received rents from their tenants but were still institutional tenants of the bishop, paying him small annual fees such as quitrents (unfortunately these fees are not detailed in the bishop's financial accounts; *e.g.* NRO, DCN/2/1/46). Next on the social ladder were the yeomen or tenants 'in fee'. Men and women such as Thomas Geben (in Tenement 1) and Elizabeth Constantine (in Tenement 24) owned their lands but, like the institutional tenants, still had some financial obligations to the lord.

Below the free tenants were the leasehold or customary tenants such as Edmund Bawsey (in Tenement 25) or John Fisher (in Tenement 14) who were usually paying the bishop an annual rent of a shilling an acre on their two- to six-acre plots (note, however, people like Elizabeth Constantine who held some land in fee but paid rent on other fields). Further down the social scale were the semi-free tenants, such as Richard Willis who was a sub-tenant of St Margaret's Priory in Tenement 11. There must have been several cottars (cottagers) and landless labourers in this part of Gaywood, although they remain invisible in the 1487 manorial survey, which is organised around land tenancy (NRO, BL/MA 2/1). Documents such as military musters allow the study of this social group in another Norfolk manor, Hevingham Bishops (Whittle and Yates 2000, 5–7, 21–2).

All these men and women lived their lives in a social world of largely unwritten custom and precedent. The tenants must have had, for example, established manorial rights of pasture in the common to the north of the Ea stream, along with other rights such as the lopping of firewood from the manor's woods. The bishop too had rights, such as grazing rights in his tenants' arable fields after harvest. These rights, along with the payment of rents and other fees, were administered through the manorial court, presumably held at the bishop's moated palace at Gaywood (Page 1906, 226; Fig. 1.4, NHER 5555). No medieval manorial court records appear to survive; the earliest surviving court rolls are from the 1540s (NRO, KL/C 56/18).

The nomenclature of salterns
The term used most frequently to describe a saltern in the Gaywood documentary sources is the Latin *salina*, which is used in several 13th- to 15th-century documents (*e.g.* NRO, BL/O J3/70 [first quarter of 13th century] (Fig. 5.1); DCN 44/42/16 [in 1432]; KLBA, KL/C 50/643 [in 1497]). The other Latin term used is *salsagana*, apparently with the same meaning as *salina*, but used in a single document in 1295 (NRO, DCN 44/42/7). The English term is usually 'salt(e)cote' (NRO, DCN 44/42/19 [in 1480] (see below); KLBA, KL/C 56/16 [in 1534]), a term which also appears in local place-names such as the lane called Saltcotegate (beyond the study area to the south; KL/C 50/639).

Several documents give some further topographic description of the salterns or former salterns. One consistent aspect is the sense of these features being raised above their marshy landscape. There are several place-names that refer to hills: Salthushill and Middolcotehill beyond the study area to the north, Gannishill in Tenement 1, Goryshille in Tenement 3, Fenkinhill in Tenement 7 and Lancelotehill in Tenement 11 (KLBA, KL/C 56/4; NRO, BL/MA 2/1, f. 4v–5; KL/C 50/658). The term 'nattocks' (usually plural) is frequently used, often in conjunction with other terms and in mixed Latin-English phrases, for example *cum salinis herbagiis nattokes* ('with salterns pastures nattocks'; KLBA, KL/C 50/643 [in 1497]), and 'sandhyll groves nattokkes' (KLBA, KL/C 56/16 [in 1534]). This obscure Middle English word seems to mean a mound (a former saltern?) in a marshy landscape (Mawer 1933, 198).

The saltern in the Turnecole property (Tenement 7) is described as a *grava salina*, presumably meaning this saltern was at this late date still associated with the medieval sand-washing technique of gathering salt-impregnated sand from plots or 'strikes' on the foreshore allotted to salters (see Chapter 4 on the Anglo-Norman term *grevas/greves*; KLBA, KL/C 50/643). Another document refers to a marsh with hills and strikes: '*mariscu[s] cum hillys greves*' (note the mix of Latin, English and Anglo-Norman; KL/C 50/645).

Documentary evidence for other land-use
(Figs 5.3–5.4)
The documentary evidence suggests that most of the land in the manor of Gaywood was used for animal pasture (*herbagium*), presumably with some use as meadows for summer-cut grass to provide winter hay. Even the unimproved marshland of Gaywood's North Marsh would have provided seasonal grazing as salt meadow (*prata salsa*; Tenement 7; NRO, DCN 44/42/10; Fig. 5.3). Flooded marsh channels are referred to using the English word 'goule', while a reed-bed (a valuable thatching resource) is described with the Latin word *arundinet* (NRO, DCN 44/42/19

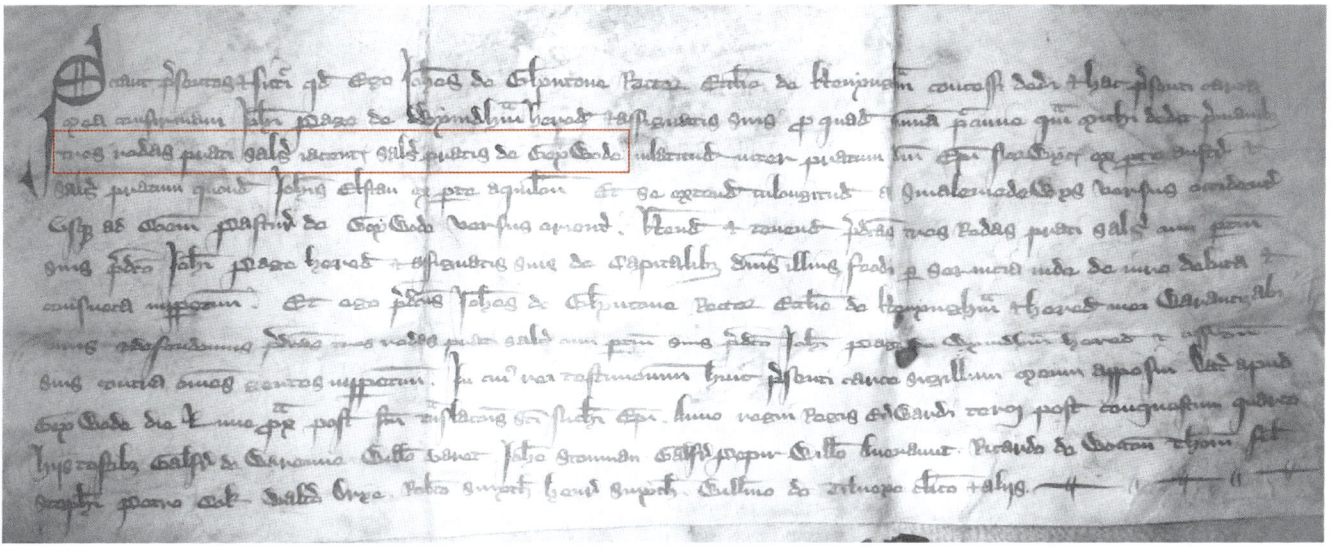

Figure 5.3 Conveyance by John de Glynton rector of church of Hevingham to John Page de Wymondham, of three roods of salt meadow in Gaywood abutting meadow of bishop of Norwich and extending from Smalemedewys to common pasture of Gaywood, 1330 (NRO, DCN 44/42/10. Reproduced by kind permission of the Norfolk Record Office)

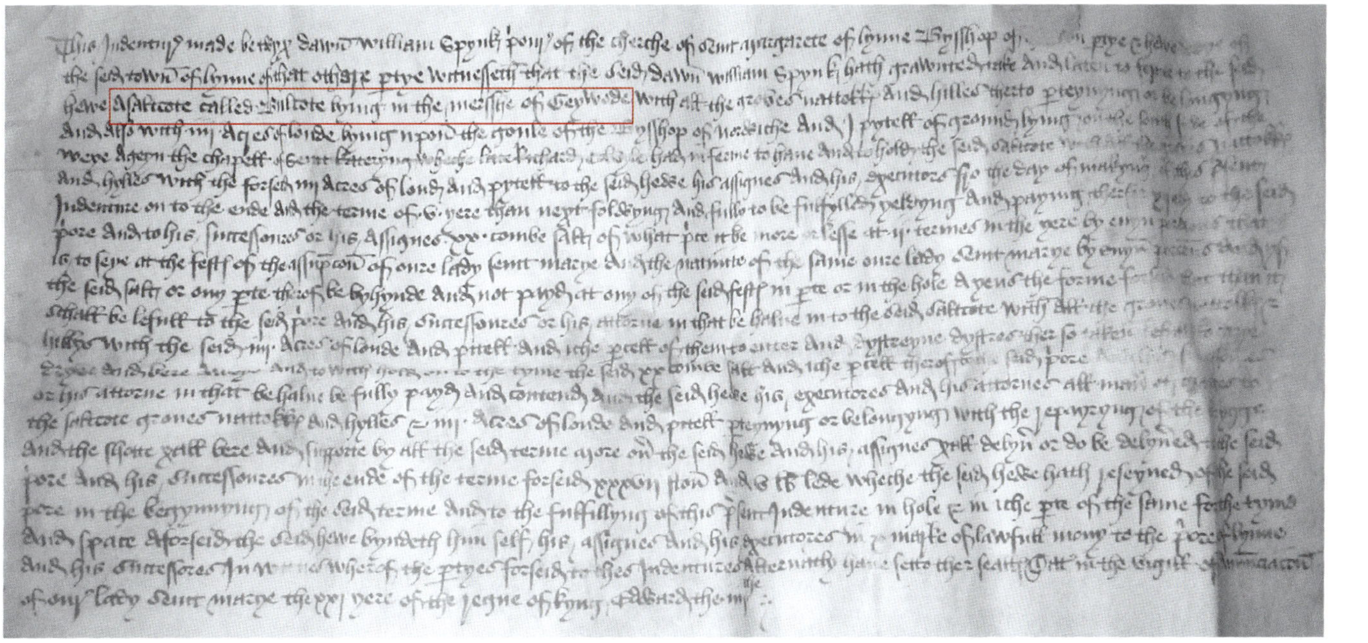

Figure 5.4 Lease by prior William Spynk of saltcote called Bulcote in marsh of Gaywood with greves, nattocks and hills, and with 4 acres of land and 1 parcel of ground lying in the south side of the way to the church of St Katherine for 5 years, paying 20 combs of salt annually, 1481 (NRO, DCN 44/42/19. Reproduced by kind permission of the Norfolk Record Office)

(Fig. 5.4); KLBA, KL/C 56/18). Although the Little Domesday survey records 'woodland for 160 pigs' in 1086, what Rackham terms wood-pasture, there is surprisingly little mention of woodland in later documents (Editions Alecto 1986, f. 191; Rackham 2000, 119–152).

Beyond the study area to the south, closer to the village of Gaywood, there are references to arable land and to orchards (*terra arabilis*; KLBA, KL/C 50/645; 'ortcyard', KL/C 50/663). One property grant of 1534 has an unusual description of a former saltern converted into a fish-drying premises with a shed and an open area: 'nowe at this present day inhabitt with chyngyll [shingle?] to drye over fyssh & a lytell house buylded upon the same' (Tenement 6; KLBA, KL/C 56/16).

III. Discussion
by Graeme Clarke

Trade in salt on the Lyn

The possibly monastic Middle Anglo-Saxon centres of Congham, Bawsey and Wormegay were no longer occupied by the time of Domesday Book. The waning of these sites and their demand for salt may be reflected in the apparent abandonment of the earlier group of salterns excavated along *Salters Waie* which did not yield any post-10th-century dating material, although such links remain highly speculative. This shift in administrative control centres is discussed at length by Hutcheson who concluded that later centres gravitated towards the formative trading sites on the Lyn. A gradual loss in the navigability of the River Gaywood (possibly also the Babingley and Nar) may have also contributed to this shift (Hutcheson 2006, 103). Considering the perhaps under-appreciated influence of salt-making in coastal change (Chapter 3), and in particular the sand-washing technique's movement of vast quantities of coastal muds (Chapter 4), it is certainly possible that Bawsey's demand for salt contributed to the silting of the river and consequently its own demise.

Although the administrative map of the hinterland shifted in the Late Anglo-Saxon period, the potential offered by the Lyn for regional trade remained. As discussed in Chapter 4, the dating evidence from the salterns suggests a second impetus for salt-making on the North Marsh (and perhaps more widely on the West Norfolk coast) which may have been instigated by a reassertion of church control after the re-establishment of the East Anglian See at Elmham in *c*.950. Perhaps reflecting a possible close relationship between Bawsey and the recently discovered evidence for a coastal 'port' on the River Gaywood (Collins 2018), the capital manors of the Late Anglo-Saxon hinterland described in Domesday Book were also linked to formative trading sites on the Lyn. South Lyn was an outlying portion of considerable land holding to the east held by Earl Harold, centred on his Westacre estate (Owen 1980, 147). North Lynn was an outlying dependency of the Abbey of Bury St Edmunds' manor of Islington. West Lynn (along with Wootton) was held by Bishop Stigand, whose administrative centre lay at the highly valued manor of Snettisham. Lynn itself (later Bishop's Lynn) lay at the western end of the more compact manor of Gaywood, held by the East Anglian bishops (Owen 1984, 7; Taylor 1844, 3).

A foothold on the Lyn was clearly of some importance to the major landholders of West Norfolk prior to the Norman Conquest. Each of these minor lordships included only a handful of salterns between them compared to the large numbers of salterns which faced the Wash between the Gaywood and Babingley rivers. Owen (1984, 7) considered salt to be the main attraction for traders to the Lyn at this time. The large numbers of pre-Conquest salterns listed in Domesday Book demonstrates that bishops who held the West Norfolk coast from Gaywood to Snettisham (Wootton was later held by King William by 1086) were producing salt at an industrial scale intended for trade with wider markets (Owen 1984, 8). In the years approaching the Norman Conquest Gaywood's manor of Lynn appears to have become the dominant place of trade for the area, with a portion of its tolls paid to the bishops (Blomefield 1808, 476–533; Hutcheson 2006, 99; Hutcheson 2009, 288). The King's Lynn Survey found little evidence for settlement at Lynn prior to the late 11th century (Clarke and Carter 1977; Hutcheson 2006, 100; Hutcheson 2009, 289). However, it can be inferred from Bishop Losinga's charter for his 'new' town at Lynn that a beach or 'sand market' and fair were already in existence where Lynn's Saturday Marketplace now stands (Clarke and Carter 1977, 412). Owen (1980, 146) describes this charter as a deliberate attempt by the bishop to monopolise informal trade in goods such as salt on the Lyn and to suppress neighbouring markets. However, competition and stimulus to the local economy continued in the 11th century. It has been postulated that the changing geography of competing ecclesiastical interests gave rise to the pottery production centres of North Lynn and Grimston, held by Bury St Edmunds and Bishop Stigand respectively (Hutcheson 2009, 290).

After the Norman Conquest there was a further shift in the constellation of administrative centres in the hinterland with Snettisham giving way to (Castle) Rising, held by Bishop Odo of Bayeux in 1086. However, Wootton, split into North and South during the later medieval period (Keen 1988, 140), passed into the King's hands and Gaywood became the capital manor of the East Anglian bishops of Norwich (Owen 1984, 8). The continued boom of salt-winning in the pre- and post-Conquest landscape suggested by the excavated salt-making remains on Gaywood's North Marsh seems to support the historical narrative for this period.

Granting the new priory and Saturday market at Lynn to the cathedral priory of Norwich in *c*.1101–19, Bishop Herbert included a new mill and all the salterns on the Gaywood North Marsh 'except those in which he has his leads' (Owen 1984, 68). With this deliberate separation of rights between salterns on the demesne and tenanted lands, salt must have continued to play an important part of the income of the bishop and in the trade of the rapidly growing town and port of Lynn across the 12th century. However, records of trade through the port after 1200 show that imported Bay-salt from the Bay of Biscay had replaced the need for locally-produced salt (Owen 1984, 41–3). This lower quality 'rough' or 'gross' salt was the cheapest salt available at the time, although finer quality English salt was still being exported from English ports (Keen 1987, 28). Figures extrapolated from the customs accounts show that in 1304–5, £50 worth of (locally-produced) salt was being exported and £10 imported to Lynn although twenty years later this had declined to just over £37 exported and £58 worth of salt imported (Owen 1984, 41–43). Furthermore, following the rise of the textile revolution of the 14th century, salt-workers in East Anglia instead turned to the cloth industry for employment from this time (Keen 1987, 28). From the 14th century onwards Bay-salt brought into Lynn by ships from Holland and Zeeland was being traded for the major export of wool (Owen 1984, 45). The effect of the diversion of the River Great Ouse to the Lyn on the viability of salt-winning in the 13th century is presented in Chapter 3. It is possible that the changes its arrival may have wrought on the physical environment of the inlet could have contributed to the destruction of North Lynn through flooding in 1271 (NHER 5531; see also the 17th-century poem by Ben Adam reproduced by Chambers (1829) and Hillen (1907, 249)). This event may have been confused by antiquarians who refer to a great part of West Lynn as having succumbed to the widening channel (*e.g.* Richards 1812, n.22–23).

A list of tenants of land in the Newland incorporated into the borough before 1296 lists rents paid in money and salt (Owen 1984, 181, no.174). The growing influence of the burgesses of Lynn in the affairs of the North Marsh across the 13th and 14th centuries is demonstrated by grants between them and the priory concerning salterns, with rents rendered in cash and/or salt measured in combs, bushels and quarters (Owen 1984, 87 nos 52–8). There is even mention of a 'saltern called Bulkote' (see Fig. 5.4); the clearest reference to the North Marsh of Gaywood. Bushels occur as a measure for salt elsewhere, with four bushels being equal to an amber (Holden and Hudson 1981, 127). These measurements of salt appear to have been universal from the Wash to the channel coast of Normandy where there are similar records of medieval salt rents paid in bushels, quarters and '*ambras*' (Carpentier 2010, 14).

This documentary evidence is perhaps at odds with the Bayesian modelling of the excavated *Bullcote Waie* salterns which determined they were probably abandoned around the late 11th/early 12th century. It can only be surmised that, although there may have been a contraction of this industry resulting from the changing environmental conditions, the salt-making activities did not cease. The latest phase of salt-winning on the North Marsh probably involved a final seaward migration to the former mouth of the Gaywood river (referred to variously as le Ea, le Salt Ea or le Seadyke). The river was diverted along the southern margins of the North Marsh in 1425 where it became known as the 'common trench', further changing the physical geography of the North Marsh. This suggestion is perhaps supported by the documentary evidence of the Gaywood Dragge survey of 1487 which lists Tenements 1, 2 and 3 encompassing the salterns of Gannishill, Hibbronds and Goryshille on the westernmost limits of the North Marsh still paying salt rents (see above and Fig. 5.2). There are, however, instances in the Adur Valley, Sussex, where old salterns turned over to pasture still continued to pay salt rents, so references to such in the Gaywood Dragge should perhaps be treated with caution (Holden and Hudson 1981, 127). This rationale was also applied to early modern salt-making on the Dives, Normandy where the latest records of salt rents dating from the late 18th century are not considered necessarily to imply production (Carpentier 2010, 19). On balance, however, considering their situation and as the only group of land parcels paying salt rents, these salterns appear to have still been active in the late 15th century as the rents were paid in measures of combs, bushels and quarters. In addition, wide tracts of the North Marsh also still lay further north between the old course of the River Gaywood and St Katherine's Fleet which divided Gaywood from Wootton, known as *Moltismarsh* and *Wraggismarsh*; the first name perhaps reminiscent of the salt-makers *mould* – salt-rich muds. Although a decline in locally produced salt is evident, this was still clearly an important local industry in the late medieval period, with the end of salt production in the region seemingly occurring in the late 16th/early 17th century (Bridbury 1955). The final reference is of Queen Elizabeth I granting 'Casper Seeler the sole privilege of making white salt for a term of twenty years...the next year similar licence to 'a stranger born' Frances Bertie of Antwerp, the Crown claiming one-tenth of the profit' (Hillen 1907, 736). It is perhaps fitting that this salter brought to a close an industry whose continued theme of continental influence was apparent with its first-named salter – Leofric son of Limburgh – almost 500 years before (Dugdale *et al.* 1846, 462).

Salt-making labour

As described in Chapters 3 and 4, although salt could theoretically be made all year, it was predominantly a seasonal activity in the summer months after the high spring tides had deposited their bed of salt on the lower saltmarsh which had been dried to a crust through the actions of the sun and wind and was then ready to be parcelled out into 'strikes' or *greves*. The salt season began at the beginning of May when it was possible to cultivate the beaches either using part-time labour freed from cultivating the fields, or full-time salters who derived their incomes solely from salt. Hocquet postulated 'three servants per stove: a wood carrier, a salt worker overseeing the broth and pulling the salt, a salt carrier...' (1984, 63). The fragile nature of the salterns, which had been abandoned since the previous year, meant that the clay floors of filtration units and hearths required repair or construction anew. The 18th-century text on the Normandy coastal saltworks referred to ovens lasting no more than two months before they became unstable and were broken up (Diderot *et al.* 1765, vol. 9, 550; Appendix 4). At the end of the salt production season, salt rents were paid on both northern French and southern English coasts on Michaelmas day, 29 September (Keen 1988, 142; Carpentier 2010, 8).

Salt-winning on the North Marsh to produce salt at a sufficient scale to provide a surplus for sale to incoming traders would have required a similarly scaled effort of organisation of the workforce to carry out the task. The supply of labour was as key to the continued economic viability of salt-making on the North Marsh as the supply of fuel and a high spring tide. It has been conjectured that an Anglo-Saxon estate comprised both an *inland* which provided for the lord and an *utland* cultivated by peasants who rendered tribute in kind or labour services to the lord. Both these lands were populated by peasants 'liable to 'public' burdens such as taxation, military service and construction work' (Baxter 2011, 100). It was this model which migrated into the post-Conquest landscape of manors comprising both the lord's demesne and his tenanted lands, held 'in fee' (as fiefs) by peasants (Baxter 2011, 100; Dyer 2002, 119).

Rather unusually for medieval Norfolk the parish of St Faith Gaywood was coterminous with the manor, suggesting that the village had a strong single identity across religious, tenurial and judicial spheres of life (Bradfer-Lawrence 1932, 147). The reconstructed map of the late 15th-century survey of the marsh shown on Fig. 5.2 suggests that the demesne salterns perhaps lay to the north of the old course of the River Gaywood with the land to the south held 'in fee' of the bishop. The reclamation of coastal marshland in the Norfolk Siltlands to the west of the Lyn during the medieval period created a large tract of new holdings of enfeoffed tenants rather than adding to the manorial demesne lands (Dodwell 1967, 54). Perhaps there was also a tendency to enfeoff parcels of reclaimed saltmarsh east of the Lyn. The many small parcels of land described by the Gaywood Dragge survey suggests reclamation of the North Marsh was a piecemeal process rather than an individual large plot or croft having been carved out of the saltmarsh in a single embankment event. The extent of the common marsh which lay to the north of the river is probably best 'fossilised' in Faden's map of 1797 (Tenements 26 and 28 on Fig. 5.2; see also Fig. 1.4).

Within the specialised sphere of salt production it is perhaps possible to perceive that the manorial system was able partly to provision salterns on the demesne with labour services solely for the lord's benefit. Tenanted salterns worked by peasants would render a proportion of their output to the lord in kind. Tithes also provided an important further stream of income for the church which could also have been produced in kind as a salt render from peasants working salterns. It was apparently the norm for lords to lease out their salterns with payment in kind (Holden and Hudson 1981, 127). In this regard, a 12th-century survey of the salt-works of Arne held by Shaftesbury Abbey on Poole Harbour, Dorset provides a useful parallel to the labour arrangement that may have existed at Gaywood (Keen 1987, 25–8). The salt-workers there paid a rent for each *plumbum* (leaden vat) which varied from as little as 2s 1d to as much as 3s or 4s. In addition to the rent of the pans, each salt-worker had to provide a *wikeworc*, or load of salt for each *plumbum* to the abbey. Keen postulates that 'one *wikeworc* was the equivalent to one *summa salis*' (1987, 27), and if correct that one *summa salis* generally consisted of eight level bushels of salt; the equivalent of one quarter of salt. This was the tithe due to the abbey, literally a tenth of total production for the salt-winning season. One *plumbum* may therefore have produced 10 quarters of salt in a season. However, this reckoning is at odds with a further record detailed by Keen from a salt-works in Hampshire that suggested a *wikeworc* may rather have equalled two quarters of salt rather than one (Keen 1987, 27). Darby also provides a useful example of the situation of a salt-worker and his obligations on the Lincolnshire fenland at Fleet (1940, 41).

In Normandy, the medieval salterns of Descanneville on the River Orne offer a further rare insight to the 'salt service' owed by certain tenants. Records there also tell of the tithes and 'obligations' of salt exacted on salt-workers by the abbey of La Trinité de Caen (Carpentier 2010, 14). The relative value and benefits of labour services versus tax in kind in providing the lord's income from the trade of surplus salt would have changed over the course of the medieval period. There was a gradual erosion over the course of the early medieval period of rights to labour services on the demesne land. There was also a steady increase in the payment of cash rents from an increasing number of 'free' tenants, rather than providing labour (see Dyer 2002, 178–83). In this way the changing social situation of peasants probably exacerbated the decline of 'institutional' salt-making by the bishop on the North Marsh as much as a result of the increasing imports of Bay-salt. As stated above, Keen (1987, 28) highlights the shift in emphasis in the East Anglian economy towards cloth production which from the 14th century turned the labour force away from salt-working. By the time of the Gaywood Dragge survey of 1487 the plots of land surveyed on that part of the North Marsh encompassing the investigation areas were almost universally held as valuable plots of pasture, most likely for flocks of sheep, held 'in fee' of bishops who continued to profit from the North Marsh in this new economic reality. As described in Chapter 3, the salterns themselves offered elevated areas for the placing of hayricks (evident as 'Riley circles') to dry grass cut for animal fodder. Of course, a further accelerating factor for 14th-century change in the availability of labour was the Black Death which probably resulted in too few labourers to work the demesne land and tenant the remaining land. The rising wages for labour after this point would also reduce the profitability of salt-making.

The role of women in salt-making remains a question to be answered. Across the North Sea in this period, the 'zoutwinning' process in the Netherlands involved men cutting the salt-impregnated peat which was burned by women to create salt in special huts (Hybel and Poulsen 2007, 219). Although speculative, the sand-washing technique employed on the Wash may also have witnessed a similar separation of tasks with men carrying out the heavier work of gathering and *sleeching* sand after which the women boiled the brine and oversaw the drying of the salt. Further afield, in modern-day Benin, women clearly undertake some of the tasks – notably brine boiling (see Fig. 4.43).

Chapter 6. Overall Discussion and Conclusions

I. Overall discussion

Overview
(Fig. 6.1)

The sand-washing technique for the extraction of salt has been shown by this study and that of the previous work on the Marsh Lane saltern (Clarke and Clarke 2018) to have been ideally suited to the environmental conditions of the Norfolk Wash from as early as the mid-8th century until perhaps the 13th century. It is significant that the *Salters Waie* group of salterns (dated to between the 8th and 10th centuries) corroborate the evidence of the previous excavation at Marsh Lane for Middle to Late Anglo-Saxon salt-making on the North Marsh which employed this method of salt production. It is conceivable that both this routeway and that of Marsh Lane, which pass along the southern and northern fringes of the marsh respectively, were founded during this early period and defined the salt-making zones established in the Middle Anglo-Saxon period (Fig. 6.1). On archaeological grounds, the Middle Anglo-Saxon focus of administration in this area was the 'productive site' of Bawsey, located *c*.3km to the east of the North Marsh, which, after Ipswich, has produced the largest collection of 8th- and 9th-century coins in East Anglia (see Chapter 2 and Hutcheson 2006, 101). Whether Bawsey represents a monastic site or aristocratic centre is discussed by Pestell (2004, 61 and 224) and Blair (2005, 210 and 318). However, the presence of a salt-making tradition at this early date on the North Marsh does perhaps weight the argument further into an ecclesiastical domain, which is described by Blair (2005, 256–8) as being better equipped in this period to exploit the necessary labour and invest in new infrastructure and equipment for more specialised commodities.

Of equal significance was the recent discovery, during a garden test pit survey by Access Cambridge Archaeology, of a substantial group of Ipswich-type ware pottery sherds (date range *c*.AD 720–850) and other artefacts on Wootton Road, a short distance to the south of the Gaywood river (Collins 2018). The early importance of the Gaywood river in providing a sheltered anchorage where trade in commodities could take place was first suggested by Owen (1980, 146). Although there is evidence that Bawsey also served as a market during the 8th and 9th centuries, this latter find clearly suggests that there was a significant settlement and probable coastal port close to where Wootton Road currently crosses the river, and which appears to have had a cardinal trading relationship with Ipswich (Collins 2018, 75). This pottery assemblage bolsters other material found in the parish belonging to this period, including a brooch associated with an otherwise undated cemetery site and a Byzantine coin (Hutcheson 2006, 101). The location of a high-status site (and the broader community) consuming imported goods from Ipswich and possibly beyond would provide the necessary impetus for salt-making, both for domestic consumption and for trade; in turn perhaps facilitating the North Marsh becoming part of a well organised estate.

It is not possible, based on the stratigraphic sequences or few secure dates gathered from Salterns 1 and 2, to speculate on any possible hiatus in salt-making between the Danish invasion of *c*.AD 855 and the English reconquest of the Eastern Danelaw in *c*.917. However, the scientific dating assay and pottery sherds gathered from the *Bullcote Waie* group of salterns (dated to between the late 10th and early 12th centuries) is suggestive of renewed church influence on salt-winning here from the second half of the 10th century. It is certainly worth noting that the latter may correspond with the reestablishment of the East Anglian See at North Elmham in *c*.950, whose capital manor by the time of Domesday lay at Gaywood (see Chapter 5). It is conceivable that this act of renewal and continuity of the See may also have included the reclamation of endowments of land such as Gaywood in the years immediately after its re-founding. It has previously been recognised that this manor may represent a vestige of the wider estate centred on Bawsey discussed above, whose focus had now shifted closer to the Lyn and which may have been contiguous with the bishop's soke over fifteen parishes in the Freebridge Hundred (Pestell 2004, 187–8; Hutcheson 2006, 101–2 and 2009, 289). The *Bullcote Waie* itself may therefore represent a re-founding of the salt-making industry by the bishops but on a slightly different geographical footing than what had gone before, reflecting the evolving environmental situation of the North Marsh.

As explored in Chapter 3, sea levels had gradually regressed to a low point by *c*.1000, which is reflected by the lower heights at which this latter group of salterns commenced. However, taking into account the possible later 10th-century hiatus of activity at the Marsh Lane saltern, this neat interpretation should also take into account the probable re-establishment of salt-making on at least some of the more landward locations beside *Salters Waie* and Marsh Lane. The dating evidence gathered from the *Bullcote Waie* group corroborates Domesday Book in that the most intensive period of salt-making on the North Marsh lay in the centuries and decades either side of the Norman Conquest. As has been shown in Chapter 3, the eventual decline of this industrial output of salt was probably a result of a combination of factors peculiar to the situation of the North Marsh.

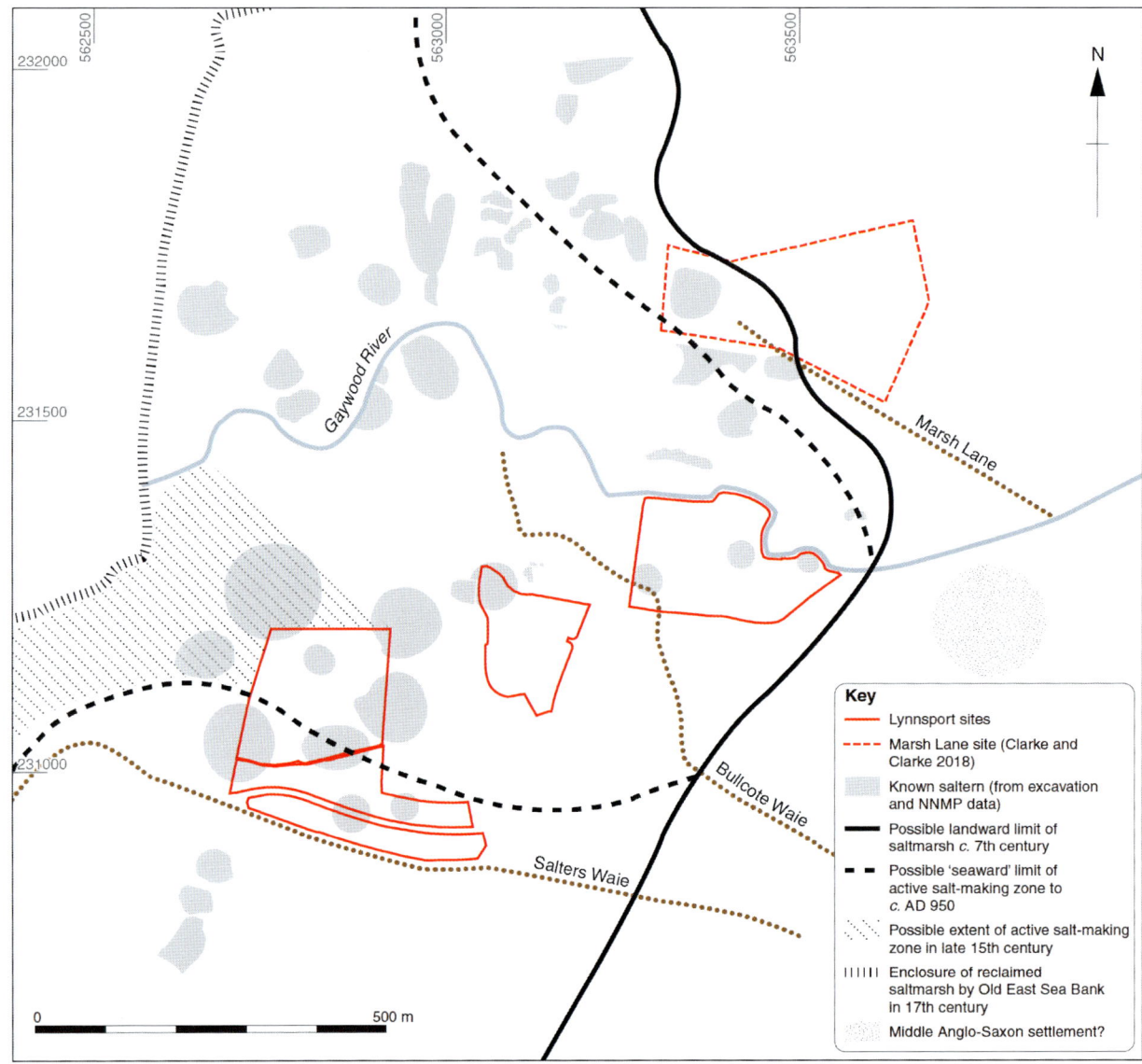

Figure 6.1 Interpretive map showing suggested reclamation of Gaywood's North Marsh

Most of the salterns forming part of this investigation were probably largely abandoned by the early/mid-12th century, although salt-making may have continued into the later medieval period on nearby salterns. The return of rights to profits rendered from salt-making in the North Marsh to bishop John de Grey (r.1200–14) by the St Margaret's Priory, Lynn at the time of the erection of his sumptuous palace at Gaywood demonstrates continued salt production on the North Marsh as late as the beginning of the 13th century (Blomefield 1808; Taylor 1844, 10–11). The dramatic 13th-century change in environmental conditions of the Lyn from a salt-water inlet to the freshwater estuary of the River Great Ouse was probably the final dominant factor in this, alongside deteriorating conditions associated with progressively rising sea levels. The changing economic situation due to the arrival of cheap imports of salt from the Bay of Biscay and changing social conditions of the 13th century, with its potential impact on the availability of labour services to the bishop on his demesne lands, as a contributing factor is explored in Chapter 5.

Although the 1487 Gaywood Dragge survey of the North Marsh demonstrates that this salt-making landscape had evolved into a valuable tract of pasture, the few mentions of salterns and payments of rent in salt nonetheless indicate that salt-making probably persisted on some of the more seaward plots into the 15th century (see Chapter 5 on Tenements 1–3; Fig. 5.2).

A shared sand-washing tradition from the Wash to the English Channel
(Fig. 6.2)

Working outwards from the Wash, a more wide-ranging overview of sand-washing for the extraction of salt is given below to demonstrate the multi-regional use of this technique across the Anglo-Saxon and medieval periods and to highlight the significance of the early dates achieved for the salterns at King's Lynn. Over 1200 *salinae* are recorded by Domesday along the coast from Lincolnshire to Cornwall (Keen 1987, 25). The clear implication is that within the widespread distribution of medieval salterns there are at least some locations which probably belie an earlier origin stretching back into the latter part of the 1st millennium AD (Fig. 6.2). For example, within Norfolk the group of saltern mounds recorded by the NNMP within the easternmost parts of the Broads, on the margins of the medieval period's Great Estuary (and Breydon Water) on the eastern seaboard have long been assumed to be of medieval origin (Albone *et al.* 2007, 21; Hill 1981, map 189; Fig. 6.2, no. 2). There is currently an absence of salt-making evidence on the North Norfolk coast. Perhaps the best candidate for future discoveries is the River Burn near to the Middle Anglo-Saxon settlement at Burnham, variously described as a 'productive site', *wic* or beach market (Davies 2010, 126–7; Loveluck and Tys 2006, 151–2).

The evidence gained by the current crop of excavations for the Anglo-Saxon origins of sand-washing is an important contribution to higher discussions previously made into the interrelations, affinities and identities of coastal societies along the Channel and southern North Sea shores across this period (see Loveluck and Tys 2006). Within the Norfolk Wash, three sherds of a possible Lincoln Kiln-type Sandy ware jar (dated to between the late 10th and 11th centuries) were recovered from Saltern 5 as part of the current investigations. Any links with Lincolnshire are clearly of interest considering the possible extent of a shared salt-winning tradition extending northwards from the Wash along the Lindsey coastline (see below and Hallam 1960; Rudkin and Owen 1960). Groups of salterns are well represented on this coast: as far north as a known concentration at Grimsby on the Humber estuary which has been subject to aerial survey (Hurst 1988, 922 citing Beresford and St Joseph 1979; Grady 1998; Fig. 6.2, no. 3). Excavation work at Marshchapel unearthed pieces of fired clay associated with an arrangement of pits (remains of settling tanks), a ditch and water channel dated to the 10th century but more reminiscent of the Romano-British method of boiling seawater than sand-washing. Nevertheless, the swathe of mounds to the east of that site beyond the parish's old sea bank are clearly a result of *sleeching* (Fenwick 2001, cited in Lane 2018, 84 and 113). The earliest securely dated Lincolnshire examples of filtration units date from the 11th/12th century at Bicker Bends (Healey 1988, 44; Lane 2018, 87) and from the 14th century at Bicker Haven (Healey 1975 and 1999; Fig. 6.2, no. 4). Considering the Late Anglo-Saxon sherds recovered from a saltern north of Quadring (McAvoy 1994, 160; Fig. 6.2, no. 5) more ancient filtration sites, contemporaneous with the North Marsh salterns on the Lincolnshire coast, probably only await future discovery.

The pre-requisite of this salt-winning technique for stretches of coastal saltmarsh fronting onto mudflats is not unique to the Wash or the Lindsey saltmarshes. The much-indented coastline of Essex had many salterns recorded at Domesday, with notable groups of probable post-Roman mounds listed by Wilkinson and Murphy (1995, 197) situated on marshes near to salt-making toponyms such as Saltcoats Farm near South Woodham Ferrers on the River Crouch and Saltcote Hall near Maldon on the Blackwater (Fig. 6.2, nos 6 and 7). Early in the 20th century these two groups were investigated when *c.*20 mounds still survived as the 'Hullbridge Group' on the River Crouch and as many as *c.*50 formed the 'Barrow Hills Group' on the Blackwater. These mounds had been marked out for investigation due to their steeper profiles and deposits lacking the burnt 'red-hills' appearance which typifies the extensive Iron Age and Roman salt-making sites of that county. Excavations into the 'Hullbridge Group' found them to be composed almost entirely of 'marsh-clay' with patches of dark peaty material and some pieces of burnt clay and wood (Christy and Dalton 1925, 36). Pottery sherds, including green-glazed earthenware, recovered from these deposits were identified as being from vessels such as cooking pots and pitchers 'all of the medieval period' (*ibid.*, 37). These early investigators reported on the unfortunate destruction of the 'Barrow Hills Group' in their publication (*ibid.*, 44). In 2002, English Heritage carried out an archaeological survey of surviving medieval salt-making earthworks east of South Woodham Ferrers (Barker 2003).

Further south, there is the single instance of a *sealtern* mentioned in a 9th-century charter on the Kent coast at Faversham (Robertson 1939, no. X; Fig. 6.2, no. 8), although the techniques employed in salt-winning at this site are unknown. To the east of Faversham a group of salterns (coastal mounds known locally as Coterells) investigated on Seasalter Level, near Whitstable in 1955 produced exclusively 13th-century pottery (Thompson 1956; Fig. 6.2, no. 9). As discussed in Chapter 2, there is a further documentary record of Anglo-Saxon salt-works associated with a religious house on the English Channel at Lyminge, Kent (Blair 2005, 258, n.58; Fig. 6.2, no. 10).

An archaeological study into salterns flanking the estuary of the River Adur on the Sussex coastline considered that sand-washing on the Channel coast was the 'standard method during the Middle Ages' (Holden and Hudson 1981, 117–48; Fig. 6.2, no. 11). The authors postulated that sand-washing on the Sussex coast began with the arrival of the new Anglo-Saxon immigrants as salterns are present in the historical record of the Adur valley by Domesday (Holden and Hudson 1981, 123). The earliest dating evidence came from a small excavation into a saltern which recovered sherds of Portchester ware dating to the 10th century which displayed scale on their surfaces considered to be indicative of this ware's use in brine boiling. Domesday records more salterns in Sussex than any other English county and, as with those at Gaywood, most of those within the Adur valley belonged to religious houses (Holden and Hudson 1981, 126–30). The remaining pottery evidence from other salterns excavated as part of this investigation demonstrates that salt-making continued into Saxo-Norman and medieval times. A further excavation into a saltern within this valley confirmed its intermittent use between the 13th and 16th centuries (Ridgeway 2000). The later chronology of salt-making on that estuary follows that of the North Marsh on the Gaywood river with its story of decline due to changing environmental and economic conditions, along with embankment of the river, from at least the 13th century onwards. Recent excavation work on the Hampshire coast has also brought to light 12th- to 13th-century pottery from extant mounds upon Pennington Marshes, Lymington facing the Solent, which corroborated early references to salt-

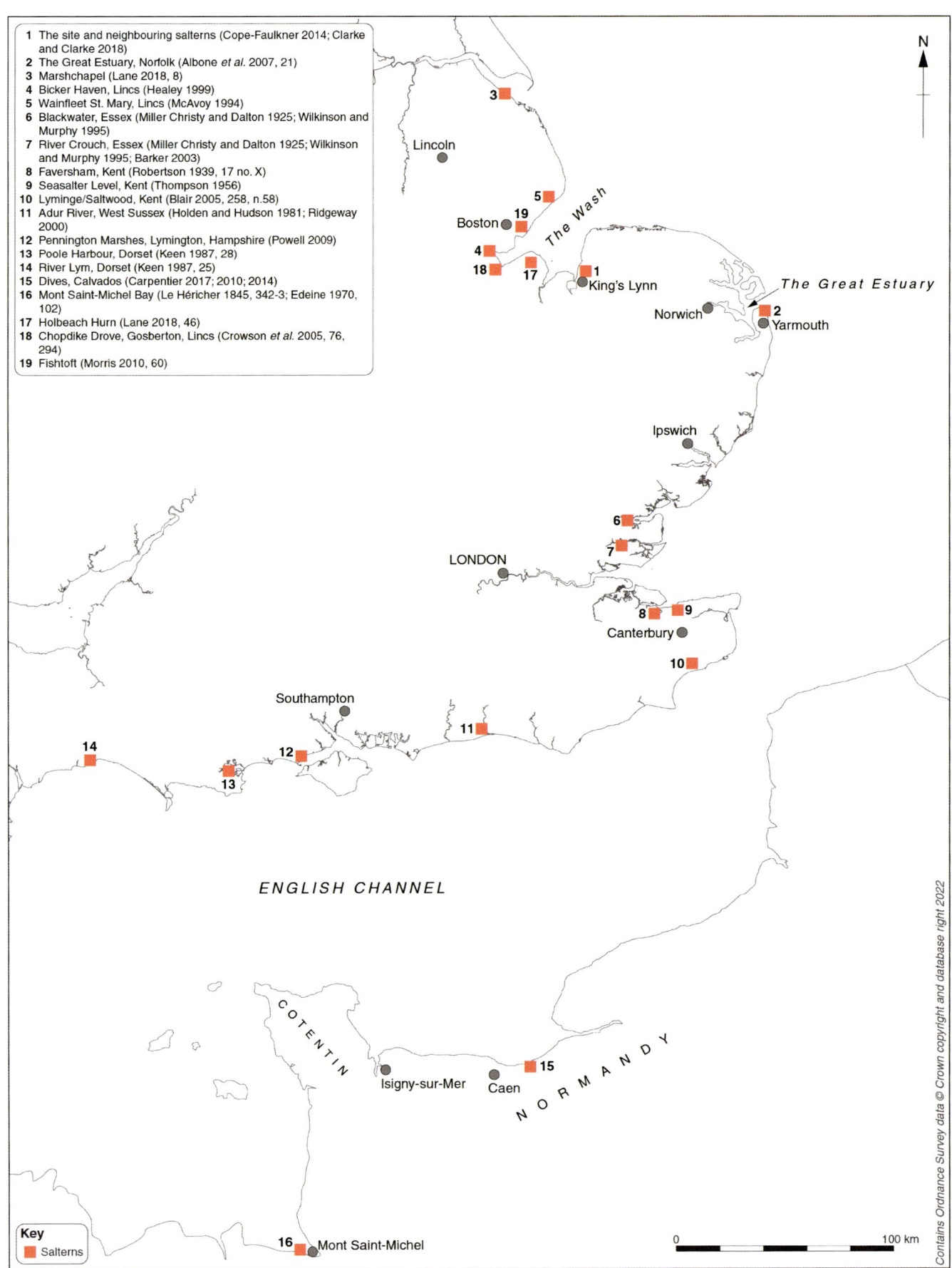

Figure 6.2 Anglo-Saxon or medieval salterns and related sites referred to in this volume

making tithes there granted to Quarr Abbey on the Isle of Wight (Powell 2009, 32; Fig. 6.2, no. 12). There is also documentary evidence for extensive salt-working activity during the medieval period in the bay of Poole Harbour and on the River Lym, Dorset associated with religious houses (Keen 1987, 25 and 28; Fig. 6.2, nos 13 and 14). Although sand-washing was probably the method employed at each of the above-mentioned sites there remains a paucity of evidence for the processes involved and whether these were refined over time or varied across the geographical extent of this tradition.

Historical studies into salt-making on the French side of the Channel have also brought to light a similar picture. Religious houses had established their control over salt-production on the Normandy coast from Carolingian times. Coastal salt flats were widely exploited by the 11th century at Mont-Saint-Michel, the west coast of Cotentin, d'Isigny-sur-Mer and on the estuaries between the Orne and Seine (Carpentier 2010, 2). Some of the ecclesiastical dealings with salt have been explored in detail such as at the abbeys of Caen and Troarn on the Dives (Fig. 6.2, no. 15). The description of medieval salt production there is also a story of scraping up of the salt-encrusted coastal sands for washing and boiling of the resultant concentrated brine. *Greves* (strikes) of salt-rich sand were allotted to each saltworks and marked out into long narrow plots perpendicular to the shore (Carpentier 2010, 15 and 17–18). A 12th-century charter relating to the monk's saltworks at Mont-Saint-Michel proves the use of the sand-washing technique (Edeine 1970, 102; Fig. 6.2, no. 16). Medieval 'Salicoles' (salt-cotes) have been extensively studied by Musset between the estuaries of the Rivers Dives and Orne where a considerable network of trackways extended as a result of this industry (Musset 1956; 1983; 1995; 1998). Significantly, considering the origins of the sand-washing technique, the antiquity of the saltworks on that estuary has been further illuminated by documentary research which shows that on the eve of the Viking incursions of the 9th to 11th centuries there were already habitations associated with '*salicoles*', '*salines*' and '*grava*' (Carpentier *et al.* 2012, 94; Carpentier 2010, 4; 2014, 202).

A consequence of the Norman Conquest of England may have been the introduction of some of the Norman-French nomenclature for sand-washing described by Keen (1988) in his study of salt-making in Anglo-Norman England. Indeed, two of the bishops who shaped the early history of King's Lynn came from salt-making regions of Normandy. Herbert de Losinga's career began as a monk at Fécamp Abbey on the Valmont River estuary and Jon de Grai's family came from Calvados on the Normandy coast (Crosby 2013, 140 and 146). Whereas Keen describes the Anglo-Norman *hogga* as the waste heap or saltern mound itself (1988, 143), the term *hogue* or *houguechon* (otherwise known as a *moie*, see Chapter 4) is here described as the small hill of salt-rich surface crust which was first scraped together and which was also surrounded by a ditch before the process of filtration took place. It has been postulated that both of these terms originate from the Norse *haugr*, which designates a height or promontory (Carpentier 2014, 209). Mention of this toponym also appears in the medieval Lincolnshire saltmarsh (Darby 1940, 41). Due to this term's documented earlier use in England as far back as at least the 10th century, Carpentier considers it possible that the use of this term entered France from England during the same century (Carpentier 2014, n.60). A shared tradition in the measurement of salt in combs, bushels, quarters and ambers also applied to both the Wash and the Channel coasts (Holden and Hudson 1981, 127; Carpentier 2010, 14). From Normandy to the Wash, salt rents were due at the end of the salt-making season at Michaelmas Day, 29 September (Keen 1988, 142). Within the context of salt-making in Normandy, its fortunes were greatly affected by warfare, the Great Plague of 1348 and the cooler and wetter climate of the 14th and 15th centuries (Carpentier 2010, 19–21; Carpentier *et al.* 2012, 172 and 174). Nevertheless, sand-washing persisted as a viable technique for winning salt until the 18th and 19th centuries within the larger shallow coastal basin of the Bay of Mont-Saint-Michel which mirrors its late usage adjacent to the extensive mudflats of Lancashire and the Solway Firth (Holden and Hudson 1981, 123) and the Lincolnshire Wash (McAvoy 1994, 160).

It must also be mentioned that on the opposing North Sea coast of the Netherlands different salt-winning techniques – zoutwinning – were employed in the post-Roman period. Salt was produced by leaching the ashes of salt-impregnated peat flooded by the sea (van den Broeke 1996, 59; van der Zwaluw 2018). There is evidence for medieval salt-making by the burning of Eel-grass (*Zostera marina* L.) in the Netherlands after salt-containing peat had become difficult to obtain (van Geel and Borger 2005). The digging of salt peat extended to northern Friesland, present day Schleswig. Once the peat was cut, women took over the work and burned the ashes to salt in special huts. Further to the north, on the west coast of Jutland there is evidence that during the 16th century salt crusts were gathered from the beaches reminiscent of the sand-washing tradition described above. However, within Denmark the salt-rich groundwater on the island of *Læsø* was the principal source there (Hybel and Poulsen 2007, 219).

II. The King's Lynn salterns: a view from Lincolnshire
by Tom Lane

Introduction
Confirmation of the Middle Anglo-Saxon origin of at least some of the salterns employing the sand-washing technique at King's Lynn has prompted a reconsideration of the dates of examples across the Wash, in Lincolnshire.

On the positive side in Lincolnshire, very many of the medieval salterns survive relatively intact as significant mounds, confirming the scale of salt-making and indicating the precise locations of the industry. Most now occupy positions within arable farmland and, unlike those in the urban setting of King's Lynn, do not succumb to 'development' (a positive), but, therefore, neither do they undergo the archaeological investigations that precede such works. These industrial sites, although surviving as considerable earthworks, are often not protected as

Scheduled Monuments, although the site at Wainfleet St Mary investigated by McAvoy (1994) is a notable example that is scheduled. Moreover, in the Fenland region in particular, the arable land is highly fertile (Grade I and II) and the agricultural regime is one of high intensity with frequent cultivation which gradually levels out the mound surfaces and damages/destroys any former mound-top structures. Not only that, but the mounds themselves can be regarded by farmers as detrimental to good agriculture and may be levelled/removed altogether. This practice has a long history and was noted by Wheeler (1896, 7) when, in discussing 'Fen Mounds', he noted that 'Several of the mounds have been levelled [recently]'. More were levelled as part of the thrust for increased and more efficient arable agriculture ahead of World War II, for example at Saracen's Head, north of Holbeach (Lane 2018, 117; Fig. 6.2, no. 17). A site at Quadring (Healey 1999) was another example of levelling of mounds in the 1960s, although in that case some archaeological investigation took place at mid-mound level. Therefore, Lincolnshire has numerous sites, many largely intact, but little can be done to record and understand their associated features and workings. In particular, the date they were first created remains unknown. For this reason, the work at King's Lynn could prove crucial in prompting a reassessment of the salt industry in Lincolnshire.

Bicker Haven
In seeking likely early (Middle Anglo-Saxon?) salterns that used the sand-washing technique, those furthest inland along the creeks and havens attract interest. Of particular significance seems to be Bicker Haven, a medieval arm of the sea into which flowed at least two streams. At the head of the Haven, Domesday records salterns at Bicker (22), Donington (27), Drayton (8) and Stenning (10). The two last-named are now in Swineshead parish. The supposed earliest reference to salt-making in Bicker Haven (and in Lincolnshire) is of four salt pans in Sutterton, further down the Haven on the east side. This was recorded in a charter of Crowland purported to be from the 9th century (Wheeler 1896, 293), although this is now known to be a late forgery (*e.g.* Roffe 1995, 93). Just to the north of Sutterton and 1.5km east of the Haven, Middle Anglo-Saxon pottery including Ipswich ware has been located at Burtoft (Healey 1979, 80) and at sites in Quadring, including a scatter round the church less than 2km west of the Haven (Hayes and Lane 1992, 31). Middle Anglo-Saxon sites are also known west of the Haven at Gosberton (*e.g.* Crowson *et al.* 2005, 92; Fig. 6.2, no. 18). Ipswich ware was also among the Middle Anglo-Saxon pottery found in ditches during trial trenching and a watching brief on land west of High Street in Swineshead (Albone 1999), all confirming a Middle Anglo-Saxon presence in the region (see also Hayes 1988).

Little archaeological investigation has taken place on the Donington/Bicker/Swineshead salterns, other than some dyke survey following creation of roadside ditches at Bicker. In the section was recorded paired hearths, pits filled with red peat ash and remains of filtration units. Associated pottery sherds were dated to the 11th to 12th century (Healey 1988, 44). Just to the west of Drayton, work on an exposed dyke section beside the A17 Swineshead bypass enabled radiocarbon dating of peat layers. At transgressive overlaps, dates of cal AD 315–425 and 395–535 signified a return there of marine conditions (Waller and Alderton 1994, 295), further implying the feasibility of salt-making in the vicinity during the Middle Anglo-Saxon period.

In considering a possible early start date for the Donington/Bicker/Swineshead salterns at the head of the Haven the relationship between the Middle Anglo-Saxon sites at King's Lynn to the nearby 'productive' site at Bawsey, 3km inland, must be addressed. Bawsey has been suggested as either a monastic or ecclesiastical site, with Blair (2005) arguing ecclesiastical organisations would be best equipped to exploit labour and invest in new (salt-making) infrastructure. In Lincolnshire, on a promontory on the fen edge, some 6km north-west from the Swineshead salterns is the notable 'productive' site of Garwick. This link between potentially early salterns and a nearby Middle Anglo-Saxon productive site mirrors that at Lynn/Bawsey. Garwick is a remarkable site, yielding plentiful continental metalwork, in particular coinage, and was in use before the late 7th century and possibly earlier (Green 2020, 192; see also Blair 2020). All the artefacts from Garwick to date have been found by metal detectorists and no fieldwalking, thus no pottery collection, has taken place.

As with the *Salters Waie* between Lynn and Bawsey there is an old and obvious route linking the Bicker Haven salterns and the productive site. The link through the Fenland between Swineshead and Garwick is a roddon (raised banks of an extinct creek and location of the modern-day A17) making a high overland routeway. Indeed, it is not impossible that this former creek/stream was still active in the Middle Anglo-Saxon period, allowing boats up to Garwick.

John Blair has argued for an intimate relationship between the site at Garwick and a putative ecclesiastical centre at Sleaford, a further 10km to the north-west (Blair 2020, 393). However, there is no concrete evidence to link Garwick with a monastic or ecclesiastical setting there or elsewhere – in fact, little at all is known about the site, other than its remarkable collection of finds. Moreover, David Roffe does not see salt-making on an industrial scale in Lincolnshire as necessarily a seigneurial or ecclesiastical activity (D. Roffe, pers. comm.). Thus, there is no sign of a large dependent population in the area that such a model would presuppose. To the contrary, the overwhelming predominance of sokage tenure suggests that salt production, at least in the Fenland part of the county, was a freeholder industry. Indeed, the apparent dearth of salterns in the Domesday accounts of Elloe and Skirbeck indicates that they did not turn a profit for lords but were worked by sokemen for sokemen (D. Roffe, pers comm; see also Roffe 2005, 286). So, while the configuration of sites at Swineshead/Garwick resembles those at Lynn/Bawsey the control of the sites may not have followed the same model.

The Lindsey marshland
A second productive site in Lincolnshire, this time on the Lindsey Marshland at Little Carlton, is also located just upstream from salterns. The Little Carlton site is on a former small island in the marsh south-

east of Louth and lies between the Beck and the Old Eau streams. These streams converge further seaward and jointly flow into the North Sea 12km from Little Carlton at Saltfleet Haven. Many metal finds come from the plough-zone, most of which could be dated to the Middle Anglo-Saxon period (*c*.AD 710–850). Coins, mostly sceattas, span *c*.AD 680–790 and are complemented by several thousand sherds of both Ipswich ware and Continental ceramics, along with items both domestic and luxurious, from whetstones and loom-weights to fragments of glass (Daubney *et al*. 2016). The Ipswich ware represents the largest collection outside of East Anglia and London of this distinctive pottery (Green 2020, xlviii). Excavation at Little Carlton revealed occupation, industrial and high-status activities, such as writing and commerce, and tempted the excavators to suggest that they might have discovered a previously unknown monastic or trading centre (Daubney *et al*. 2016).

Salterns are known at Saltfleet (Grady 1998, 90, fig. 6), downstream from Little Carlton, and others nearby may be or have been obliterated by the creation subsequently of a storm beach and blown sands from the Haven northwards towards Tetney. Saltfleet is at the southern end of the extensive belt of saltern mounds which continue some 18km north to Humberston and include the well-known examples at places such as Tetney and Marshchapel (*e.g*. Lane 2018, fig. 36). Other than a presence at Domesday (Maybury 2011, 21) there is little dating evidence for these salterns as, again, there is little development taking place in this agricultural setting. However, a recent investigation ahead of a cable route yielded pottery dated to AD 1050–1100 from the firing chamber of a hearth on a mound in Tetney (Network Archaeology, forthcoming), the earliest known date directly associated with the mounds on the Lindsey coast. Whether any of these mounds, particularly in Saltfleet/Skidbrooke, downstream from Little Carlton, are potentially of Middle Anglo-Saxon origin, like the King's Lynn examples, remains conjecture.

In seeking Anglo-Saxon, or at least pre-Domesday salt-making in Lincolnshire it should be noted that two sites have been part-excavated which are interpreted as salt-making sites but not using the sand-washing technique. At Burnt Hill, Marshchapel, a 10th-century date was inferred for what appeared to be evidence of a Roman style of salt-making with briquetage (Fenwick 2001). East of Boston, at Fishtoft, briquetage was found at Clampgate Road in contexts dated to the 8th to 9th centuries (Morris 2010, 60; Fig. 6.2, no. 19). Briquetage at both sites predominantly consisted of supports and hearth/oven remains. These sites suggest a method of Middle/Late Anglo-Saxon salt-making in Lincolnshire other than sand-washing. Fishtoft also has known Middle Anglo-Saxon pottery elsewhere in the village including Ipswich ware. It may also be of significance that Fishtoft was one of the sites described by Wheeler (1896, 7) where fen mounds had been destroyed. Therefore, it is not out of the question that the scattered briquetage at Fishtoft may have originated at a sand-washing site, the mound of which has been removed.

Conclusion

The excavations at King's Lynn have indicated that the sand-washing method of salt-making was clearly in use on the east coast of England during the Middle Anglo-Saxon period. While this volume argues that the productive site at Bawsey remains the most likely candidate for the organisation and control of salt production in the King's Lynn area from the end of the 7th century onwards, it also acknowledges that it remains unknowable if this scenario holds true, as no charters or grants of Middle Anglo-Saxon salterns survive from that part of Norfolk.

For Lincolnshire, David Roffe suggests salt-making was more of a freeholder enterprise, but again, evidence is scant. The Anglo-Saxon villages along the siltlands bordering the Wash would have been good candidates for engaging in salt-making and the new dating information within this volume only strengthens this supposition. That the Lyn sites were engaged in this industry in the Middle Anglo-Saxon period, using this method, would not have been lost on their Lincolnshire neighbours to the north. Whoever was in control at the sites aside, the potential for salt-making in the Middle Anglo-Saxon period, as confirmed in this volume at King's Lynn, gives a fresh impetus to saltern studies in Lincolnshire.

III. General conclusions

It is hoped that this volume will further raise the profile of the salterns of the Norfolk Wash coast with their potential to inform on the wider sphere of archaeological and historical research into post-Roman salt-making on these shores. The Lynnsport housing and school developments provided a valuable opportunity to investigate and compare the remains of multiple sites in a single landscape setting. Indeed, the relict saltmarshes of the West Norfolk coast stretching from King's Lynn to Castle Rising are perhaps uniquely available for study considering the current boom in house building in these parts of Norfolk. As this study progressed it became apparent that many relict salt-making landscapes along the riverine estuaries of eastern and southern England had been destroyed historically through embankment and levelling of earthworks to make way for farmland and other development. This is a sad irony for an industry which this study has highlighted probably itself impacted greatly the natural development of saltmarshes. The wider search for parallel archaeological investigations into Anglo-Saxon and medieval sand-washing sites within the shallow coastal bays and estuaries of eastern England and the Channel only further heightened the sense of the rare opportunity the current sites presented to this field of study.

One of the primary objectives of this work was to establish a firm chronology for salt-making on the North Marsh, underscored by the application of Bayesian modelling. There was a question as to whether the evidence for an 8th-century (or perhaps earlier) origin for salt-making gained from the Marsh Lane excavation was indicative of only localised production or alluded to a more widespread industry involving higher levels of production at this early date. Both the scientific dates and the few sherds of pottery from the salterns' deposits and *in situ* features from two of the salterns in the *Salters Waie* group demonstrated salt-making was indeed present at multiple locations from at least the 8th century. These salterns had appeared on the saltmarshes east of the Lyn during the same dynamic period that saw settlement (re)advance in the Middle Anglo-Saxon centuries onto more coastal reaches of the Norfolk Siltlands to the west. Consideration of this wider setting also necessitated investigation of any possible correlation between the emergence of salt production at an industrial scale with the appearance of 'productive sites' established in the nearby coastal hinterland, or the possible role of salt in attracting early trade to this region. The discovery of early salt-making has an impact on the understanding of how the social geography of this part of Norfolk evolved. Substantial resources of labour, fuel and other materials were evidently orientated towards seasonal salt-winning campaigns which presumably involved higher levels of control, by aristocracy or church.

A further overarching objective of this publication was to explore the salterns in their natural landscape setting to build on the earlier work carried out at Marsh Lane. Reconstruction of the wider salt-making environment encompassing its West Norfolk hinterland highlights the probable central importance of the belt of woodland that lay upon the acidic soils of the escarpment to the rear of the saltmarsh in providing fuel to the brine-boiling hearths of Gaywood and Wootton to the north (see Fig. 3.7). Further exploration of the theme on changing environmental conditions over the period in question found a possible correlation between change in sea level with an apparent drift in the active salt-making zone. Through the movement of great quantities of coastal muds the growing number of saltern mounds contributed to change in the physical environment of the saltmarsh. It was recognised at the outset that — building on the previous Marsh Lane excavation — there was an opportunity to map the rate of any 'seaward' advance through the determination of date ranges for multiple salt-making sites. Comparing the range of dates recovered from seven salterns with their geographical spread highlighted an interesting chronological link between distinct groups of salterns and the three known ancient trackways that formerly advanced onto the marsh from Gaywood (Fig. 6.1). It is proposed that the more 'landward' routes of Marsh Lane and *Salters Waie* commuted the necessary materials, manpower and fuel to their respective groups of salterns between the 8th and 10th centuries. It is further proposed that during the 10th century a new trackway — *Bullcote Waie* — struck out towards the hitherto wetter central part of the saltmarsh alongside the river at a time when sea level had reached a point of maximum regression. This century witnessed both the decline of the 'productive sites' and the arrival of East Anglian bishops who by Domesday were the dominant landholders east of the Wash, the bishops of Norwich maintaining their dominance throughout the medieval period. The chronologically later group of *c.* late-10th- to early-12th-century (or later) salterns within that part of the marsh serviced by *Bullcote Waie* played its part in the income of the bishops and the funding of their new priory of St Margaret's at Bishop's Lynn.

In addition to establishing a firm chronology for salt-making on the North Marsh, this study also aimed to provide a better understanding of how salt-winning techniques may have changed over time. Sand-washing methods have been postulated to be diagnostic of post-Roman salt-making in the cooler latitudes of the English Channel and the shallow bays of the British coastline generally. The central finding of this investigation was of a remarkably consistent use of technologies involving filtration tanks and open-pan hearths across the Middle and Late Anglo-Saxon periods and well into medieval times. Both the conservative character of salt-making and its longevity demonstrate the persistence of well-suited environmental conditions, notwithstanding times of flood from the river or sea, for the continual supply of salt with each spring tide. The microbotanical remains confirm salt-rich muds were gathered from sand strikes or *greves* along the intertidal zone of the lower saltmarsh and upper tidal mudflats. This *c.*500 year-long cycle of salt-winning was probably dramatically affected by the diversion of the River Great Ouse to the Lyn with a probable fall in salinity in the coastal waters at its outflow. Although the accumulations of each saltern mound were laid down in saltmarsh, they had since at least the 13th century lain within reclaimed dryland pastures which were, based on the surviving records of conveyances and survey, divided into a complex patchwork of jealously guarded plots of valuable grazing land and meadow. By the time of the late 15th-century Gaywood Dragge survey of this fossilised salt-making landscape of '-hills' and '-cotes', there had clearly been a final seaward advance of the active salt-making zone on the saltmarsh west of the current excavations. It is hoped that the opportunity for future excavations within this historic and dynamic saltmarsh will further flesh out this narrative and test these conclusions.

Appendix 1: Glossary

Allec (*alecium, allecum, etc.*)	A medieval Latin term referring to herring whether fresh, dried, smoked, salted, or pickled. Widespread use of this term in northern Europe.
Allochthonous	Denoting a deposit or formation that originated at a distance from its present position.
Allochem	A term used to describe a grain larger than 0.25mm within a carbonate rock.
Amber (*ambras, etc.*)	A medieval English and French measure for salt.
Autochthoneity (autochthonous)	Indigenous rather than descended from migrants or colonists.
Bitters	The non-sodium chloride content. Unpalatable salt residues, unsuitable for food preservation, separated (skimmed) from brine during boiling.
Bushel	A medieval English and French measure for salt.
Briquetage	French word thought to have been used first in describing the ceramic debris from Iron Age salt-making in the La Salle valley. It now incorporates all the ceramic remains from salt-making including fragments of the ceramic containers, pedestals, clips, slabs and structural remains from hearths or ovens.
Cloughs (clowzes)	From the Latin *clusi/clusum* – to shut water in or out.
Comb	A medieval English and French measure for salt.
Coterells	A local Kent name for coastal mounds/salterns.
Dragge	A rarely used medieval name for a land survey.
Dyke	A raised embankment or sea wall.
Fen mounds	A modern English name for former salterns.
Filtration unit	A modern name given to clay-lined tanks (with probable wooden superstructures) used to wash coastal muds of their sand content.
Foraminifera	Single-celled marine animals (protozoa) that usually secrete a carbonate shell.
Greva (*greve, grava, etc.*)	An Anglo-Norman name for a sand-strike or coastal plot allotted to a salter upon the mudflats for the gathering of salt-rich mud.
Grimston Thetford-type ware	A Thetford-type coarseware pottery produced at Grimston, Norfolk between the late 10th to 11th centuries.
Hap	An early modern British word for a large rake drawn by a horse or oxen for gathering salt-impregnated coastal mud.
Haugr	A medieval Norse name for a height or promontory.
Haveau (*banneau, etc.*)	An early modern French word for a large rake drawn by a horse or oxen for gathering salt-impregnated coastal mud.
Herbagium	A medieval Latin name for animal pasture.
Hogga	An Anglo-Norman name for a saltern mound.
Hogue (*houguechon, etc.*)	A medieval French name for a heap of salt-impregnated coastal mud gathered for sand-washing.
Ipswich ware	A coarseware pottery produced at Ipswich, Suffolk between *c.* late 7th to 9th centuries. Synonymous with the Middle Anglo-Saxon period of East Anglia.
Filtration unit	A pair of clay-lined tanks used to process the salt-impregnated coastal muds: a shallower, flat-based rectangular filtration tank into which the mud was heaped above a filter bed of turves and a deeper, circular tank which acted as a cistern for the resultant brine. These tanks were connected by a narrow clay-lined channel to drain the brine from the filtration tank to the cistern.
Kinch	A medieval name for a clay-lined filtration unit.
Littoral	Coastal region such as the shore zone between high tide and low tide.
Lyn (*Lym, lena, etc.*)	A coastal toponym of the English Channel and eastern coasts denoting a saltwater inlet or marshy river location.
Mesohaline	Brackish water with a salinity of between 5 and 18 parts per thousand (‰).
Micropalaeontology	The study of the microscopic remains of animals, plants and protists generally less than 1mm in size.
Moie (*mouée(s)*)	An early modern French word for a heap of salt-impregnated coastal mud gathered for sand-washing.
Mould	An Anglo-Norman name for salt-impregnated coastal muds. The raw material heaped into kinches/filtration units.
Muldefange	A medieval name for sand-washing on the Lincolnshire coastline.
Nattokes (*nattokkes, etc.*)	An obscure medieval English name, probably for a mound or former saltern
Neap-tide	A period of smaller tides when the sun and moon are at right angles to each other.

Oligohaline	Characterised by very low salinity, in the range 0–0.5%; brackish.
Open-pan hearth	A modern name given to brine boiling hearth used during Anglo-Saxon and medieval times. Brine was boiled within a lead pan placed above a clay-built hearth and supported by clay wedges or soft-fired clay bricks.
Ostracods (Ostracoda)	From the Greek '*ostrakon*', which means 'a shell', and refers to the bi-valved carapace that is characteristic of these tiny crustaceans, which resemble water fleas. They are found commonly as fossils and are still living today in all aquatic habitats from the deep sea to small temporary ponds.
Plumba (*plumbum*, *etc.*)	A medieval Latin name for a lead pan.
Prata salsa	A medieval Latin name for a saltmarsh meadow.
'Productive' site	A term describing locations yielding concentrations of Middle Anglo-Saxon coinage and metalwork.
Quarter	A medieval English and French measure for salt.
Quin	An early modern French name for a reservoir or basin from which salt workers take water for sand-washing.
Red herring	Herring cured through smoking.
Red Hills	Iron Age and Roman coastal salt-making sites in Essex.
Riley circles	D.N. Riley's interpretation of ring ditches in the silt fens being the remains of ditched haystacks.
Roddon	Dried raised siltbeds and levees of former natural tidal creeks, their raised elevation above the surrounding marshland making them suitable historically for later settlement and farming.
Saeltearn (sealtern, *etc.*)	An Anglo-Norman word for a saltern or salt-cote.
Salicole	French equivalent name for a salt-cote.
Salina	A medieval Latin name for a saltern.
Salsagana	A medieval Latin name for a saltern.
Salt-cote (salt(e)cote, *etc.*)	A medieval English name for salt-working houses or shelters which enclosed open-pan brine boiling hearths.
Salt-slag	Fragments of vitrified saline silicate with fired clay hearth-lining material often attached, representing accumulations of spatter residues from boiling brine.
Saltern	Salt-making site of any period. On Anglo-Saxon and medieval sites the term is used for the extant and relict mounds of de-salted sands, along with hearth waste, often interspersed with remains of clay-lined filtration units and hearths. On earlier sites the word usually refers simply to the site where salt is made.
Sandhyll	A medieval English name for a saltern or former saltern.
Sand-washing	An umbrella term for post-Roman salt-making techniques whereby salt-impregnated coastal muds were stripped of their salt content using filtration methods.
Siltlands	Region of reclaimed saltmarsh on the Norfolk and Lincolnshire Wash coast.
Sleech	A medieval name for salt-impregnated coastal muds. The raw material heaped into kinches/filtration units.
Sleeching	A medieval name for sand-washing on the Cumbrian/Lancashire coastline.
Spring-tide	The 'springing forth' of the tide during new and full moon.
Stockfish	Unsalted fish, especially cod, dried by cold air and wind on wooden racks.
Thetford ware	A coarseware pottery produced at Thetford, Norfolk between *c.* mid/late 9th to 11th centuries. Synonymous with the Late Anglo-Saxon period of East Anglia.
Toponym	A place name, especially one derived from a topographical feature.
White herring	Herring cured through salting.
Wikeworc	A medieval English name for a load of salt, or salt-rent provided to the lord.

Appendix 2. Radiocarbon Dating and Chronological Modelling
by Derek Hamilton (SUERC)

Ten samples from archaeological contexts associated with salt-processing at *Salters Waie* and *Bullcote Waie* were processed for radiocarbon dating by accelerator mass spectrometry (AMS). Brought together with these are four samples from salt-processing evidence at Marsh Lane. The samples consisted of single entities (Ashmore 1999) of charcoal, charred plant remains, and charred grains. The samples were submitted to the Scottish Universities Environmental Research Centre (SUERC), East Kilbride where they were pre-treated and measured as described by Dunbar *et al*. (2016).

The SUERC lab maintains rigorous internal quality assurance procedures, and participation in international inter-comparisons (Scott 2003; Scott *et al*. 2010) indicate no laboratory offsets; thus, validating the measurement precision quoted for the radiocarbon ages.

The results are presented (Table A2.1) as conventional radiocarbon ages (Stuiver and Polach 1977). They have been calibrated using the internationally agreed terrestrial calibration curve (IntCal20) of Reimer *et al*. (2020) and the OxCal v.4.4 computer program (Bronk Ramsey 2009). Simple calibrated results are presented at 95% confidence intervals (unless otherwise noted) in plain text and rounded outward to ten years. The *italicised* dates presented in the text below are posterior density estimates derived from mathematical modelling of archaeological problems and have been rounded outward to five years. These dates can change with the addition of new data or when the modelling choices are varied.

Methodological approach

A Bayesian approach (Buck *et al*. 1996) has been applied to the interpretation of the chronology of some of the salt-making evidence at *Salters Waie*, *Bullcote Waie*, and Marsh Lane. Although simple calibrated dates are accurate estimates of the radiocarbon age of samples, this is not, usually, what archaeologists really wish to know. It is the dates of the archaeological events represented by those samples that are of interest. For example, the start and end of the salt production at the excavated salterns is of particular interest. The chronology of salt-making can be estimated not only by using the absolute dating derived from the radiocarbon measurements, but also by using stratigraphic relationships between samples and the relative dating information provided by the archaeological phasing.

The methodology used here allows the combination of these different types of information explicitly, to produce realistic estimates of the dates of archaeological interest. The posterior density estimates produced by this modelling are not absolute, rather they are interpretative estimates, which can and will change as further data become available and as other researchers choose to model the existing data from different perspectives. The technique used is a form of Markov Chain Monte Carlo sampling and has been applied using the program OxCal v4.4 (http://c14.arch.ox.ac.uk/). Details of the algorithms employed by this program are available in Bronk Ramsey (1995; 1998; 2001; 2009) or from the online manual. The algorithm used in the models can be derived from the OxCal keywords and bracket structure shown in Fig. A2.1.

Models and results
(Figs A2.1–A2.2)

The samples all come from contexts and features associated with salterns, primarily from hearth waste and the filtration units. An initial model was created that treated the radiocarbon dates from each of the three sites as unordered groups of dates (*e.g.* no stratigraphic or phase relationships between any individual dates), with the model following the type described in Hamilton and Kenney (2015). The model has good agreement between the radiocarbon dates for each site and the assumption that in each instance they could belong to a period of discrete and relatively continuous activity (Amodel=100). A second model was generated that included radiocarbon dates from two phases in a sequence, but there was no appreciable difference between this model and the slightly more conservative model presented below.

Salters Waie

The model estimates the dated activity at *Salters Waie* began in *cal AD 500–890 (95% probability*; Fig. A2.1; *start: Salters Waie*), and probably in *cal AD 735–870 (68% probability)*. The dated activity here ended in *cal AD 775–1190 (95% probability*; Fig. A2.1; *end: Salters Waie*), and probably in *cal AD 835–985 (68% probability)*. The overall span of the dated activity covered *1–625 years (95% probability*; Fig. A2.2; *span: Salters Waie*), and probably *1–215 years (68% probability)*.

Bullcote Waie

The model estimates the dated activity at *Bullcote Waie* began in *cal AD 885–1030 (95% probability*; Fig. A2.1; *start: Bullcote Waie*), and probably in *cal AD 970–1020 (68% probability)*. The dated activity here ended in *cal AD 1035–1230 (95% probability*; Fig. A2.1; *end: Bullcote Waie*), and probably in *cal AD 1040–1165 (68% probability)*. The overall span of the dated activity covered *15–315 years (95% probability*; Fig. A2.2; *span: Bullcote Waie*), and probably *40–185 years (68% probability)*.

Marsh Lane

The model estimates the dated activity at Marsh Lane began in *cal AD 230–930 (95% probability*; Fig. A2.1; *start: Marsh Lane*), and probably in *cal AD 645–865 (68% probability)*. The dated activity here ended in *cal AD 1025–1645 (95% probability*; Fig. A2.1; *end: Marsh Lane*), and probably in *cal AD 1040–1240 (68%*

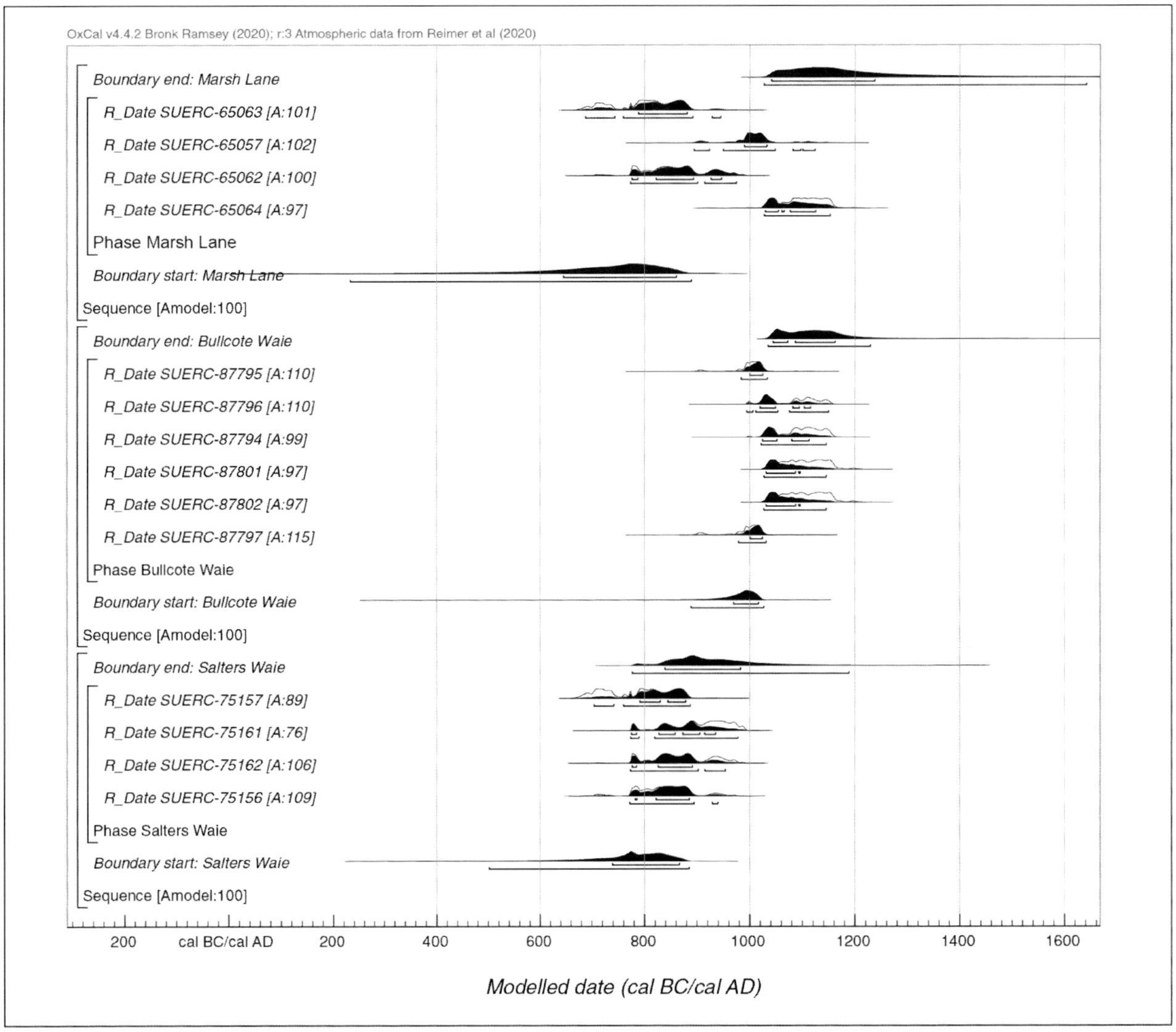

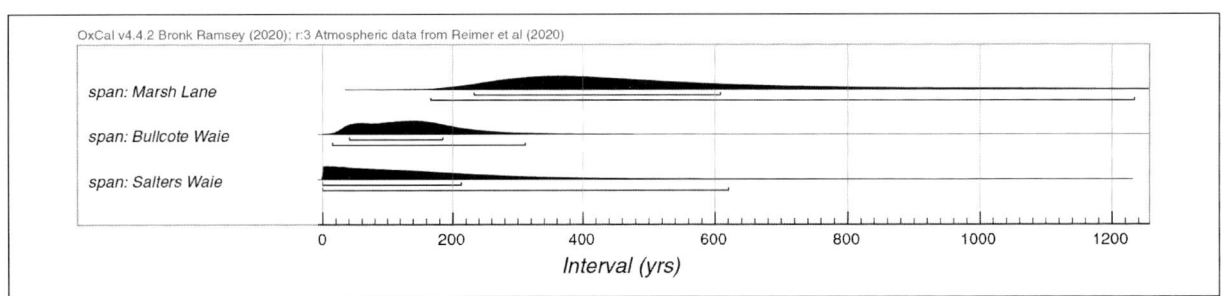

Figure A2.1 Chronological model for the salt production activity at Salters Waie, Bullcote Waie, and Marsh Lane. Each distribution represents the relative probability that an event occurred at some particular time. For each of the radiocarbon measurements two distributions have been plotted, one in outline, which is the result of simple radiocarbon calibration, and a solid one, which is based on the chronological model use. The other distributions correspond to aspects if the model. For example, 'start: Salters Waie' is the estimated date that activity began at the site, based on the radiocarbon dating results. The large square 'brackets' along with the OxCal keywords define the overall model exactly

Figure A2.2 Span of the activity for each of the three sites in the primary model shown in Figure A2.1

Lab ID SUERC-	Context	Context description	Material dated	$\delta^{13}C$ (‰)	Radiocarbon age (BP)	Calibrated radiocarbon date (95% confidence)	Modelled date (95% probability)
Salters Waie							
75156	Saltern 1, Phase III	Hearth waste rake-out 85 from pit 83	Charred rhizome/ tuber fragment	−26.4	1191 ± 31	cal AD 700–960	*cal AD 770–895 (94%) or cal AD 925–945 (1%)*
75162	Saltern 1, Phase III	Hearth waste rake-out 91 from pit 128	Charcoal: *Corylus avellana*	−25.6	1166 ± 31	cal AD 770–980	*cal AD 770–955*
75161	Saltern 1, Phase IV	Soil 89	Charcoal: *Salix/ Populus* sp.	−25.6	1136 ± 31	cal AD 770–1000	*cal AD 770–790 (8%) or cal AD 820–980 (87%)*
75157	Saltern 2, Phase IV	Fill 118 in filtration unit 117	Charcoal: Maloideae	−26.6	1239 ± 31	cal AD 670–890	*cal AD 705–890*
Bullcote Waie							
87797	Saltern 4, Phase II	Hearth waste 1035	Charcoal: roundwood; *Calluna vulgaris/Erica* sp.	−27.3	1052 ± 26	cal AD 900–1030	*cal AD 975–1035*
87802	Saltern 5, Phase IV	Rake-out pit 1011	Charcoal: roundwood; *Calluna vulgaris/Erica* sp.	−27.6	939 ± 26	cal AD 1020–1170	*cal AD 1025–1150*
87801	Saltern 5, Phase IV	Hearth waste 958	Charcoal: roundwood; *Quercus* sp.; <5 growth rings	−24.4	939 ± 26	cal AD 1020–1170	*cal AD 1025–1150*
87794	Saltern 11, Phase II	Hearth waste 676	Charcoal: cf. *Betula* sp.	−28.4	965 ± 26	cal AD 1020–1160	*cal AD 1020–1150*
87796	Saltern 12, Phase IV	Filtration unit 451	Charcoal: roundwood; cf. *Quercus* sp.	−28.1	984 ± 26	cal AD 990–1160	*cal AD 995–1150*
87795	Saltern 12, Phase IV	Filtration unit 457	Charcoal: Maloideae	−28.2	1045 ± 26	cal AD 900–1040	*cal AD 985–1035*
Marsh Lane							
65064		189 (Cut/ Group 187)	Charred grain	−27.6	952 ± 26	cal AD 1020–1170	*cal AD 1025–1155*
65062		200	Charred root/tuber	−27.5	1177 ± 35	cal AD 770–980	*cal AD 770–975*
65057		218	Charcoal	−25.6	1033 ± 35	cal AD 900–1040	*cal AD 895–1050 (90%) or cal AD 1080–1125 (4%)*
65063		266 (Cut/ Group 253)	Charcoal	−27.0	1225 ± 35	cal AD 670–890	*cal AD 685–895 (94%) or cal AD 925–945 (1%)*

Table A2.1 Radiocarbon dates from *Salters Waie*, *Bullcote Waie*, and Marsh Lane

probability). The overall span of the dated activity covered *165–1235 years* (*95% probability*; Fig. A2.2; *span: Marsh Lane*), and probably *230–610 years* (*68% probability*).

Discussion
(Fig. A2.3)
It should first be pointed out that all three sites have a relatively low number of results, when compared to the potential length of time the associated salt-making spanned. This can result in lower precision in the resulting probability estimates (Steier and Rom 2000). Nevertheless, the results do provide some insights into the chronology of these three salt-manufacturing areas. Firstly, it is highly probable that salt-making at both *Salters Waie* and Marsh Lane began prior to activity at *Bullcote Waie* (probabilities >99%). There is also a 71% probability *end: Salters Waie* occurred prior to *start: Bullcote Waie*. There is a 66% probability that *start: Marsh Lane* occurred prior to *start: Salters Waie* and a 70% probability that *end: Bullcote Waie* occurred prior to *end: Marsh Lane*. A closer visual comparison of the probabilities (Fig. A2.3) shows that the low number of dates associated with Marsh Lane and the fact that it appears to run for nearly the entire span of both *Salters Waie* and *Bullcote Waie*, suggests the possibility that activity at Marsh Lane is roughly coeval with the activity at *Salters Waie* and *Bullcote Waie*. The modelling would suggest salt-making at Marsh Lane and *Salters Waie* began in the *8th or 9th century cal AD*. In the *10th century cal AD* at *Salters Waie* the activity ended, while it started up at about this time at *Bullcote Waie*. Salt production then ceased at *Bullcote Waie* and Marsh Lane in the *latter half of the 11th century or in the 12th century cal AD*.

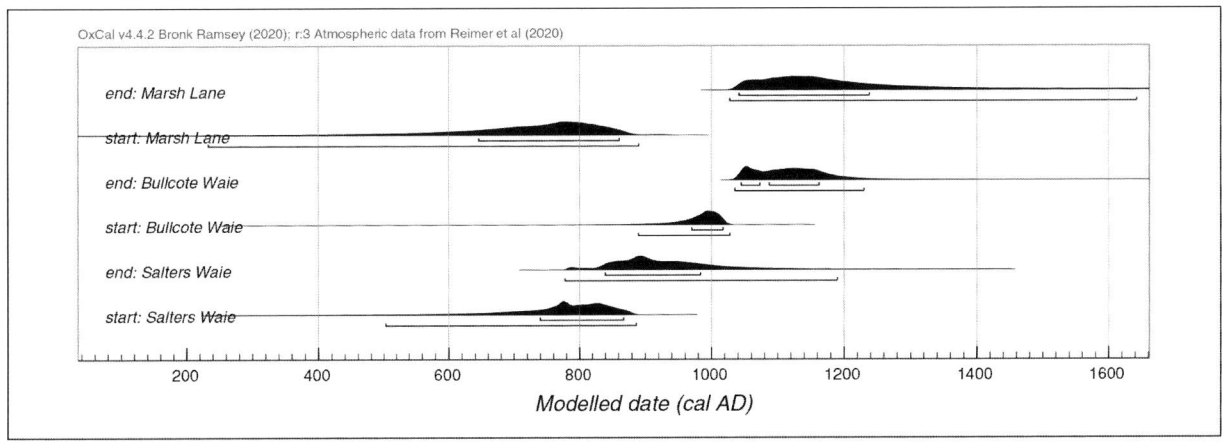

Figure A2.3 The boundaries of the three site elements that form the chronological model presented in Figure A2.1

Appendix 3. Methodologies

Iron slag
by Simon Timberlake
The slag was identified visually using an illuminated x10 magnifying lens, and compared where necessary with an archaeological reference collection. The pieces were tested with a magnet to determine the presence of free iron or wustite.

Fired clay
by Ted Levermore
The assemblage was quantified by context, fabric and form and counted and weighed to the nearest whole gramme. Fabrics were examined using a x20 hand lens and were described by main inclusions present. The quantified data and fabric descriptions are presented on an Excel spreadsheet held with the site archive

Briquetage
by Simon Timberlake
The assemblage was identified visually using an illuminated x10 magnifying lens, and compared where necessary with an archaeological reference collection. The pieces were tested with dilute hydrochloric acid to determine the presence of carbonate and then (where possible) fitted together, and the fabric composition and original sizes determined.

Pottery
by Sue Anderson
Quantification was carried out using sherd count, weight, minimum number of vessels (MNV) and estimated vessel equivalent (eve) based on rim diameters and percentages. All fabric codes were assigned from the Norfolk post-Roman fabric series (based on Jennings 1981). Form terminology follows MPRG (1998). Other attributes (such as decoration, abrasion, sooting, limescale) were recorded as appropriate. The catalogue was input directly into an MS Access database, which forms the archive catalogue.

Charred plant remains
by Rachel Fosberry
A sub-sample of each of the samples was processed by tank flotation using modified Siraf-type equipment for the recovery of preserved plant remains, dating evidence and any other artefactual evidence that might be present. The floating component (flot) of the samples was collected in a 0.3mm nylon mesh and the residue was washed through 10mm, 5mm, 2mm and a 0.5mm sieve.

A magnet was dragged through each residue fraction for the recovery of magnetic residues prior to sorting for artefacts. Any artefacts present were noted and reintegrated with the hand-excavated finds.

The dried flots were subsequently sorted using a binocular microscope at magnifications up to x60 and recorded in an Excel spreadsheet. Identification of plant remains was with reference to the Digital Seed Atlas of the Netherlands (Cappers *et al.* 2006) and the author's own reference collection. Nomenclature is according to Stace (2010).

Following standard environmental processing and assessment any charcoal fragments larger than 2mm in size were extracted for charcoal assessment, primarily to determine its suitability for providing radiocarbon dating material, but also to assess its potential for providing information on fuel use.

Charcoal
by Denise Druce
Charcoal assessment was carried out using a binocular microscope at up to x40 magnification, whereby fragments were fractured to reveal transverse sections and preliminary species identifications were made. In particular, the presence of any small roundwood, sapwood, and short-lived wood species was noted, for the purpose of providing suitable material for radiocarbon dating. The results were recorded on an assessment pro-forma, kept with the site archive. Fragments considered suitable for radiocarbon dating were then fractured to reveal both

radial and tangential sections, which were examined under a Meiji incident-light microscope at up to x400 magnification. Identifications were made with reference to Hather (2000), and modern reference material. Characteristics, such as possession of tyloses in hardwoods, any insect damage, or radial splitting were also noted as an aid to assessing wood maturity and condition prior to charring.

Pollen and diatoms
by Frances Green
Sub-samples of 1cm^3 were cut from the cleaned faces of the monoliths. Preparations followed the standard method: acetolysis and removal of silicates using HF (Fäegri and Iversen 1975; Moore and Webb 1991). Two grammes of sediment were desegregated by boiling in 10% potassium hydroxide for 5–10 minutes and passed through a 180μm sieve. Silicates were removed by heating at 80°C in concentrated hyrodrofluoric acid (HF), the high sand content requiring prolonged treatment (more than 24 hours). Acetolysis was performed to remove cellulose. The remaining material was stained, mixed with silicone fluid and mounted on slides using large square coverslips. A count of a minimum of 200–300 land pollen types per sample was attempted under a magnification of x400 and x1000. Pollen identifications were assisted by reference to Moore and Webb (1991) and Andrew (1984), with fungal spores referred to Van Hoeve and Hendrikse (1998). Diagrams were drawn using TILIA (Grimm 1993) with most data expressed as a percentage of total land pollen (tlp *i.e.* trees, shrubs and terrestrial herbs). Note that aquatics, spores and unidentified are, for example, expressed as a percentage of tlp + aquatics. Algae and fungi are expressed independently as a percentage of tlp (*i.e.* not including algae or fungi in the final sum). Plant nomenclature follows Fitter *et al.* (1985) with minor amendments from Stace (1997).

Diatom samples were prepared by boiling 3–4cm^3 of sediment in 10% hydrogen peroxide for seven hours or until all the organic material had disappeared. Two drops of supernatant were placed on a coverslip with 4–5 drops of water and dried on a hot plate. The coverslip was then mounted onto a slide using Naphrax. Routine counting under x1000 magnification attempted to count 200 frustules.

Ostracods
by Simon Timberlake
Standard processing of the environmental samples by flotation was undertaken by OA East Archaeobotanist Rachel Fosberry using Endecott sieves (see above, Charred plant remains), the only variation in the technique being that the >0.5mm <1mm fraction was collected from samples where ostracods were noted to recover the larger juvenile and adult valves and carapaces where present. For samples from Saltern 5, the fractions examined were limited to: 1–2mm (generally without ostracods), 0.5–1mm, and 0.25–0.5mm and <0.25mm (containing most of the ostracods). The smallest size fraction was examined to record the presence of juveniles, hence to establish an idea of population structure and thereby determine the degree of autocthoneity of the species recovered. The reporting of juvenile instars to the flot fractions may well be linked to the ability of some of these shells to float, but perhaps also to an entrapment of these within fibrous material such as roots or algae. The recovery of ostracods by this method is never going to be complete, yet it is conceivably representative of the assemblage present.

Initial assessment involved a count then removal of all the identified valves and carapaces into separate numbered petri dishes. For Saltern 5, the examination of the four fractions involved a whole count where this was practically possible within the timescale allowed (*i.e.* only when looking at volumes of residues up to 2g in weight). If this was not possible then a carefully measured fraction of the sediment was counted and the final numbers calculated (*i.e.* estimated) accordingly. The ostracods were examined using an illuminated stage Vickers binocular microscope with x10 eyepiece and a x1–x3 objective, with individual ostracods being removed using an extra-fine camel-hair brush. Standard texts plus a reference collection of published SEM images were used for the purposes of ostracod identification.

The numbers of male and female adult valves and carapaces were counted, and wherever possible those of the sexually dimorphic later instars also. Notes were made concerning the presence or absence of noded and smooth polymorphs of some of these species, as well as the range of smaller juvenile instars that could be seen within this assemblage. Some information was also recorded on the accompanying foraminifera and mollusc fauna. However, these notes were intended purely to be an indication of the palaeoenvironment, and as such these generic identifications require confirmation.

Foraminifera
by Simon Timberlake
Standard processing of the environmental samples by flotation was undertaken by OA East Archaeobotanist Rachel Fosberry using Endecott sieves (see above, Charred plant remains). The only variation here was in the counting technique, which for the purposes of assessment was only undertaken for the 0.25–0.5mm size fraction; the size range which contained most of the better-preserved tests. This approach was in response to the overall quantity of forams within the sample(s), although the results are considered to be representative of the types and abundance present.

The examination involved a whole count of this fraction if this was practically possible within the timescale allowed, but if this was not possible then a carefully measured fraction of the sediment was counted and the final numbers calculated (estimated) accordingly. The cut-off point in terms of the volume/weight of sediment which could be looked at in total was approximately 2g.

The forams were examined using an illuminated stage Vickers binocular microscope with x10 eyepiece and a x1–x3 objective with individual ostracods being removed using an extra-fine camel-hair brush. Standard texts plus a reference collection of published SEM images were used for the purposes of identification. These were identified only to generic level except where these could be rapidly and accurately assessed to species level within the timescale.

Micromorphological analysis of laminar deposits
by Charles French

A soil block was sub-sampled from monolith <421> (Saltern 5) provided for micromorphological analysis at the McBurney Laboratory, Department of Archaeology, University of Cambridge (after Murphy 1986; Courty *et al.* 1989; French 2015, app. 3). The sub-sample was taken across the central zone of the monolith which exhibited multiple finely laminar sediments (contexts 1004 and 1005; basal horizon deposit beneath Saltern 5) and context 1002 above (waste filtration silt, Group 1039). The monolith thin sections were described using the accepted terminology of Bullock *et al.* (1985), Stoops (2003) and Stoops *et al.* (2010; sections C.1.910).

Appendix 4. Translation of the 'Encyclopédie'

Text on the 18th-century coastal salt-works of Lower Normandy which employed the sand-washing process
Translated by Séverine Bézie
From Diderot *et al.* 1765, Volume XIV, 549–50, Available: http://enccre.academie-sciences.fr/encyclopedie/

Summary description of the way artificial white salts are made in the *sauneries* [salt-works or salt pans] of Lower Normandy. The *sauneries* must be established on low-lying areas around the muds and mouths of the rivers, so that the mud continually carried by the tide, can better salt the shorelines, and make them more suitable for the making of this kind of salt, from which the preparation and the labour are usually done everywhere in the way that we will explain; sometimes some of the shorelines are washed several times during the high tides, more or less, depending on where the *sauneries* are located; but it is necessary for the shorelines to be covered by the saltwater at least during high tide, which would be every fortnight.

When those who want to establish a *saunerie* have found a suitable place, they level it and make it as flat and horizontal as possible; whether this place is old or new, it is ploughed with an ordinary plough drawn by horses or oxen, starting with the edge of the shore and ending in the centre, always turning; after which it is harrowed like any other land, by homogenising it as much as possible with a tool they call *haveau* ['a sort of scraper formed from a six-foot-wide board armed with a metal blade' (Ménard 2005)]; this preparation is usually done on the eve of the spring tides in March, allowing the saltwater to cover the shore...so as it becomes saltier. When the shorelines are so prepared, and dried out by the heat, we can see on a clear and sunny day, the surface of the sand or the shore white with salt, we can also notice on the surface thick strikes [or *lignes*; 'one *ligne* equals 2.25mm' (Edeine 1970, 106)], depending on the degree of whiteness there; we can also observe ripples or small furrows on the sand called *havelées* by the *sauniers* [salt-workers]; with intervals of six or seven feet [or '*pied du Roi* equals 32.4cm' (Edeine 1970, 106)] at the most between each; this part of the work is called *haveler*, with help of the *haveau* that we have already used to homogenise the bed of the first preparation, it takes one person to drive the head of the *haveau*, and another one to drive and lift the *haveau*, always putting the collected material at the end of the last scraped bands.

After the *havelées* are scraped, they are collected in small heaps, which are called *mêlées* [mixtures], spaced six or seven feet apart; after which we hitch a small dumper [tip-cart] which they call *banneau*, to one or two beasts, usually one or two oxen, which are driven between the furrows; four people, two in front and two behind, pick up or load the sand from the furrows into the dumper, and a fifth one leads it to the big heap, which is the main deposit of the saltworks or salterns.

Near the large heap is the *quin*, reservoir or tank, from which the salt-workers draw out the water to wash the sand; this water of the *quin* is replenished by the tide which brings back all the saltwater during the high tides, covering the shores and filling the *quin*.

When the salt-workers want to make their brine, they take the sand from the big heap and put it in the [filtration] pits, which are small circular hollows measuring about two and a half feet in diameter, 12 to 14 inches deep at most; the bed of these pits is lined with clay and ground hay, so that the water flowing on it does not get lost, but falls directly into the *tuvau* [or pipe] that leads from each [filtration] pit to the *tonée* [tank or reservoir] of the brine, around the bottom there are small *jentes* or *douvelles* [staves] of beech wood about one inch high, which surround the base of the pit, and upon which are placed raised staves, separated from each other by not more than one line ['equals 2.25mm', (Edeine 1970, 106)]; *glu* [pitch] about one inch thick is spread out on the staves, upon which is put the sand, which is compacted as much as possible.

When the filtration tank is prepared and full of sand, the *relai* or 'second water' is taken from a barrel buried within range of the pits, that is water which was previously filtered from the sand already wetted twice. The pits are usually loaded [with sand] twice a day; the 'first water' is added, producing the pure brine, [the sand] is filtered completely after 4 to 6 hours, depending on how well the sand is compacted, after which the action is repeated with the *relai* or 'second water' filtered on the same sand of the pits, and which becomes the good water [brine] for the salt worker, from the first pits that are then recharged; water filters through the pitch in the bottom of the pits, the process uninterrupted during day and night.

It has been said that the 'first water' is the real brine; it flows directly through the channels of each [filtration] pit into the brine barrel, which is placed next to the stoves [brine-boiling hearths]; during the process to make the *relai* or second water, the pipe is drilled so that the water falls only into the barrel of the *relai* next to the pits; the rains, as can be seen, do a great deal of damage to this activity; they also destroy the *havelées* on the shores, which are thus completely lost. Once the 'first water' and the *relai* 'second water' have been extracted from the [filtration] pits, there is only a kind of mud left, discarded by the salt-makers, and washed away by the tide.

To check if the brine is good and strong, a small lead ball is used, as big as a *poste à loup* [perhaps a reference to the size of a token used to play the 'game of the wolf' (mentioned in Guérin 1837, 131)], covered with wax, which makes it as big as a musket ball; it must float on the surface of this brine; then it is poured into *plombs* [*plumbas* or lead pans] placed on stoves; the *plombs* or boilers, which are three (and more often some salt works have only two) are of rectangular shape, being two and a half feet of length by two feet of width and the height of the edges is two inches, all together are six *lignes* thick ['equals 13.5mm', (Edeine 1970, 108)]; they are placed above the stove, from which the opening is at the front. They each have two vents on the back; the fire is continuous from Monday at dawn, until Sunday at dawn.

When you start the week, and once you light the fire in the stove, you fill the *plombs* with brine that you boil continuously until the salt is ready, which lasts about two and a half hours, three hours at most; after all the water has evaporated, the salt is quickly collected with a *rabot* [or rake], and it is removed with a small shovel similar to those with which the sand of the *havelées* is lifted, and salt is thrown into baskets, which are called *marvaux à égoutter* [draining baskets]; these baskets [possibly equivalent to a *boisseau* or bushel] are cone shaped like the ones used to strain sugar; after the salt is left to strain for about five or six hours, the salt cakes are put in *colombiers* [lofts in a barn] ... it takes several months before the salt cakes are ready in their final form; one *plomb* can only make at most two per annum.

The lead-pans must be picked up every two days at least to re-beat them, and to repair them, because the action of the fire and the accumulation of grime make them sag, and they must be straightened and cleaned to allow an easier boiling. The salt-makers call this work *corroyer les plombs* [or to trim, to prepare the lead-pans]; this is done with a hammer. The stoves cannot last more than two months, after which they are removed to be rebuilt again, because they have become too clogged from salt residues; the materials are crushed as small as possible, and placed in [filtration] pits, if the salt-makers realise that the mixture is not strong enough.

Small logs and firewood bundles are burned in the stoves. Beech wood for logs and oak for bundles are considered the best woods, in places where wood is scarce, marine rushes are also used. The salt-makers take turns with each other to watch over the stoves, and always maintain the fire in a state of boiling; salt is scoured when it begins to boil with a *rabot*, with which it is picked up.

The custom of the owners of these salt flats and the salt-makers who work there is to share in this way; the owner supplies all the utensils and tools and sand, and the salt-makers have only the seventh part of the sale price. ... The salt manufactured, as we have just said, must be consumed in the countries of the surrounding area, being elsewhere forbidden, and smuggled, it will be dispatched only to four to five leagues at most. It is of poor quality, which is especially noticeable in the meat that is prepared from it, and which cannot be well preserved; that's why when we want to make good quality cured meats, we only use, when we can, salts that are much softer, instead of these ones which are very acrid and very corrosive.

Appendix 5. Extract from Dugdale *et al.* (1846) on the Endowment of St Margaret's Priory, Bishop's Lynn

Dugdale *et al.* 1846, Monasticon Anglicanum, vol. 4, 462
At the foundation [of the Benedictine Priory of Lynn in c.1100], Bishop Herbert de Losinga gave the monks here all that he possessed, as far as the church which belonged to William the son of Stanquin, on the other side of Sewaldesfeld, in rents, lands, and men; except Seman and his land and the salt-work which the mother of Seman held. He likewise granted them a market on Saturdays, and a fair on St Margaret's day; but made both the cell of Lynn and its possessions subordinate to his priory of the Holy Trinity in Norwich. Bishop Herbert also gave them a new mill in Gaywode Marsh, together with that marsh; the churches of Gaywode and Mintling; the priest of Mintling; the tithes of his demesne of Gaywode; a villan named Edward, with his land; all his salt-works in that town, except two, and that which Leofric the son of Limburgh held, and the mother of Seman; the church of Sedgford, with the tithes, and all that Walter the archdeacon had, as he held it; the church of Thornham, with the tithes, and all belonging to it; his land at Freinges; seventy acres of land in Secheford, free of every service; and the land which had belonged to Owen of Lakesle.

Bishop Turbe [1147–74], in the time of Henry II, confirmed to this priory the church of Wigenhale St Germans, the gift of William Gifford earl of Bucks, with two parts of the tithe of North Rungton and Middleton. He also confirmed this place as a cell to the priory of Norwich, reciting its endowments, with an addition of 'quandam grevam' (which Parkyn interprets a place on the sands by the water-side) between the two bridges.

In the beginning of King John's reign, William, who was the prior of Norwich, with his convent, granted to John de Grey bishop of Norwich [1200–14] the fair of Lynn, the Saturday market, and all the pleas and profits whatsoever which they held, by virtue of a lay fee, with a messuage near the chapel of St Nicholas to the west, and a messuage near Surflete bridge, with all their salt-pits in the villages of Lynn and Gaywode, and the toll which they held there, in exchange for the manor of Cress Magna and Sedgford in Norfolk.

Bishop John de Grey afterwards confirmed to the monks of Norwich the church of St Margaret here, with the chapels of St James and St Nicholas, the church of Mintling, and all the tithes of his demesne lands at Gaywode, except those that belonged to the church of St Faith of Gaywood, dated 11th kal. April, in the fifth year of his pontificate.

In Henry the Third's reign, William de Lewis gave to the priory of Lynn twelve acres of his land in Wigenhale…

Bibliography

Adounkpè, J., Agboton, C., Hounkpatin, W.A., Kounouhewa, B., Ahouannou, C. and Sinsin, B., 2021
'Qualitative assessment of table salt production techniques in Southern Benin Republic, and related mangrove destruction and health issues', *Food and Nutrition Sciences* 12(7), 759–73

Albone, J., 1999
Archaeological Field Evaluation Report. Land west of High Street, Swineshead, Lincolnshire (SWH 99), Pre-Construct Archaeol. (unpubl.)

Albone, J., Massey, S. and Tremlett, S., 2007
The Archaeology of Norfolk's Coastal Zone. Results of the National Mapping Programme. English Heritage Project No. 2913. Norfolk Landscape Archaeology/English Heritage (unpubl.)

Andrew, R., 1984
A Practical Pollen Guide to the British Flora, Technical Guide No. 1 (Cambridge, Quaternary Research Assoc.)

Andrews, M., 2017
'Bead', in Clarke, G., *Lynnsport 4 & 5: Middle to Late Saxon Salterns on Land Adjacent to Greenpark Avenue, King's Lynn, Norfolk. Post-excavation Assessment and Updated Project Design*, OA East Rep. No. 2078, 61 (unpubl.)

Armstrong, J., 1725
The History of the Ancient and Present State of the Navigation of the Part of King's Lynn and of Cambridge (London, J. Roberts)

Ashmore, P.J., 1999
'Radiocarbon dating: avoiding errors by avoiding mixed samples', *Antiquity* 73, 124–30

Athersuch, J., Horne, D.J. and Whittaker, J.E., 1989
'Marine and brackish water ostracods (superfamilies Cypridacea and Cytheracea)', in Kermack, D. and Barnes, R.S.K. (eds), *Synopses of the British Fauna*, new series, 43, 343 (Leiden, E.J. Brill)

Bagyaraj, D.J. and Varma, A., 1995
'Interaction between arbuscular mycorrhizal fungi and plants. Their importance in sustainable agriculture in arid and semi-arid tropics', in Jones, J.G. (ed.), *Advances in Microbial Ecology* 14, 119–36 (New York, Plenum Press)

Baird, W. 1843
'Travels in New Zealand with contributions to the geography, geology, botany and natural history of that country', *Dieffenb. Trav. New Zeal.* 2, 268

Barker, L., 2003
Morris Farm, Stow Maries, Essex: A Medieval Salt-Working Complex, English Heritage Archaeol. Investigation Rep. Series No. AI/22/2003 (unpubl.)

Baxter, S., 2011
'Lordship and labour', in Crick, J. and van Houts, E. (eds), *A Social History of England: 900–1200*, 98–114 (Cambridge, Cambridge Univ. Press)

Bayley, J., Dungworth, D. and Paynter, S., 2001
Archaeometallurgy (London, English Heritage)

Bell, A., Gurney, D. and Healey, H., 1999
Lincolnshire Salterns. Excavations at Helpringham, Holbeach St Johns and Bicker Haven, E. Anglian Archaeol. 89 (Sleaford)

Beloe, E.M., 1899
Our Borough and Our Churches, King's Lynn, Norfolk. With the Art of the Renaissance in King's Lynn (Cambridge, Macmillan & Bowes)

Behre, K.E., 2007
'A new Holocene sea-level curve for the southern North Sea', *Boreas* 36, 82–102

Beresford, M.W. and St Joseph J.K.S., 1979
Medieval England: An Aerial Survey, 2nd ed. (Cambridge, Cambridge Univ. Press)

Blackbourn, K., 2019
Late Saxon to Early Medieval Salterns at Lynnsport 1: Land South of Aconite Road, King's Lynn, Norfolk. Post-Excavation Assessment and Updated Project Design, OA East Rep. No. 2305 (unpubl.)

Blair, J., 2005
The Church in Anglo-Saxon Society (Oxford, Oxford Univ. Press)

Blair, J., 2018
Building Anglo-Saxon England (Woodstock, Princeton Univ. Press)

Blair, J., 2020
'Beyond the Billingas: from lay wealth to monastic wealth on the Lincolnshire Fen-edge', in Langlands, A.J. and Lavelle, R. (eds), *The Land of the English Kin. Studies in Wessex and Anglo-Saxon England in Honour of Professor Barbara Yorke*, 387–406 (Leiden, Brill) Available: https://doi.org/10.1163/9789004421899_021 Accessed 8 February 2022

Blinkhorn, P., 2005
'Pottery', in Crowson A., Lane T., Penn K. and Trimble D., *Anglo-Saxon Settlement on the Siltland of Eastern England*, Lincolnshire Archaeol. Heritage Rep. Ser. 7, 213 (Heckington)

Blinkhorn, P., 2012
The Ipswich Ware Project: Ceramics, Trade and Society in Middle Saxon England, Medieval Pottery Res. Group Occ. Pap. 7 (London)

Blomefield, F., 1808
'Freebridge Hundred and Half: Gaywode', in *An Essay towards a Topographical History of the County of Norfolk: Volume 8*, 419–25. Available: http://www.british-history.ac.uk/topographical-hist-norfolk/vol8/pp419-425 Accessed 1 November 2017

Bloomer, I., Frenzl, P. and Faike, M., 2016
'Salinity-driven size variability in *Cyprideis torosa* (Ostracoda, Crustacea)', *J. Micropalaeontology* 36, 63–9. Available: https://doi.org/10.1144/jmpaleo2015-043 Accessed 1 November 2022

Borer, O., 1939
'Changes in the Wash', *Geog. J.* 93, 491–6

Bradfer-Lawrence, H.L., 1932
'Gaywood Dragge', *Norfolk Archaeol.* 24, 46–83

Brady, G.S., 1868
'IX. A Monograph of the Recent British Ostracoda, Communicated by Dr Sclater, F.L.S. &c.', *Trans. Linnean Soc. London* 26(2), 353–495

Brasier, M.D., 1980
Microfossils (London, George Allen and Unwin)

Bridbury, A.R., 1955
England and the Salt Trade in the Later Middle Ages (Oxford, Clarendon Press)

British Geological Survey, 2023
BGS Geology Viewer, https://www.bgs.ac.uk/map-viewers/bgs-geology-viewer/

Bronk Ramsey, C., 1995
'Radiocarbon calibration and analysis of stratigraphy: the OxCal program', *Radiocarbon* 37, 425–30

Bronk Ramsey, C., 1998
'Probability and dating', *Radiocarbon* 40, 461–74

Bronk Ramsey, C., 2001
'Development of the radiocarbon calibration program', *Radiocarbon* 43, 355–63

Bronk Ramsey, C., 2009
'Bayesian analysis of radiocarbon dates', *Radiocarbon* 51, 337–60

Brown, N. and Glazebrook, J. (eds), 2000
Research and Archaeology: A framework for the Eastern Counties 2: research agenda and strategy, E. Anglian Archaeol. Occ. Pap. 8 (Norwich)

Brownrigg, W., 1748
The Art of Making Common Salt, As Now Practised in Most Parts of the World: With Several Improvements Proposed in that Art, For the Use of the British Dominions (London, C. Davis)

Brudenell, M. and Clarke, G., 2017
Lynnsport 1–5: The emerging historical salt-making landscape of Gaywood, King's Lynn, Norfolk. Overarching Written Scheme of Investigation, OA East (unpubl.)

Brushfield, T.N., 1890
'Notes on the Parish of East Budleigh', *Trans. Devonshire Assoc. Advancement of Science, Literature, and Art* 22, 260–316

Buck, C.E., Cavanagh, W.G. and Litton, C.D., 1996
Bayesian Approach to Interpreting Archaeological Data (Chichester, John Wiley & Sons)

Bullock, P., Fedoroff, N., Jongerius, A., Stoops, G. and Tursina, T., 1985
Handbook for Soil Thin Section Description (Wolverhampton, Waine Research)

Cappers, R.T.J, Bekker R.M, and Jans, J.E.A., 2006
Digital Seed Atlas of the Netherlands, Groningen Archaeological Studies 4 (Eelde, The Netherlands, Barkhuis Publishing)

Carpentier, V., 2010
'Trois documents inédits sur les salines de la Dives (XIIe–XIVe siècles)', *Tabularia: Sources écrite du monde normands médiévaux*. Available https://doi.org/10.4000/tabularia.2542 Accessed 16 October 2020

Carpentier, V., 2014
'Du mythe colonisateur à l'histoire environnementale des côtes de la Normandie à l'époque viking : l'exemple de l'estuaire de la Dives (France, Calvados), IXe–XIe siècles', in Baduin P. and Musin A.E. (eds), *Vers l'Orient et vers l'Occident; regards croisés sur les dynamiques et les transferts culturels des Vikings à la Rous ancienne*, actes des colloques internationaux de Saint-Pétersbourg-Novgorod-Staraja Russa et Caen (2009), 199–213 (Caen, Presses universitaires de Caen, Publications du Crahm)

Carpentier, V., Ghesquière, E. and Marcigny, C., 2012
Grains de Sel. Sel et salines du littoral bas-normand de la Préhistoire au XIXe siècle (Bayeux, OREP ed.)

Chambers, J., 1829
A General History of the County of Norfolk, Intended to Convey all the Information of a Norfolk Tour, Vol. II, 465–66 (Norwich, Longman, Rees, Orme, Brown and Green),

Chris Blandford Associates, 2007
King's Lynn and West Norfolk Borough Landscape Character Assessment (King's Lynn and West Norfolk Borough Council) Available: https://www.west-norfolk.gov.uk/downloads/download/77/landscape_character_assessment Accessed January 2021

Christy, M. and Dalton, W.H., 1925
'On two large groups of marsh-mounds on the Essex coast. By incorporating reports by the Morant Club, by Francis W Reader & S Hazledine Warren; also an Appendix of similar works by Francis W Reader', *Trans. Essex Arch. Soc.*, new series, 18 (1), 27–56

Clarke, G., 2016
A Late Saxon to Medieval Saltern at Marsh Lane, King's Lynn, Norfolk. Archaeological Excavation, OA East Rep. No. 1820 (unpubl.)

Clarke, G., 2017
Lynnsport 4 & 5: Middle to Late Saxon Salterns on Land Adjacent to Greenpark Avenue, King's Lynn, Norfolk. Post-Excavation Assessment and Updated Project Design, OA East Rep. No. 2078 (unpubl.)

Clarke, G. and Clarke, R., 2018
'A Tale of Two Salterns: recent excavations at Walpole St Peter and Gaywood, King's Lynn', *Norfolk Archaeol.* 48, 1–24

Clarke, G. and Clarke R., 2020
Salt-Winning on The Lyn. Anglo-Saxon and medieval industry at Gaywood's North Marsh, King's Lynn. Publication Proposal, OA East (unpubl.).

Clarke, H. and Carter, A., 1977
Excavations in King's Lynn, 1963–1970, Soc. Medieval Archaeol. Monogr. Ser. 7 (London)

Clarke, R., 2009
Medieval and Later Salt-working and Channel Management at Walpole St Peter, Norfolk: Post-Excavation Assessment, OA East Rep. No. 1116 (unpubl.)

Coles, J. and Hall, D., 1998
Changing Landscapes: The Ancient Fenland (Cambridge, Cambridgeshire County Council and Wetland Archaeology Research Project)

Collins, C., 2018
Archaeological Test Pit Excavations in Gaywood, King's Lynn, Norfolk, in 2010, 2011 and 2013, Access Cambridge Archaeology Rep., Univ. Cambridge (unpubl.)

Cope-Faulkner, P., 2012
Clampgate Road, Fishtoft. Archaeology of a Middle Saxon Island Settlement in the Lincolnshire Fens, Lincolnshire Archaeol. Heritage Rep. Ser. 10 (Heckington)

Cope-Faulkner, P., 2014
'A medieval salt-making complex in King's Lynn: investigations at the former Queen Mary's Nursing Home, 2002–2003', *Norfolk Archaeol.* 47, 67–86

Crosby, E., 2013
The King's Bishops: The Politics of Patronage in England and Normandy, 1066–1216 (London, Palgrave and Macmillan)

Crowson A., Lane T., Penn K. and Trimble D., 2005
Anglo-Saxon settlement on the Siltland of Eastern England, Lincolnshire Archaeol. Heritage Rep. Ser. 7 (Heckington)

Curtis, R.I., 1984
'*Negotiatores Allecarii* and the Herring', *Phoenix* 38 (2), 147–58 (Classical Association of Canada)

Courty, M-A., Goldberg, P. and Macphail, R.I., 1989
Soils and Micromorphology in Archaeology (Cambridge, Cambridge Univ. Press)

Darby, H.C., 1940
The Medieval Fenland, Cambridge Studies in Economic History (Cambridge, Cambridge Univ. Press)

Daubney, A., Townend, P., Vickers G. and Willmott, H., 2016
'The mystery in the marsh: Exploring an Anglo-Saxon island at Little Carlton', *Current Archaeol.* 313, 28–34

Davidson-Arnott, R.G.D., Bauer, B.O. and Houser, C., 2019
Introduction to Coastal Processes and Geomorphology, 2nd edn (Cambridge, Cambridge Univ. Press)

Davies, G., 2010
Settlement, Economy and Lifestyle: The changing social identities of the coastal settlements of West Norfolk, 450–1100AD (unpubl. D. Phil thesis, Univ. Nottingham) Available: https://eprints.nottingham.ac.uk/12002/1/GDavies_Thesis_2.pdf, Accessed 18 February 2021

Diderot, D., d'Alembert, J. le R., Papillon, J.M. and Mouchon, P., 1765
'Salines', in *Encyclopédie, ou, Dictionnaire raisonné des sciences, des arts et des métiers*, Vol. XIV, 549–50 (Neufchastel, Samuel Faulche), Available: http://enccre.academie-sciences.fr/encyclopedie/ Accessed 25 September 2020

Diderot, D. and d'Alembert, J. le R., 1768
'Histoire naturelle. Minéralogie. Travail du Sel. Saunerie de Normandie, Plate I', in *Supplément à l'Encyclopédie ou Dictionnaire raisonné des sciences, des arts et des métiers*, Planches tome VI (Paris, Briasson, David & Le Breton) Available: http://enccre.academie-sciences.fr/encyclopedie/ Accessed 25 September 2020

Diderot, D. and d'Alembert, J. le R., 1778
Grande Encyclopédie, Vol. 29, 795 (Genève)

Dodwell, B., 1967
'Holdings and inheritance in medieval East Anglia', *Economic Hist. Rev.*, new series, 20 (1), 53–66 doi:10.2307/2592035

Dunbar, E., Cook, G.T., Naysmith, P., Tripney, B.G. and Xu, S., 2016
'AMS ^{14}C dating at the Scottish Universities Environmental Research Centre (SUERC) Radiocarbon Dating Laboratory', *Radiocarbon* 58, 9–23

Dugdale, W., Bandinel, B., Ellis, H. and Caley, J., 1846
Monasticon Anglicanum: a history of the abbies and other monasteries, hospitals, frieries, and cathedral and collegiate churches.... New edn. (London) Vols 4 and 5 HathiTrust Digital Library, available: https://babel.hathitrust.org accessed 18 February 2021; Vol. 3 Internet Archive, available: https://archive.org/details/MonasticonAnglicanumAHistoryOfTheA accessed 18 February 2021; Vol. 6 Part 3, Google Books, available: https://books.google.com/ Accessed 18 February 2021

Duncan, H., 1812
'On the mode of manufacturing salt from sea-sand or sleech. Practised in Annandale, along the Coast of the Salway Firth', in Singer, W., *General View of the Agriculture, State of Property, and Improvements in the County of Dumfries*, The Board of Agriculture, 527–33 (Edinburgh, James Ballantyne and Co.)

Dyer, C., 2002
Making a Living in the Middle Ages. The People of Britain 850–1520 (Newhaven, Yale Univ. Press)

East Anglian Coastal Group, 2010
'Appendix C: Baseline Processes' in Environment Agency *et al.* (eds), *The Wash Shoreline Management Plan 2. Gibraltar Point to Old Hunstanton* (unpubl) Available: https://www.eastangliacoastalgroup.org/assets/img/1441139.pdf Accessed 11 January 2023

Edeine, B., 1970
'La technique de fabrication du sel marin dans les sauneries protohistoriques', *Annales de Bretagne et des pays de l'Ouest* 77(1), 95–133

Editions Alecto, 1986
Little Domesday, online version Available: https://www.nationalarchives.gov.uk/help-with-your-research/research-guides/domesday-book/#6-accessing-domesday-online Accessed 18 March 2020

Fäegri, K. and Iversen, J., 1975
Textbook of Pollen Analysis, 3rd edn (Oxford, Blackwell Scientific Publications)

Fenwick, H., 2001
'Medieval salt production and landscape development in the Lincolnshire Marsh', in Ellis, S., Fenwick, H., Lillie, M. and Van de Noort, R., *Wetland Heritage of the Lincolnshire Marsh. An Archaeological Survey*, 231–41 (Kingston-upon-Hull, Humber Wetlands Project)

Fielding, A. and Fielding, A., 2006
The Salt Industry (Princes Risborough, Shire Publications)

Fitter, R., Fitter, A. and Blamey, M., 1985
The Wild Flowers of Britain and Northern Europe, 4th edn (London, Collins)

Forester, T. (trans.), 1854
The Chronicle of Florence of Worcester with the two continuations: comprising annals of English history, from the departure of the Romans to the reign of Edward I (London, Bohn's Antiquarian Library)

French, C., 2015
A Handbook of Geoarchaeological Approaches for Investigating Landscapes and Settlement Sites, Studying Scientific Archaeology 1 (Oxford, Oxbow)

Frenzl, P., Schulz, I. and Pint, A., 2012
'Noding of *Cyprideis torosa* valves (Ostracoda) – a proxy for salinity? New data for field observations and a long-term microcosm experiment', *Hydrobiology* 97 (4), 314–29

Gallois, R.W., Cox, B.M., Morter, A.A., Wood, C.J., Cornwell, J.D. and Kimbell, S.F., 1994
The Geology of the Country around King's Lynn and The Wash. Memoir of the British Geological Survey, Sheet 145 and part of 129 (England and Wales)

Gardiner, M., 2005
'Archaeological evidence for the exploitation, reclamation and flooding of salt marshes', in Klapste, J. (ed.), *Ruralia V: Water Use and Management in Europe*, 73–83 (Prague, Institute of Archaeology)

Gidon, F., 1939
'Une technique préhistorique de la saunerie: l'extraction du sel néritique par lavage des sables salés', *Extrait du compte rendu sommaire des séances de la Société de Biogéographie* 16, nos 138 et 139, séance du 20 octobre 1939, 79–82

Grady, D.M., 1998
'Medieval and post-medieval salt extraction in North-East Lincolnshire' in Bewley, R.H. (ed.), *Lincolnshire's Archaeology from the Air*, Occ. Pap. Lincolnshire Hist. Archaeol. 11, 81–95

Green, C., 2020
Britons and Anglo Saxons: Lincolnshire AD 400–650, 2nd edn. (Lincoln, History of Lincolnshire Committee)

Grimm, E., 1993
TILIA: a Pollen Program for Analysis and Display (Springfield, Illinois State Museum)

Guérin, E. de, 1837
Lettres, Available: https://www.lalanguefrancaise.com/dictionnaire/definition/loup Accessed 22 November 2022

Guido, M., 1999
The Glass Beads of Anglo-Saxon England c.AD 400–700. A Preliminary Visual Classification of the More Definitive and Diagnostic Types (Woodbridge, Boydell & Brewer)

Hall, D. and Coles, J., 1994
Fenland Survey: An Essay in Landscape and Persistence, English Heritage Archaeological Report 1 (London)

Hallam, H.E., 1960
'Salt-making in the Lincolnshire Fenland during the Middle Ages', *Lincs. Architect. Archaeol. Soc. Reports and Papers* 8, 85–112

Hallam, H.E., 1988
'New Settlement: Eastern England', in Hallam, H.E (ed.), *The Agrarian History of England and Wales Vol. II, 1042–1350*, 139–73 (Cambridge, Cambridge Univ. Press),

Hamilton, D. and Kenney, J., 2015
'Multiple Bayesian modelling approaches to a suite of radiocarbon dates from ovens excavated at Ysgol yr Hendre, Caernarfon, North Wales', *Quaternary Geochronology* 25, 72–82

Harper-Bill, C., 2004	'Losinga, Herbert de (d. 1119), abbot of Ramsey and bishop of Norwich', *Oxford Dictionary of National Biography*, Oxford; online edn: <doi:10.1093/ref:odnb/17025> Accessed 16 March 2020	Hutcheson, A.R.J., 2009	*The Origins of East Anglian Towns: Coin Loss in the Landscape, AD 470–939* (unpubl. D.Phil thesis, Univ. East Anglia) Available: https://ueaeprints.uea.ac.uk/19100/1/ARJ_Hutcheson_Thesis.pdf Accessed 11 January 2023
Harris, S.J., 2003	'Ælfric's Colloguy' in Kline, D.T. (ed.), *Medieval Literature for Children*, 112–30 (London, Routledge)	Hybel, N. and Poulson, B., 2007	*The Danish Resources c.1000–1550: Growth and recession* (Leiden/Boston, Brill)
Harrod, H., 1874	*Report on the Deeds and Records of the Borough of King's Lynn* (King's Lynn, Thew & Son)	Innes, J.B. and Blackford J.J., 2003	'The ecology of Late Mesolithic woodland disturbances: model testing with fungal spore assemblage data', *J. Archaeol. Sci.* 30(2), 185–94
Hather, J.G., 2000	*The Identification of the Northern European Woods. A Guide for Archaeologists and Conservators* (New York, Routledge)	Jennings, S., 1981	*Eighteen Centuries of Pottery from Norwich*, E. Anglian Archaeol. 13 (Norwich)
Hayes, P.P., 1988	'Roman to Saxon in the south Lincolnshire Fens', *Antiquity* 62 (235), 321–6	Johnson, A. and Collcutt, S., 2008	*Land off Bergen and Hamburg Way, North Lynn Industrial Estate, Kings Lynn, Norfolk. A desk-based archaeological assessment*, Oxford Archaeological Associates (unpubl.)
Hayes, P.P. and Lane, T.W., 1992	*The Fenland Project, Number 5: Lincolnshire Survey, The South-West Fens*, E. Anglian Archaeol. 55 (Sleaford)	Jones, T.R., 1850	'Description of the Entomostraca of the Pleistocene Beds of Newbury, Copford, Clacton, and Grays', *Annals and Magazine of Natur. Hist.* 6 (Series 2), 25–8
Healey, R.H., 1975	'A medieval salt-making site in Bicker Haven, Lincolnshire', in de Brisay, K.W. and Evans, K.A. (eds), *Salt – The Study of an Ancient Industry*, 36 (Colchester, Colchester Archaeol. Group)	Keen, L., 1987	'Medieval salt-working in Dorset', *Dorset Natur. Hist. Archaeol. Soc. Proc.* 109, 25–8
		Keen, L., 1988	'Coastal salt production in Norman England', in Allen Brown, R. (ed.), *Proceedings of the Battle Conference on Anglo-Norman Studies XI*, 133–180 (Woodbridge, Boydell Press)
Healey, R.H., 1979	'Recent Saxon finds from South Lincolnshire', *Lincs Hist. Archaeol.* 14, 80–1		
Healey, H., 1988	'Bicker Bends', *Fenland Research* 5, 44–5		
Healey, H., 1999	'A medieval salt making site in Bicker Haven, Lincolnshire', in Bell, A., Gurney, D. and Healey, H. (eds) *Lincolnshire Salterns, Excavations at Helpringham, Holbeach St Johns and Bicker Haven*, E. Anglian Archaeol. 89, 82–101 (Sleaford)	Kestner, F.J.T., 1962	'The old coastline of The Wash', *Geog. J.* 128, 457–71
		Kilyeni, T.I. and Whittaker, J.E., 1974	'On *Cyprideis torosa* (Jones 1850)', in Sylvester-Bradley, P.C. and Siveter, D.J. (eds), *A Stereo-Atlas of Ostracod Shells 2*, 21–32 (Dept. Geology, Univ Leicester)
Hill, D., 1981	*An Atlas of Anglo-Saxon England* (Oxford, Basil Blackwell)	Knight, T. and Clarke, G., 2019	*Late Saxon to Early Medieval Salterns on Land North of Greenpark Avenue, Kings Lynn, Norfolk. Post-Excavation Assessment and Updated Project Design*, OA East Rep. No. 2308 (unpubl.)
Hill, D. and Cowie, R. (eds), 2001	*Wics. The Early Mediaeval Trading Centres of Northern Europe*, Sheffield Archaeol. Monogr. 14 (Sheffield Academic Press)		
Hillen, H.J., 1907	*History of the Borough of King's Lynn*, Vol. I (Norwich, East of England Newspaper Co.)	Kwiatkowska, M., 2020	*Late Saxon to Early Medieval Salterns at Lynnsport 3: Land South of Front Way, King's Lynn, Norfolk. Post-Excavation Assessment and Updated Project Design*, OA East Rep. No. 2380 (unpubl.)
Hocquet, J.C., 1984	'Sedes et effusio métrologie et histoire religeuse durant la 'phase ecclésiastique' de la production du sel', *Cahiers de Civilisation Médiévale* 27, 57–69		
Hodges, R., 1982	*Dark Age Economics: the Origins of Towns and Trade AD 600–1000* (London, Duckworth)	Lane, T., 2018	*Mineral from the Marshes: Coastal Salt-Making in Lincolnshire*, Lincolnshire Archaeol. Heritage Rep. Ser. 12 (Sleaford, Heritage Trust of Lincolnshire)
Hodges, R., 1989	*The Anglo-Saxon Achievement. Archaeology and the Beginnings of English Society* (London, Duckworth)	Lane, T. and Morris, E.L. (eds), 2001	*A Millennium of Saltmaking: Prehistoric and Romano-British Salt Production in the Fenland*, Lincolnshire Archaeol. Heritage Rep. Ser. 4 (Sleaford, Heritage Trust of Lincolnshire)
Holden, E. and Hudson, T., 1981	'Salt making in the Adur Valley', *Sussex Archaeol. Collections* 119, 117–48		
Horne, D.J. and Boomer, I., 2000	'The role of Ostracoda in saltmarsh meiofaunal communities', in Sherwood, B.R., Gardiner, B.G. and Harris, T. (eds), *British Saltmarshes*, 182–202 (Cardigan, Forrest Text, for the Linnean Society of London)	Le Héricher, E., 1845	*Avranchin Monumental et Historique*, Vol. 1 (Avranches)
		Lindbo, D., Stolt, M. and Vepraskas, M., 2010	'Redomixorphic features', in Stoops, G., Marcelino, V. and Mees, F. (eds), *Interpretation of Micromorphological Features of Soils and Regoliths*, 129–47 (Oxford, Elsevier)
Hurst, J.G., 1988	'Rural building in England and Wales: England', in Hallam, H.E (ed.), *The Agrarian History of England and Wales Vol. II: 1042–1350*, 854–930 (Cambridge, Cambridge Univ. Press),	Loveluck, C.P. and Tys, D., 2006	'Coastal societies, exchange and identity along the Channel and southern North Sea shores of Europe, AD 600–1000', *J. Maritime Archaeol.* 1(2), 140–69
Hutcheson, A.R.J., 2006	'The origins of King's Lynn? Control of wealth on the Wash prior to the Norman Conquest', *Medieval Archaeol.* 50, 71–104	Mawer, A., 1933	'The study of field-names in relation to place-names', in Edwards, J.G., Galbraith, V.H. and Jacob, E.F. (eds), *Historical Essays in Honour of James Tait*, 189–200 (Manchester, Manchester Univ. Press)

Maybury, T., 2011	*A Century of Change on the Lindsey Marshland. Marshchapel 1540–1640* (Unpubl. DPhil thesis, Univ. Hull)		Owen, D.M., 1984	*The Making of King's Lynn, a Documentary Survey,* Records of Social and Economic History (New Series) 18 (Oxford, Oxford Univ. Press)
McAvoy, F., 1994	'Marine salt extraction: the excavation of salterns at Wainfleet St. Mary, Lincolnshire', *Medieval Archaeol.* 38, 134–63		Page, W. (ed.), 1906	*A History of the County of Norfolk, Vol. 2* (London, Victoria County History)
Ménard J-L., 2005	*La révolte des nu-pieds en Normandie au XVIIe siècle* (Ouistreham, Editions Dittmar), Available/cited: https://www.lalanguefrancaise.com/dictionnaire/definition/haveau Accessed 22 November 2022		Paquet, N., 2018	'Bénin: À la découverte de l'extraction du sel de sable à Djègbadji', *Nouvelle Afrique* 26, March 2018
			Pestell, T., 2004	*Landscapes of Monastic Foundation: The Establishment of Religious Houses in East Anglia c.650–1200* (Woodbridge, Boydell Press)
Milligan, B., 1982	'Pottery', in Coad, J.G. and Streeten, A., 'Excavations at Castle Acre Castle, Norfolk, 1972–77: country house and castle of the Norman earls of Surrey', *Archaeol. J.* 139, 138–301		Powell, A.B., 2009	'Two thousand years of salt making at Lymington, Hampshire', *Proc. Hampshire Field Club Archaeol. Soc.* 64, 9–40
Moore, P.D. and Webb, J.A., 1991	*Pollen Analysis* (Oxford, Blackwell)		Powell-Smith, A., 2011	'Open Domesday', online version of Hull Domesday project, Available: https://opendomesday.org/ Accessed 13 February 2020
Morris, E.L., 2010	'The Briquetage', in Cope Faulkner, P., *Clampgate Road, Fishtoft. Archaeology of a Middle Saxon Island Settlement in the Lincolnshire Fens,* Lincolnshire Archaeol. and Heritage Reports Ser. No. 10, 60–8		Rackham, O., 1996	*The History of the Countryside* (London, Dent and Sons)
			Rackham, O., 2000	*The History of the Countryside: The classic history of Britain's landscape, flora and fauna* (London, Phoenix Press)
MPRG, 1998	*A Guide to the Classification of Medieval Ceramic Forms,* Medieval Pottery Res. Group Occ. Pap. 1 (London)		Regnouf de Vains, M., 1840	'Mémoire sur les salines de la Basse-Noirmandie et particulièrement sur celles de l'Ancien Pays Avranchin', *Annuaire des cinq départements de la Normandie* 6, 207–19
Murphy, C.P., 1986	*Thin Section Preparation of Soils and Sediments* (Berkhamsted, A.B. Academic)			
Musset, L., 1956	'La fabrication du sel blanc en Basse-Normandie par ebullition', *Annales de Normandie* 6(2), 192–93		Reimer, P.J., Austin, W.E.N., Bard, E., Bayliss, A., Blackwell, P.G., Ramsey, C.B., Butzin, M., Cheng, H., Edwards, R.L., Friedrich, M., Grootes, P.M., Guilderson, T.P., Hajdas, I., Heaton, T.J., Hogg, A.G., Hughen, K.A., Kromer, B., Manning, S.W., Muscheler, R., Palmer, J.G., Pearson, C., Plicht, J.v.d., Reimer, R.W., Richards, D.A., Scott, E.M., Southon, J.R., Turney, C.S.M., Wacker, L., Adolphi, F., Büntgen, U., Capano, M., Fahrni, S.M., Fogtmann-Schulz, A., Friedrich, R., Köhler, P., Kudsk, S., Miyake, F., Olsen, J., Reinig, F., Sakamoto, M., Sookdeo, A. and Talamo, S., 2020	'The IntCal20 Northern Hemisphere Radiocarbon Age Calibration Curve (0–55 cal kBP)', *Radiocarbon* 62(4), 725–57
Musset, L., 1983	'Sur les chemins sauniers de la Normandie médiévale', *Annales de Normandie* 33, 175–9			
Musset, L., 1995	'Aspects de la production du sel sur la côte entre Dive et Orne du XIIe au XIVe siècle', in *Les Normands et la Mer,* Actes du XXVe Congrès des Sociétés Historiques et Archéologiques de Normandie (Communauté urbaine de Cherbourg, 4–7 oct. 1990), 188–91 (Saint-Vaast-la-Hougue, Musée Maritime de l'Île Tatihou)			
Musset, L., 1998	'Une grande saline oubliée: 'Escanneville [Descanneville] (à Merville,Calvados), du XIII e au XVIII e siècle', *Bulletin de la Société des Antiquaires de Normandie* 61 (an. 1990–1993, Proc.-verb. de la séance du 5 mai 1990), 291–4			
National Ocean Service, 2021	'What are spring and neap tides' Available: https://oceanservice.noaa.gov/facts/springtide.html Accessed 6 Jan 2023			
Neale, J.W. and Delorme, L.D., 1985	'*Cytheromorpha fuscata,* relict Holocene marine ostracode from freshwater inland lakes of Manitoba, Canada', *Revista Espanola de Micropaleontologia* 17, 41–64			
Network Archaeology, forthcoming	*Hornsea Offshore Windfarm Project 2* (unpubl.)			
Neville, J., 2014	*Norfolk Mills website* Available: http://www.norfolkmills.co.uk/ Accessed 18 March 2020			
Oosthuizen, S., 2017	*The Anglo-Saxon Fenland* (Oxford, Windgather Press)		Richards, W., 1812	*The History of Lynn* (London, R. Baldwin)
Owen, D.M., 1980	'Bishop's Lynn: the first century of a new town?', in Brown, R.A. (ed.), *Proceedings of the Battle Conference on Anglo-Norman Studies,* Vol. II, 141–53 (Woodbridge, Boydell)		Ridgeway, V., 2000	'A medieval saltern mound at Millfields Caravan Park, Bramber, West Sussex'. *Sussex Archaeol. Collections* 138, 135–52
			Rippon, S., 2000	*The Transformation of Coastal Wetlands* (Oxford, Oxford Univ. Press)

Robertson, A.J., 1939	*Anglo-Saxon Charters*, reprinted 2009 (Cambridge, Cambridge Univ. Press)	Steier, P. and Rom, W., 2000	'The use of Bayesian statistics for ^{14}C dates of chronologically ordered samples: a critical analysis', *Radiocarbon* 42, 183–98
Roffe, D.R., 1995	'The Historia Croylandensis: a plea for reassessment', *English Hist. Rev.* 110, 93–108	Stevenson, J. (ed.), 1996	*The Chronicle of Florence of Worcester with a continuation and appendix* (Felinfach, Llanerch Publishers)
Roffe, D.R., 2005	'The historical context', in Crowson, A., Lane, T., Penn. K. and Trimble, D., *Anglo-Saxon Settlement on the Siltland of Eastern England*, Lincolnshire Archaeol. Heritage Rep. Ser. 7, 264–88	Stuiver, M. and Polach, H.A., 1977	'Reporting of ^{14}C data', *Radiocarbon* 19, 355–63
Rogerson, A. and Silvester, R.J., 1986	'Middle Saxon occupation at Hay Green, Terrington. St Clement', *Norfolk Archaeol.* 39, 320–2	Stoops, G., 2003	*Guidelines for Analysis and Description of Soil and Regolith Thin Sections* (Wisconsin, Soil Science Society of America)
Rosenfeld, A., 1977	'Die rezenten Ostracoden-Arten in der Ostsee', *Meyniana* 29, 11–49	Stoops, G., Marcelino, V. and Mees, F. (eds), 2010	*Interpretation of Micromorphological Features of Soils and Regoliths* (Amsterdam, Elsevier)
Rudkin, E.H. and Owen, D.M., 1960	'The medieval salt industry in the Lindsey marshland', *Lincs. Architec. Archaeol. Soc. Reports and Papers* 8, 76–84	Tansley, A.G., 1939	*The British Islands and Their Vegetation* (Cambridge, Cambridge Univ. Press)
Rutledge, P., 1993	'Ecclesiastical jurisdictions', in Wade-Martins, P. (ed.), *An Historical Atlas of Norfolk*, 90–91 (Norwich, Norfolk Museums Service)	Taylor, W., 1844	*The Antiquities of King's Lynn* (Kings Lynn, J. Thew)
Saunders, H.W., 1930	*An Introduction to the Obedientiary and Manor Rolls of the Norwich Cathedral Priory* (Norwich, Jarrold and Sons)	Thompson, M.W., 1956	'A group of mounds on Seasalter Level, near Whitstable, and the medieval embanking in this area', *Archaeologia Cantiana* 70, 44–67
Seppings, E.R., c.1961	*Soil Salinities*, Notes prepared for Nottingham University Extra-Mural Class (unpubl.)	Thorp, J.H. and Covich, A. (eds), 2001	*Ecology and Classification of North American Freshwater Invertebrates* (San Diego, Academic Press)
Scott, E.M., 2003	'The Third International Radiocarbon Intercomparison (TIRI) and the Fourth International Radiocarbon Intercomparison (FIRI) 1990–2002: results, analysis, and conclusions', *Radiocarbon* 45, 135–408	Timberlake, S., 2008	*Plot 13, Hamburg Way, North Lynn Industrial Estate, King's Lynn, Norfolk*, Cambridge Archaeol. Unit Rep. No. 832 (unpubl.)
Scott, E.M., Cook, G.T. and Naysmith, P., 2010	'A report on phase 2 of the Fifth International Radiocarbon Intercomparison (VIRI)', *Radiocarbon* 52(3), 846–58	Timberlake, S. and Haylock, K., 2016	'Chemical analysis (by pXRF) and characterisation of the salt slags, and other materials' in Clarke, G., *A Late Saxon to Medieval Saltern at Marsh Lane, King's Lynn, Norfolk. Archaeological Excavation*, OA East Rep. No. 182, 65–81 (unpubl.)
Shennan, I., 1986	'Flandrian sea-level changes in the Fenland. II: tendencies of sea-level movement, altitudinal changes, and local and regional factors', *J. Quat. Sci.* 1, 155–79	Tröels-Smith J., 1955	'Characterisation of unconsolidated sediments', *Danmarks Geologiske Undersølgelse*, Ser. IV, 3, 38–73
Silvester, R.J., 1988	*The Fenland Project Number 3: Marshland and the Nar Valley, Norfolk*, E. Anglian Archaeol. 45 (Norwich)	Tylecote, R.F. and Owles, E., 1960	'A second-century iron smelting site at Ashwicken, Norfolk', *Norfolk Archaeol.* 32, 142–62
Simmons, I.G., 2015	*Margins of the East Fen; Historic Landscape Evolution.* (Unpubl. PhD thesis, Univ. Durham) Available https://www.dur.ac.uk/east-lincs-history/ Accessed 13 February 2020	van den Broeke, P.W., 1996	'Turfwinning en zoutwinning langs de Noordzeekust. Een verbond sinds de ijzertijd?', *Tijdschrift voor Waterstaatsgeschiedenis* (themanummer Turfwinning in Laag Nederland voor 1530) 5, 48–59
Smith, D.M., Zalasiewicz, J.A., Williams, M., Wilkinson, I.P., Scarborough, J.J., Knight, M., Sayer, C., Redding, M. and Moreton, S.G., 2012	'The anatomy of a Fenland roddon: sedimentation and environmental change in a lowland Holocene tidal creek environment', *Proc. Yorks. Geol. Soc.* 59(2), 145–59	van Geel, B. and Borger, G.J., 2005	'Evidence for medieval salt-making by burning Eel-grass (*Zostera marina* L.) in the Netherlands', *Netherlands J. Geosciences (Geologie en Mijnbouw)* 84(1), 43–9
		Van Hoeve, M. and Hendrikse, M. (eds), 1998	*A Study of non-pollen objects in pollen slides: the types as described by Dr Bas van Geel and colleagues* (Unpubl. compilation, Univ. Utrecht, Netherlands)
Smith, D.M., 2013	*The Ancient Channel 'Roddon' networks of the Fenland of Eastern England and their significance as indicators of palaeoenvironmental change during the Holocene* (Unpubl. DPhil thesis, Univ. Leicester)	van der Zwaluw, A.T.J., 2018	*Zoutwinning in West-Friesland in de Bronstijd, Een oplossing en nieuw gevormde benadering voor archeologische vraagstukken over zout* (Unpubl. Bachelor's thesis, Univ. Leiden)
Smith, P., 2012	*Petitionary Negotiation in a Community in Conflict: King's Lynn and West Norfolk c.1575 to 1662* (Unpubl. DPhil thesis, Univ. E. Anglia)	Waller, M., 1994	*The Fenland Project Number 9: Flandrian Environmental Change in Fenland*, E. Anglian Archaeol. 70 (Cambridge)
Stace, C., 1997	*New Flora of the British Isles,* 2nd edn (Cambridge Univ. Press)	Waller, M. and Alderton, A., 1994	'Swineshead', in Waller, M., *The Fenland Project, Number 9: Flandrian Environmental Change in Fenland*, E. Anglian Archaeol. 70, 288–95 (Cambridge)
Stace, C., 2010	*New Flora of the British Isles,* 3rd edn (Cambridge, Cambridge Univ. Press)		

Went, D., 2011 — *Introduction to Heritage Assets: Pre-Industrial Salterns* (Historic England). Available: https://historicengland.org.uk/images-books/publications/iha-preindustrial-salterns/heag225-pre-industrial-salterns Accessed: 09 November 2020

Wheeler, A.J., 1995 — 'Saltmarsh development from fen: analysis of late Holocene deposits from north-central Fenland, U.K', *Quat. Int.* 26, 139–45

Wheeler, W.H., 1896 — *A History of the Fens of South Lincolnshire*, 2nd edn (Boston, J.M. Newcomb, Simpkin, Marshall & Co.)

White, C.H.E., 1893 — 'Losinga, Herbert de (1054?–1119)', *Dictionary of National Biography*, 34 (Oxford) Available: https://www.oxforddnb.com/view/10.1093/odnb/9780192683120.001.0001/odnb-9780192683120-e-17025 Accessed 16 March 2020

Whittle, J. and Yates, M., 2000 — "Pays réel or pays légal'? Contrasting patterns of land tenure and social structure in eastern Norfolk and western Berkshire, 1450–1600', *Agr. Hist. Rev.* 48(1), 1–26

Wilkinson, T. and Batt, C., 2019 — 'Archaeomagnetic dating', in Knight, T. and Clarke, G., *Late Saxon to Early Medieval Salterns on Land North of Greenpark Avenue, Kings Lynn, Norfolk. Post-Excavation Assessment and Updated Project Design*, OA East Rep. No. 2308, 82–91 (unpubl.)

Wilkinson, T. and Murphy, P., 1995 — *Archaeology of the Essex Coast, Volume I: The Hullbridge Survey*, E. Anglian Archaeol. 71 (Chelmsford)

Young, J., Vince, A. and Naylor, V., 2005 — *A Corpus of Anglo-Saxon and Medieval Pottery from Lincoln*, Lincoln Archaeol. Stud. 7 (Oxford, Oxbow)

Index

Page numbers in *italics* denote illustrations.

Abell, Richard 83
Aconite Road 1
Adam, Ben, poem by 13, 88
Adur Valley (W. Sussex), salt-winning 74, 77, 89, 93
Ælfric 33
Aethelmoth, bishop of Sherborne 17
Almar, bishop of Elmham 9, 80
archaeomagnetic dating 59
Arne (Dorset) 89
Arundel, earls of 81
Ashly, John 82
Ashwicken (Norfolk) 14
d'Aubigny, Hugh, earl of Arundel 81

Babingley, River 14, 16, 19, 88
Baker, John 83, 84
Bardike sea wall 13, 15, 19
Barker, John 82
Barrow Hills Group (Essex) 93
basketwork 36, *75*, 77, 78–9
Bawsey (Norfolk), productive site
  decline 32, 87–8
  market 16
  pottery 14
  research questions 11
  status and connection to salt trade 15, 88, 91, 96, 97
Bawsey, Edmund 82, 83, 84, 86
Baxter, Henry 83, 84
Bay-salt 88, 90, 92
bead, glass 43
beamslot 58, 73
Beaufeu, William de, bishop of Thetford 80
Bertie, Frances 89
Bewsher (Bewshere), Richard 83
Bicker Bends (Lincs) 93
Bicker Haven (Lincs), saltern 96
  dating 93
  filtration unit 41, 77
  hearths 5, 35, 74, 76
  salt-cote 73–4
Bilney, John 84
bitters 74–5
Black Death 90, 95
Blackwater 93
Braibroke, John 84
Bramber (W. Sussex) 74
Breydon Water (Norfolk) 93
briquetage
  excavation evidence
    Saltern 5 59–65, *64*, *65*, 74
    Wash salterns 1, 5
  methodology 104
Brow-of-the-Hill (Norfolk) 14
Brownrigg, W. 35, 64, 76
Bulcote 87, 89
Bulecote 58
le Bull 30
Bullcote Waie (Salters Lode), trackway
  dating 38, 98
  function 32, 53, 91
  location 33, *36*, *37*
Bullcote Waie (Salters Lode) group
  dating *36*, 38, 53–7, 101–3, *102*, *104*
  discussion 89, 91, 98
  excavation evidence 34, 52–73, *53*
  see also Salterns 4–12
Burmond, John 83
Burn, River 93
Burnham (Norfolk) 93
Burtoft (Lincs) 96
Bury St Edmunds abbey (Suffolk) 88

Caen (France)
  St-Étienne 76, 95
  La Trinité 90
Caldecott, Thomas 83, 84
Calvados (France) 95
Castle Acre (Norfolk) 57
Castle Rising (Norfolk) 14, 15, 81, 88
charcoal 49, 68, 104–5
chronology
  dating framework 36–8, *36*
  research agenda 9, 11
  salterns
    Bullcote Waie group 53–7
    Salters Waie group 39
  see also archaeomagnetic dating; radiocarbon dating
church, influence of 11, 15–16, 91, 93, 96
Clenchwarton (Norfolk) 13, 19, 27
Coatham (N. Yorks) 16
Collyng, Richard 84
Congham (Norfolk) 16, 87
Constantine, Elizabeth 82, 83, 84, 86
Constantine, Thomas 82, 83, 84
coppicing 76
Cotentin (France) 95
Crabhouse Nunnery (Norfolk) 22
creeks *27*, 30–1
Cress Magna (Norfolk) 108
Cressingham (Norfolk) 80
Crouch, River 93
Crowland Abbey (Lincs) 96
Curson, Walter 83
Curteys, Isabella 83
Curteys, John 83
Curts, John 82
Cynewulf, King 17

le Dale 30
Denmark, salt-winning 95
Descanneville (France) 90
diatoms 52, 105
Diderot, D. 35, 106–7
Dives (France) 89, 95
Djègbadji (Benin), salt-winning 74, *75*, 77, 90
Domesday Book 5, 9, 13, 80, 91, 93
Donington (Lincs) 96
Donne, William 80
Dowdy, John 81
Dowshill 80
Drayton (Lincs) 96
Duncan, H. 35, 64, 76

Le Ea 89
East Anglia, bishops of 5
Eau Brink 19, 22, *22*
economy, importance of salt to 10
Edward 107
Edward the Confessor, King 17
Elizabeth I 89
Elloe (Lincs) 96
Elmham, diocese of 9, 15, 88
Emneth estate 13
Encyclopédie 106–7
Esk, River 19
Evesham Abbey (Worcs) 17

Faversham (Kent), *sealtern* 76, 93
Fécamp Abbey (France) 95
Fenkinhill 82, 83, 85, 86
filtration units
  background and nomenclature 33, 34, 35
  discussion 76–8, *78*
  excavation evidence
    Bullcote Waie group 56, 57–8, *57*, *58*, *59*
    Salters Waie group 41, 42, *44*, *45*, 50
filtration waste 34–5, 51, 72–3
fired clay 35, 44, 104
fish, preserving 16–17
Fisher, John 82, 86
Fishtoft (Lincs) 1, 97

Fleet (Lincs) 90
Florence of Worcester 19
foraminifera
  methodology 105
  Saltern 1 29, 50
  Saltern 5 70–1, *70*
  Saltern 10 72, *72*
  Saltern 11 72, *72*
Freebridge Hundred 91
Freinges (Norfolk) 107
Front Way 1
fuel 17, 35, 49, 66–8, 76, 98

Gannishill 82, 85, 86, 89
Garwick (Lincs) 96
'gateway communities' 14–15, *14*, 16
Gaywood
  bishop's palace 86, 92
  hospital of St Mary Magdalene 81, 82, 83, 86
  manor 1, 15, 80, 82–6, 88, 89–90, 91
  parish 36, 89
  St Faith's church 107, 108
  settlement, Anglo-Saxon 14, 15
  tithe map *24*
  trading site 16, 32, 88, 91
  see also North Marsh
Gaywood, River
  course of 19, 31, 89
  environment 22–5, *23*, *24*, 27, 29
  navigability 88
  salterns 5, 77
  settlement, Anglo-Saxon 14
  trading site 16, 32, 88, 91
'Gaywood Dragge' 11, 31, 81–7, *81*, 89, 90, 92
Geben, Thomas 82, 86
Gedney Dyke *see* Holbeach Hurn/Gedney Dyke
Genyns, Alice 83
Genyns, Robert 83
Gervis (Gervys), Robert 83
Gifford, William, earl of Buckingham 107
Glen, River 5
Glynton, John de 83, 87
Godewyn, Richard 84
Goldwell, James, bishop of Norwich 81
le Goole 30
Goryshille (*Gorishille*) 85, 86, 89
Gosberton (Lincs) 13, 96
Great Ouse, River
  course of *18*, *19*, *21*, 23, *23*
    current 1, *2*, *6*, *19*, *24*
    diversion in C13 9–10, 22, 25, 88, 92, 98
  salinity 22
Greenpark Avenue 1
Greenpark Avenue Primary School, excavations 1, *2*, 3, *4*, *6*, 8–9
grevas/greves 29, 35, 73, 86, 89, 95, 98
Grey, John de, bishop of Norwich 80, 92, 95, 107–8
Grimsby (Lincs) 93
Grimston (Norfolk) 14, 88
gully 58

Hamburg Way 5
Harold, Earl 88
Hashecoates 58, 82
hayricks 31–2, *31*, 90
hearth bases 65–6
hearth waste
  defined 35, 36
  discussion 74
  excavation evidence 66–8, *68*,
  sedimentology 47, 49
hearths
  background and nomenclature 33, 34, 35–6
  discussion 74–6, *75*
  excavation evidence
    Saltern 1 43–4, *46*
    Saltern 5 59, *62*, *63*, *64*, 65–6
herring 16–17
Hevingham (Norfolk) 86
Hibbronds 82, 89
hoggas 36, 73, 95
hogue/houguechon 95
Holbeach Hurn/Gedney Dyke (Lincs) 5

Holt House Farm (Norfolk) 14
horse burial 32
houguechon see hogue/houguechon
Hullbridge Group (Essex) 93
Hunstanton (Norfolk) 27
Hunt, Robert 83

Icknield Way 16
Ipswich (*Gipeswic*) (Suffolk) 16, 17, 91
iron ore 14, 16
iron smelting 14, 16; *see also* slag
iron smithing 66, *66*, 74, 76, 79; *see also* slag
d'Isigny-sur-Mer (France) 95
Islington (Norfolk) 13, 88

kinches 29, 35
King's Lynn (Bishop's Lynn)
  environment 18, 19–25, *19*, *20–2*, *23*, 27
  foundation 80, 88
  manor 88
  market 88
  Old East Sea Bank 25
  Queen Mary's Nursing Home saltern
    briquetage 59, 74
    dating 5
    filtration unit 76
    fired clay 47
    hearths 7, 35, 43–4, 59, 74, 76
    salt-cote 73
    sand-washing 9, 35
  ramparts 10, 22
  St Margaret's church 80
  St Margaret's Priory
    and cathedral priory 88
    endowment of 35, 81, 98, 107–8
    rents/possessions 82, 84, 86, 89, 92
  salt trade 11
  see also Gaywood; Lyn
Kirkby, Robert 82

Lancelotehill 82, 85, 86
land reclamation
  Lyn 19–22, *20*
  North Marsh 9, 25, 89–90, 92, *92*
Langham, William 83, 84
lead waste 65, 76
Leofric 17
Leofric, son of Limburgh 89, 107
Lewis, William de 108
Lin *see* Lyn
Lincolnshire, salt-winning 95–7
Lindsey marshland 96–7
Little Carlton (Lincs) 96–7
Lomb, Alexander 84
Losinga, Herbert de, bishop of Norwich 80–1, 88, 95, 107
Lym, River 17, 95
Lyme (Dorset) 77
Lyminge (Kent) 17, 76, 77, 93
Lymington (Hants) 77, 93–5
Lyn (Lin)
  archaeological overview 13–14, *14*
  church influence 15–16
  discussion 16–17
  environment and land reclamation *18*, 19–25, *20–2*, *23*
  'gateway' communities 14–15, *14*, 16
  trade and role in salt supply 16, 87–9
Lynnsport, excavations 1, *2*, 3, *4*, *6*, 7–9

Maldon (Essex), Saltcote Hall 93
le Marish 30
Marsh Lane
  creek 30
  saltern, excavations
    background and location 1, *2*, 3, 5–7, 39
    briquetage 59, 63, 74
    dating 36–8, *36*, 53, 101–3, *102*, *104*
    filtration unit 58, 76
    fired clay/slag 7, 47
    fuel 49
    hearths 7, 44, 59, 74, 76
    pans, lead 64–5, 74
    pottery 7

sand-washing 9, 91
slag 66, 74
tank 58, 77
sea level 27
trackway 32, *37*, 38, 91, 98
Marshchapel (Lincs) 97
Merlou, John snr and jnr 84
micromorphology
  methodology 106
  Saltern 1 47
  Saltern 2 51
  Saltern 5 28–9, *29*, 72–3
Middleton (Norfolk) 14, 107
Middleton Stop Drain 19
Middolcotehill 86
minerogenic sediments 27–8, *27*
Mintlyn (Norfolk) 14, 107, 108
moies 73, *73*, 77, 78, 95
molluscs 29, 50
Moltismarsh 89
monasteries 15, 16–17, 91, 93, 95, 96
Mont-Saint-Michel (France) 78, 95
mould 34, 35, 51, 73, 89
muldefange 29, 35
Myller, Thomas 83

nail, iron 45
Nar, River 14–15, 16, 19, 88
Nene, River 22, 25
Netherlands, salt-winning 95
nomenclature 34–5
Normandy (France), salt-winning
  compared 95
    filtration units 77, 78
    fuel 76
    moies 73
    open pan hearths 74, 75, 76
    rents 89, 90
    salicole 73, *73*
Encyclopédie, translation of 106–7
North Elmham See 15, 91
North Lynn (Norfolk) 5, 27, 88
North Marsh
  archaeological/historical background 16–17
    gateway and monastic communities 14–16
    overview of environs 13–14, *14*
  environment *18*, 19, 22–5, *23*, 27–31
  excavations
    dating evidence 36–8, *36*, 39
    discussion 97–8
      excavation evidence 73–9, *73*, *75*, *78*
      Lincolnshire, a view from 95–7
      overview 91–2, *92*
      sand-washing tradition 92–5, *94*
    environmental evidence
      Bullcote Waie group 68–73, *69*, *70*, *71*, *72*
      Salters Waie group 50–2
    excavation evidence 33–5, *34*
      Period 1: *Salters Waie* group 38–52, *38*
      Period 2: *Bullcote Waie* group 52–73, *53*
    excavation and reporting strategy 7–9, *8*
    overview of previous work 1–7, *6*
    project background and location 1, *2*, *3*, *4*
    research agenda 9–11, *10*
  historical evidence
    discussion 87–90
    Domesday, charters and cartularies 80–1, *80*, 107–8
    'Gaywood Dragge' 81–7, *81*, *87*
  mills 25, 77, 88, 107
  see also Marsh Lane; saltmarsh
North Rungton (Runcton) (Norfolk) 107
North Sea Bank 19, 22
North Wootton (Norfolk) 14, 15, 88
Norwich (Norfolk)
  bishops of 9, 80–2, 84, 86, 88, 90, 98
  Holy Trinity Priory 80, 81, 88, 107, 108

Odo, bishop of Bayeux 88
Old Eau River 5
Old Wiggenall Eau 19
Oldemedewe, John 84
Oldmedell, John 82

Orne, River 95
ostracods
  methodology 105
  Saltern 1 29, 50, 51, 70
  Saltern 5 68–70, *69*
  Saltern 10 71–2, *71*
  Saltern 11 71–2, *71*
Owen of Lakesle 107
ownership and organisation, research agenda 9

Page, John 83, 87
pans
  lead 35, 59, 64–5, 74, 76, 78
  saltmarsh 30–1
pasture 31–2, 86, 90
peat 17, 68, 76
Pennington Marshes (Hants) 74
Pepper, Edmund, widow of 82, 83, 84
Philpott, William 83, 84
Pilton, William 84
pits *see* rake-out pits
plant remains
  methodology 104
  salterns 41–3, 66–8, 72
  see also vegetation
Podike 22
pollen analysis
  methodology 105
  salterns 30, 51–2, 72
Poole Harbour (Dorset) 95
post-holes 58–9, 73–4
Potter, William 83
pottery, Anglo-Saxon–early medieval
  methodology 104
  Lyn 13–14, *14*, 16
  North Marsh 37
    Bullcote Waie group 53–7
    Salters Waie group 39–41
pottery production 88
Purfleet (Essex) 77

Quadring (Lincs) 78, 93, 96
Quarr Abbey (IOW) 95

radiocarbon dates 101–3, *102*, *104*
rake-out pits
  defined 35
  discussion 75
  excavation evidence
    Saltern 1 44–7, *47*, *48*, 49
    Saltern 2 44, 47, *48*
    Saltern 5 59
Raley, William de, bishop of Norwich 81
Reffley Wood 15, 76
Reluflete 30
ridge and furrow 31
Riley circles 31–2, *31*, 90
roddons 13, 15, 27, 96
Rondshill 80

St Katherine's Fleet 89
salinity 22, 25, 29, 30, 98
le Salt Ea 30, 89
Salt Rivallett 30
salt slag 35, 65–6, *65*, 74–5
salt trade 87–9
salt workers 10, 89–90
salt-cotes 35–6, 58–9, *60*, 73–4, *73*
salt-making
  cause of coastal change 25–7, 31, 32, 88, 98
  methods 1–5, 9, 11; *see also* sand-washing (*sleeching*)
  portability 78–9
Saltcotegate 86
Saltern 1
  chronology 39
  environmental evidence
    charcoal 49
    diatoms 52
    foraminifera 50
    molluscs 50
    ostracods 50, 51, 70
    plant remains 41–3

pollen 30
sedimentology 27–8, 47, 49
excavation evidence *40, 41*
circular tanks 43, *46*, 77–8
filtration unit 41, 42, *44*, 76, 77
hearth 43–4, *46*, 74
lead 65, 76
rake-out pits 44–7, *47, 48*, 75
pottery 39–41
Saltern 2
chronology 39
environmental evidence
micromorphology 51
plant remains 41–3
pollen 51, *51*–2
sedimentology 27–8, 51, 52
excavation evidence *42, 43*
filtration unit 41, 42, *45*, 76, 77
rake-out pits 44, 47, *48*, 75
pottery 39–41
Saltern 4
chronology 53, 54
excavation evidence 31, *31*, 53, 56, *61*
pottery 53
Saltern 5
briquetage 59–65, *64, 65*, 74
chronology 37, 53, 54
environmental evidence
foraminifera 70–1, *70*
micromorphology 28–9, *29*, 72–3
ostracods 68–70, *69*
soil development 28
excavation evidence *4*, 53, *61*
filtration unit 56, 77
hayrick 31–2
hearth 59, *62, 63, 64*, 65–6, 74, 75, 76
pits 58, 59
salt slag 65–6, *65*
iron working evidence 66
pottery 57, 93
Saltern 6
chronology 54
excavation evidence 53, *61*
iron working evidence 66, *66*, 76
Saltern 7 53, 54, 56, *61*
Saltern 8 53, 54
Saltern 9 53, 54, 56
Saltern 10
chronology 54
environmental evidence 71–2, *71, 72*
excavation evidence 53, *55*
filtration unit 56, 57–8, *57, 58, 59*, 76, 77
iron working evidence 66, 76
water supply 77
Saltern 11
chronology 53, 54
environmental evidence
charcoal 68
foraminifera 72, *72*
ostracods 71–2, *71*
plant remains 66–8, 72
pollen 72
soil development 28
excavation evidence 53, *67*
filtration unit 56
hearth waste 66–8, *68*, 74
iron working evidence 66, 76
water supply 77
Saltern 12
chronology 53, 54–5
environmental evidence 68, 73
excavation evidence 52, 53
filtration unit 56
hearth waste 68, 74
salt-cote 58–9, *60*, 73–4
tanks 58, 77
fuel 68, 76
iron working evidence 59, 66, 76
pottery 53
water supply 77
salterns, cross-section *8*
Salters Waie, trackway

dating 38, 98
function 32, 91
location 33, *36, 37*
Salters Waie group
dating *36*, 39, 101–3, *102, 104*
discussion 88, 91, 98
excavation evidence *34*, 38–52, *38*
see also Salterns 1–2
Saltfleet Haven (Lincs) 97
Salthushill 86
saltmarsh
environment *18*, 19, *19*, 32
Gaywood Valley and North Marsh 22–5, *23, 24*
Lyn 13, 19–22, *19, 20*–2
formation, evidence for 25–31, *26, 27, 29*
pasture, transition to 31–2, *31*
research questions 9, 11
salt-making, effects of 25–7, 31, 32, 98
Saltwood (*Salteode*) (Kent) 76
sand-washing (*sleeching*)
discussion 91, 92–7, 98
process 35–6, 76, 77, 88, 106–7
Wash 1–5
Saracen's Head (Lincs) 96
Scarlett, Andrew 84
Scarlett, William 84
Scolt Head Island (Norfolk) 30
Sea Bank (Roman Bank) 13, 15, 19, 25
sea defences 13, 15, 19, 25
sea levels 27
Early Anglo-Saxon 15
C11 39, 53, 91
C13 22, 25, 92
research agenda 9
Seabank Estate 5
le Seadyke 22, 89
Seasalter (Kent) 79, 93
Sedgeford (Norfolk) 80, 107, 108
sedimentology
North Marsh 27–8
rake-out pits 47, 49, 51, 52
Seeler, Casper 89
Seman 107
Seman, mother of 107
Shaftesbury Abbey (Dorset) 90
Skidbrooke (Lincs) 97
Skirbeck (Lincs) 96
slag, iron
Lyn 14, *14*
methodology 104
salterns 59, 66
see also salt slag
Sleaford (Lincs) 96
sleeching see sand-washing
sleeching waste *see* filtration waste
Smyth, John 84
Snettisham (Norfolk) 15, 88
soil development 28–9, 51–2, 73
South Lyn manor 88
South Woodham Ferrers (Essex) 93
South Wootton (Norfolk) 15, 88
Spelman, Sir Henry 80
Spynk, William 87
Stallingborough (Lincs) 16
Stenning (Lincs) 96
Stigand, bishop of Elmham 88
strikes 35, 73, 86, 89, 95, 98
Sturiun, John 84
Sutterton (Lincs) 96
Swanton, Andrew 82
Swineshead (Lincs) 96

tanks
background and nomenclature 34, 35
discussion 76, 77–8
excavation evidence 43, *46*, 58
Taunton Priory (Som) 17
Tego, John 82, 84
Teignmouth (Devon) 17
Terrington (Norfolk) 13
Terrington All Saints (Norfolk) 27
Terrington St Clement (Norfolk) 13

119

Tetney (Lincs) 97
Thetford, bishops of 9
Thornham (Norfolk) 107
Tigo, John 84
Tigo, Richard 84
Tilney St Lawrence (Norfolk) 13
trackways 30, 32, *36*, *37*, 38, 98; *see also Bullcote Waie*; Marsh Lane; *Salters Waie*
Tracy, John 83, 84
trade, role of salt in 16–17, 87–9
Troarn Abbey (France) 95
turbaries 76
Turbe, William, bishop of Norwich 35, 107
Turncoults 58, 82, 83
Turnecole 83, 86
tuyère holes 66, *66*, 74, 76
Tydde, Robert 82

Upgonacre 84, 86

Vains, Regnouf de 77
vegetation, saltmarsh 29–30
villae regiae 15

Wainfleet St Mary (Lincs), saltern
  briquetage 59, 63–4, 74
  designation 96
  filtration units 5, 41, 58, 76, 77, 78
  frames/boxes, wooden 35
  hearth 74, 78
  pits 75
  salt-making method 35, 77
  spatial organisation 78
Walpole (Norfolk), 13, 15
Walpole St Peter (Norfolk) 49, 59

Walsoken (Norfolk) 13, 15
Walter the archdeacon 107
Walter, James 83
Walton estate 13
Wareyn, Robert 83, 84
Wash
  salterns 1–5, 95–7
  saltmarsh 25–6
Welland, River 5
West Lynn (Norfolk) 27, 88
West Walton (Norfolk) 13, 15
West Winch (Norfolk) 19
Westacre estate 88
Western Escarpment 13, 19, 22
Whittlesey (N. Cambs) 72
Wicks, John 81; *see also* Wyks
Wickton, Sir Edmund 82
Wiggenhall St Germans (Norfolk) 13, 19, 30, 107
Wiggenhall St Mary Magdalen (Norfolk) 13, 19–22
William I 88
William, prior of Holy Trinity 80, 107
William son of Stanquin 107
Willis, Richard 82, 86
women 90
wood 76
woodland 17, 76, 87, 98
Wootton (Norfolk) 76, 88, 98
Wootton Road, pottery 16, 91
Worlesse, William 83
Wormegay (Norfolk) 14, 15, 16, 87
Wraggismarsh 89
Wyks, John 82; *see also* Wicks

Yarmouth (Norfolk) 17
Yates, William 83, 84

East Anglian Archaeology
is a serial publication sponsored by ALGAO EE and English Heritage. It is the main vehicle for publishing final reports on archaeological excavations and surveys in the region. For information about titles in the series, visit **https://eaareports.org.uk**. Reports can be obtained from:
    Oxbow Books, **https://www.oxbowbooks.com/oxbow/eaa**
or directly from the organisation publishing a particular volume.

Reports available so far:

No.1,	1975	Suffolk: various papers
No.2,	1976	Norfolk: various papers
No.3,	1977	Suffolk: various papers
No.4,	1976	Norfolk: Late Saxon town of Thetford
No.5,	1977	Norfolk: various papers on Roman sites
No.6,	1977	Norfolk: Spong Hill Anglo-Saxon cemetery, Part I
No.7,	1978	Norfolk: Bergh Apton Anglo-Saxon cemetery
No.8,	1978	Norfolk: various papers
No.9,	1980	Norfolk: North Elmham Park
No.10,	1980	Norfolk: village sites in Launditch Hundred
No.11,	1981	Norfolk: Spong Hill, Part II: Catalogue of Cremations
No.12,	1981	The barrows of East Anglia
No.13,	1981	Norwich: Eighteen centuries of pottery from Norwich
No.14,	1982	Norfolk: various papers
No.15,	1982	Norwich: Excavations in Norwich 1971–1978; Part I
No.16,	1982	Norfolk: Beaker domestic sites in the Fen-edge and East Anglia
No.17,	1983	Norfolk: Waterfront excavations and Thetford-type Ware production, Norwich
No.18,	1983	Norfolk: The archaeology of Witton
No.19,	1983	Norfolk: Two post-medieval earthenware pottery groups from Fulmodeston
No.20,	1983	Norfolk: Burgh Castle: excavation by Charles Green, 1958–61
No.21,	1984	Norfolk: Spong Hill, Part III: Catalogue of Inhumations
No.22,	1984	Norfolk: Excavations in Thetford, 1948–59 and 1973–80
No.23,	1985	Norfolk: Excavations at Brancaster 1974 and 1977
No.24,	1985	Suffolk: West Stow, the Anglo-Saxon village
No.25,	1985	Essex: Excavations by Mr H.P.Cooper on the Roman site at Hill Farm, Gestingthorpe, Essex
No.26,	1985	Norwich: Excavations in Norwich 1971–78; Part II
No.27,	1985	Cambridgeshire: The Fenland Project No.1: Archaeology and Environment in the Lower Welland Valley
No.28,	1985	Norfolk: Excavations within the north-east bailey of Norwich Castle, 1978
No.29,	1986	Norfolk: Barrow excavations in Norfolk, 1950–82
No.30,	1986	Norfolk: Excavations at Thornham, Warham, Wighton and Caistor St Edmund, Norfolk
No.31,	1986	Norfolk: Settlement, religion and industry on the Fen-edge; three Romano-British sites in Norfolk
No.32,	1987	Norfolk: Three Norman Churches in Norfolk
No.33,	1987	Essex: Excavation of a Cropmark Enclosure Complex at Woodham Walter, Essex, 1976 and An Assessment of Excavated Enclosures in Essex
No.34,	1987	Norfolk: Spong Hill, Part IV: Catalogue of Cremations
No.35,	1987	Cambridgeshire: The Fenland Project No.2: Fenland Landscapes and Settlement, Peterborough–March
No.36,	1987	Norfolk: The Anglo-Saxon Cemetery at Morning Thorpe
No.37,	1987	Norfolk: Excavations at St Martin-at-Palace Plain, Norwich, 1981
No.38,	1988	Suffolk: The Anglo-Saxon Cemetery at Westgarth Gardens, Bury St Edmunds
No.39,	1988	Norfolk: Spong Hill, Part VI: Occupation during the 7th–2nd millennia BC
No.40,	1988	Suffolk: Burgh: The Iron Age and Roman Enclosure
No.41,	1988	Essex: Excavations at Great Dunmow, Essex: a Romano-British small town in the Trinovantian Civitas
No.42,	1988	Essex: Archaeology and Environment in South Essex, Rescue Archaeology along the Gray's By-pass 1979–80
No.43,	1988	Essex: Excavation at the North Ring, Mucking, Essex: A Late Bronze Age Enclosure
No.44,	1988	Norfolk: Six Deserted Villages in Norfolk
No.45,	1988	Norfolk: The Fenland Project No. 3: Marshland and the Nar Valley, Norfolk
No.46,	1989	Norfolk: The Deserted Medieval Village of Thuxton
No.47,	1989	Suffolk: West Stow: Early Anglo-Saxon Animal Husbandry
No.48,	1989	Suffolk: West Stow, Suffolk: The Prehistoric and Romano-British Occupations
No.49,	1990	Norfolk: The Evolution of Settlement in Three Parishes in South-East Norfolk
No.50,	1993	Proceedings of the Flatlands and Wetlands Conference
No.51,	1991	Norfolk: The Ruined and Disused Churches of Norfolk
No.52,	1991	Norfolk: The Fenland Project No. 4, The Wissey Embayment and Fen Causeway
No.53,	1992	Norfolk: Excavations in Thetford, 1980–82, Fison Way
No.54,	1992	Norfolk: The Iron Age Forts of Norfolk
No.55,	1992	Lincolnshire: The Fenland Project No.5: Lincolnshire Survey, The South-West Fens
No.56,	1992	Cambridgeshire: The Fenland Project No.6: The South-Western Cambridgeshire Fens
No.57,	1993	Norfolk and Lincolnshire: Excavations at Redgate Hill Hunstanton; and Tattershall Thorpe
No.58,	1993	Norwich: Households: The Medieval and Post-Medieval Finds from Norwich Survey Excavations 1971–1978
No.59,	1993	Fenland: The South-West Fen Dyke Survey Project 1982–86
No.60,	1993	Norfolk: Caister-on-Sea: Excavations by Charles Green, 1951–55
No.61,	1993	Fenland: The Fenland Project No.7: Excavations in Peterborough and the Lower Welland Valley 1960–1969
No.62,	1993	Norfolk: Excavations in Thetford by B.K. Davison, between 1964 and 1970
No.63,	1993	Norfolk: Illington: A Study of a Breckland Parish and its Anglo-Saxon Cemetery
No.64,	1994	Norfolk: The Late Saxon and Medieval Pottery Industry of Grimston: Excavations 1962–92
No.65,	1993	Suffolk: Settlements on Hill-tops: Seven Prehistoric Sites in Suffolk
No.66,	1993	Lincolnshire: The Fenland Project No.8: Lincolnshire Survey, the Northern Fen-Edge
No.67,	1994	Norfolk: Spong Hill, Part V: Catalogue of Cremations
No.68,	1994	Norfolk: Excavations at Fishergate, Norwich 1985
No.69,	1994	Norfolk: Spong Hill, Part VIII: The Cremations
No.70,	1994	Fenland: The Fenland Project No.9: Flandrian Environmental Change in Fenland
No.71,	1995	Essex: The Archaeology of the Essex Coast Vol.I: The Hullbridge Survey Project
No.72,	1995	Norfolk: Excavations at Redcastle Furze, Thetford, 1988–9
No.73,	1995	Norfolk: Spong Hill, Part VII: Iron Age, Roman and Early Saxon Settlement
No.74,	1995	Norfolk: A Late Neolithic, Saxon and Medieval Site at Middle Harling
No.75,	1995	Essex: North Shoebury: Settlement and Economy in South-east Essex 1500BC–AD1500
No.76,	1996	Nene Valley: Orton Hall Farm: A Roman and Early Anglo-Saxon Farmstead
No.77,	1996	Norfolk: Barrow Excavations in Norfolk, 1984–88
No.78,	1996	Norfolk:The Fenland Project No.11: The Wissey Embayment: Evidence for pre-Iron Age Occupation
No.79,	1996	Cambridgeshire: The Fenland Project No.10: Cambridgeshire Survey, the Isle of Ely and Wisbech
No.80,	1997	Norfolk: Barton Bendish and Caldecote: fieldwork in south-west Norfolk
No.81,	1997	Norfolk: Castle Rising Castle
No.82,	1998	Essex: Archaeology and the Landscape in the Lower Blackwater Valley
No.83,	1998	Essex: Excavations south of Chignall Roman Villa 1977–81
No.84,	1998	Suffolk: A Corpus of Anglo-Saxon Material
No.85,	1998	Suffolk: Towards a Landscape History of Walsham le Willows
No.86,	1998	Essex: Excavations at the Orsett 'Cock' Enclosure
No.87,	1999	Norfolk: Excavations in Thetford, North of the River, 1989–90
No.88,	1999	Essex: Excavations at Ivy Chimneys, Witham 1978–83
No.89,	1999	Lincolnshire: Salterns: Excavations at Helpringham, Holbeach St Johns and Bicker Haven
No.90,	1999	Essex: The Archaeology of Ardleigh, Excavations 1955–80
No.91,	2000	Norfolk: Excavations on the Norwich Southern Bypass, 1989–91 Part I Bixley, Caistor St Edmund, Trowse
No.92,	2000	Norfolk: Excavations on the Norwich Southern Bypass, 1989–91 Part II Harford Farm Anglo-Saxon Cemetery
No.93,	2001	Norfolk: Excavations on the Snettisham Bypass, 1989
No.94,	2001	Lincolnshire: Excavations at Billingborough, 1975–8
No.95,	2001	Suffolk: Snape Anglo-Saxon Cemetery: Excavations and Surveys
No.96,	2001	Norfolk: Two Medieval Churches in Norfolk
No.97,	2001	Nene Valley: Monument 97, Orton Longueville
No.98,	2002	Essex: Excavations at Little Oakley, 1951–78
No.99,	2002	Norfolk: Excavations at Melford Meadows, Brettenham, 1994
No.100,	2002	Norfolk: Excavations in Norwich 1971–78, Part III
No.101,	2002	Norfolk: Medieval Armorial Horse Furniture in Norfolk
No.102,	2002	Norfolk: Baconsthorpe Castle, Excavations and Finds, 1951–1972
No.103,	2003	Cambridgeshire: Excavations at the Wardy Hill Ringwork, Coveney, Ely
No.104,	2003	Norfolk: Earthworks of Norfolk

No.105,	2003	Essex: Excavations at Great Holts Farm, 1992–4
No.106,	2004	Suffolk: Romano-British Settlement at Hacheston
No.107,	2004	Essex: Excavations at Stansted Airport, 1986–91
No.108,	2004	Norfolk: Excavations at Mill Lane, Thetford, 1995
No.109,	2005	Fenland: Archaeology and Environment of the Etton Landscape
No.110,	2005	Cambridgeshire: Saxon and Medieval Settlement at West Fen Road, Ely
No.111,	2005	Essex: Early Anglo-Saxon Cemetery and Later Saxon Settlement at Springfield Lyons
No.112,	2005	Norfolk: Dragon Hall, King Street, Norwich
No.113,	2006	Norfolk: Excavations at Kilverstone
No.114,	2006	Cambridgeshire:Waterfront Archaeology in Ely
No.115,	2006	Essex:Medieval Moated Manor by the Thames Estuary: Excavations at Southchurch Hall, Southend
No.116,	2006	Norfolk: Norwich Cathedral Refectory
No.117,	2007	Essex: Excavations at Lodge Farm, St Osyth
No.118,	2007	Essex: Late Iron Age Warrior Burial from Kelvedon
No.119,	2007	Norfolk: Aspects of Anglo-Saxon Inhumation Burial
No.120,	2007	Norfolk: Norwich Greyfriars: Pre-Conquest Town and Medieval Friary
No.121,	2007	Cambridgeshire: A Line Across Land: Fieldwork on the Isleham–Ely Pipeline 1993-4
No.122,	2008	Cambridgeshire: Ely Wares
No.123,	2008	Cambridgeshire: Farming on the Edge: Archaeological Evidence from the Clay Uplands west of Cambridge
No.124,	2008	*Wheare most Inclosures be*, East Anglian Fields: History, Morphology and Management
No.125,	2008	Bedfordshire: Life in the Loop: a Prehistoric and Romano-British Landscape at Biddenham
No.126,	2008	Essex: Early Neolithic Ring-ditch and Bronze Age Cemetery at Brightlingsea
No.127,	2008	Essex: Early Saxon Cemetery at Rayleigh
No.128,	2009	Hertfordshire: Four Millennia of Human Activity along the A505 Baldock Bypass
No.130,	2009	Norfolk: A Medieval Cemetery at Mill Lane, Ormesby St Margaret
No.131,	2009	Suffolk: Anglo-Saxon Settlement and Cemetery at Bloodmoor Hill, Carlton Colville
No.132,	2009	Norfolk: Norwich Castle: Excavations and Historical Survey 1987-98 (Parts I–IV)
No.133,	2010	Norfolk: Life and Death on a Norwich Backstreet, AD900–1600: Excavations in St Faith's Lane
No.134,	2010	Norfolk: Farmers and Ironsmiths: Prehistoric, Roman and Anglo-Saxon Settlement beside Brandon Road, Thetford
No.135,	2011	Norfolk: Romano-British and Saxon Occupation at Billingford
No.136,	2011	Essex: Aerial Archaeology in Essex
No.137,	2011	Essex: The Roman Town of Great Chesterford
No.138,	2011	Bedfordshire: Farm and Forge: late Iron Age/Romano-British farmsteads at Marsh Leys, Kempston
No.139,	2011	Suffolk: The Anglo-Saxon Cemetery at Shrubland Hall Quarry, Coddenham
No.140,	2011	Norfolk: Archaeology of the Newland: Excavations in King's Lynn, 2003–5
No.141,	2011	Cambridgeshire: Life and Afterlife at Duxford: archaeology and history in a chalkland community
No.142,	2012	Cambridgeshire: Extraordinary Inundations of the Sea: Excavations at Market Mews, Wisbech
No.143,	2012	Middle Saxon Animal Husbandry in East Anglia
No.144,	2012	Essex: The Archaeology of the Essex Coast Vol.II: Excavations at the Prehistoric Site of the Stumble
No.145,	2012	Norfolk: Bacton to King's Lynn Gas Pipeline Vol.1: Prehistoric, Roman and Medieval Archaeology
No.146,	2012	Suffolk: Experimental Archaeology and Fire: a Burnt Reconstruction at West Stow Anglo-Saxon Village
No.147,	2012	Suffolk: Circles and Cemeteries: Excavations at Flixton Vol.I
No.148,	2012	Essex: Hedingham Ware: a medieval pottery industry in North Essex; its production and distribution
No.149,	2013	Essex: The Neolithic and Bronze Age Enclosures at Springfield Lyons
No.150,	2013	Norfolk: Tyttel's *Halh*: the Anglo-Saxon Cemetery at Tittleshall. The Archaeology of the Bacton to King's Lynn Gas Pipeline Vol.2
No.151,	2014	Suffolk: Staunch Meadow, Brandon: a High Status Middle Saxon Settlement on the Fen Edge
No.152,	2014	A Romano-British Settlement in the Waveney Valley: Excavations at Scole 1993–4
No.153,	2015	Peterborough: A Late Saxon Village and Medieval Manor: Excavations at Botolph Bridge, Orton Longueville
No.154,	2015	Essex: Heybridge, a Late Iron Age and Roman Settlement: Excavations at Elms Farm 1993–5 Vol.1
No.155,	2015	Suffolk: Before Sutton Hoo: the prehistoric remains and Early Anglo-Saxon cemetery at Tranmer House, Bromeswell
No.156,	2016	Bedfordshire: Close to the Loop: landscape and settlement evolution beside the Biddenham Loop, west of Bedford
No.157,	2016	Cambridgeshire: Bronze Age Barrow, Early to Middle Iron Age Settlement and Burials, Early Anglo-Saxon Settlement at Harston Mill
No.158,	2016	Bedfordshire: Newnham: a Roman bath house and estate centre east of Bedford
No.159,	2016	Cambridgeshire: The Production and Distribution of Medieval Pottery in Cambridgeshire
No.160,	2016	Suffolk: A Late Iron-Age and Romano-British Farmstead at Cedars Park, Stowmarket
No.161,	2016	Suffolk: Medieval Dispersed Settlement on the Mid Suffolk Clay at Cedars Park, Stowmarket
No.162,	2017	Cambridgeshire: The Horningsea Roman Pottery Industry in Context
No.163,	2018	Nene Valley: Iron Age and Roman Settlement: Rescue Excavations at Lynch Farm 2, Orton Longueville, Peterborough
No.164,	2018	Suffolk: Excavations at Wixoe Roman Small Town
No.165,	2018	Cambridgeshire: Conquering the Claylands: Excavations at Love's Farm, St Neots
No.166,	2018	Norfolk: Late Bronze Age Hoards: new light on old finds
No.167,	2018	Norfolk: A Romano-British Industrial Site at East Winch
No.168,	2018	Cambridgeshire: Small Communities: Life in the Cam Valley in the Neolithic, Late Iron Age and Early Anglo-Saxon Periods. Excavations at Dernford Farm, Sawston
No.169,	2019	Suffolk: Iron Age Fortification Beside the River Lark: Excavations at Mildenhall
No.170,	2019	Cambridgeshire: Rectory Farm, Godmanchester: Excavations 1988–95, Neolithic monument to Roman villa farm
No.171,	2020	Norfolk: Three Bronze Age Weapon Assemblages
No.172,	2020	Suffolk: Excavations at Stoke Quay, Ipswich: Southern Gipeswic and the parish of St Augustine
No.173,	2020	Nene Valley: Prehistoric Burial Mounds in Orton Meadows, Peterborough
No.174,	2021	Suffolk: Provisioning Ipswich: Animal Remains from the Saxon and Medieval Town
No.175,	2021	Norfolk: Crownthorpe: a Boudican Hoard of Bronze Vessels from Early Roman Norfolk
No.176,	2022	Norfolk: Fransham: people and land in a central Norfolk parish
No.177,	2022	Suffolk: Living with Monuments: Excavations at Flixton Vol.II
No.178,	2023	Cambridgeshire: Hinxton Part I, Excavations at the Wellcome Genome Campus: Late Glacial Lithics to the Icknield Way
No.179,	2023	Norfolk: Aspects of 7th- to 11th-century Norwich
No.180,	2023	Norfolk: Saltwinning on the Lyn